Edited by Angus Hall

First published in Great Britain in 1976 by
The Hamlyn Publishing Group Limited
Produced by Phoebus Publishing Company/
BPC Publishing (A Division of Macdonald
and Co (Publishers) Ltd)

This edition published in 1991 by
Treasure Press
Michelin House
81 Fulham Road
London SW3 6RB

ISBN 1 85051 170 5

Printed and bound in the UK by The Bath Press

Introduction

Crimes of Horror is a study of the chillingly unexpected in crime. The inexplicable, irrational twist in a crime that takes it beyond understanding. This book presents the rare cases in which the cold-blooded brutality, the cunning calculations behind a killing, the callous lack of motive in a murder take the crime onto another level – the dimension of horror.

In the kidnapping of Mrs McKay not only was the "wrong woman" tragically taken, but her body has never been found. The American "Mother Duncan" loved her son so possessively that she hired two men to kill his wife. The mass-murderer Peter Manuel boasted to police of killing whole families. Ghoulish Mr Robinson methodically cut up a prostitute and left the pieces in a trunk at the station luggage office. The Richardson brothers drunkenly tortured those who wouldn't "co-operate" in their protection racket.

The dossier of Horror Crimes in this book might be explained as a catalogue of madness, and it certainly makes uneasy reading.

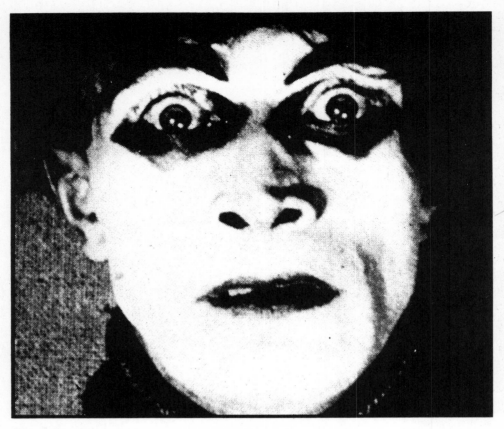

Contents

THE ACID BATH BLOOD-DRINKER

Totally emotionless killers are rarer than is generally supposed. But John George Haigh was more than this: he also drank the blood of his victims . . .

TO THE permanent residents, and especially the elderly ladies, at the genteel Onslow Court Hotel, in London's South Kensington, Mr. John George Haigh was the epitome of charm and well-bred good manners. At meal times he never failed to acknowledge his fellow guests with a warm smile and the hint of a formal bow as he threaded his way between the separate tables to his own reserved corner of the dining room. In the eyes of the widowed ladies, comfortably, if sometimes tediously, counting off the days in quiet seclusion, he was something of a favourite handsome nephew.

One of these widows, a Mrs. Durand-Deacon, was already enjoying a growing friendship with the 39-year-old, and apparently successful, self-employed engineer. They occupied adjoining tables and, as a result of mutual confidence, Haigh already knew a good deal about her. Olive Henrietta Helen Olivia Robarts Durand-Deacon was 69, a well-preserved, well-dressed, buxom woman, who was a devoted Christian Scientist and whose late husband—a colonel in the Gloucestershire Regiment—had left her a legacy of some £40,000.

She was not the sort of person who could spend her final years in total idleness. To amuse herself, and add to her invested capital, she had made some paper designs of artificial fingernails which, she hoped, could be manufactured in plastic. To her delight, the kindly Mr. Haigh suggested that he might be able to help, and they could choose the materials at his factory at Crawley, in Sussex.

Elaborate preparations

On the afternoon of Friday, February 18, 1949, Haigh drove Mrs. Durand-Deacon the 30 miles south to Crawley in his Alvis car, and at around four o'clock they were seen together in the George Hotel. From the hotel they went to a small factory in Leopold Road, Crawley—a factory that Haigh did not own, as he had said, but where he was allowed the use of a storeroom for his "experimental engineering" work.

There in the factory he had made elaborate preparations for Mrs. Durand-Deacon's visit. He had bought a carboy of sulphuric acid and a 45-gallon drum specially lined to hold corrosive chemicals. He had laid out, on a bench, a stirrup pump, of the type used for firefighting during the days of the German air raids on Britain, gloves, and a rubber apron.

It was strange equipment to assemble for what was supposed to be a discussion about artificial fingernails. But, whatever Mrs. Durand-Deacon might have thought, that was not the purpose for which Haigh had brought her to the deserted workshop.

As the elderly widow turned her back to him to search in her handbag for her paper designs, Haigh slipped a revolver from his coat pocket and killed her with a single shot through the nape of the neck. Stooping beside the body he took a knife, made an incision in an artery, gathered a few inches of the still-coursing blood in a glass, and drank it at a gulp.

Haigh then began the real work for which he had lured his victim to the factory. He stripped the body and carefully placed on one side the widow's Persian lamb coat, rings, necklace, ear-rings, and a cruciform, which had hung around the neck. That done, he moved to the second part of his plan, in which he had the benefit of previous experience: the disposal of the body by dissolving it in acid.

His own later description of the operation illustrated the workmanlike way in which this 10-stone murderer put his 15-stone victim into an acid bath.

He took an anticorrosive drum, or barrel, as he called it, laid it down lengthwise on the floor "and with a minimum of effort pushed the head and shoulders in. I then tipped the barrel up by placing my feet on the forward edge and grasping the top of the barrel with my gloved hands. By throwing my weight backwards the barrel containing the body rocked to a vertical position fairly easily and I found I could raise a 15-stone body easily.

"You may think that a 40-gallon drum standing only four feet high would be too

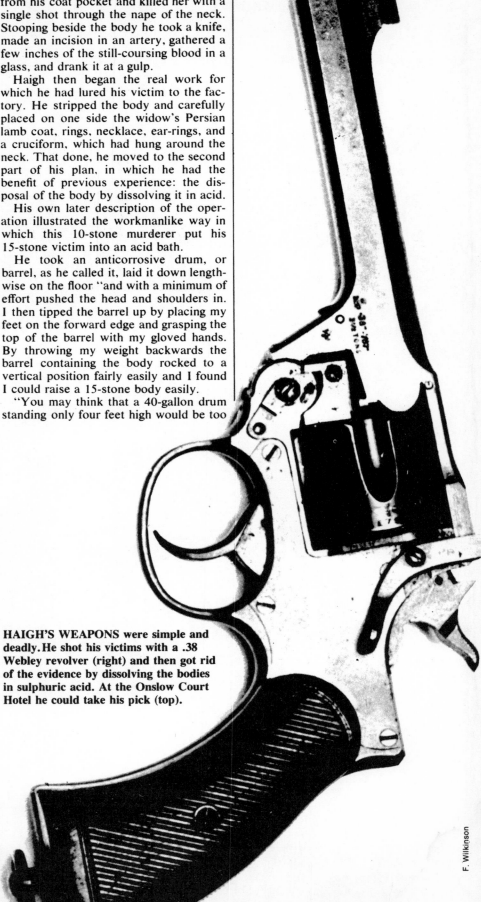

HAIGH'S WEAPONS were simple and deadly. He shot his victims with a .38 Webley revolver (right) and then got rid of the evidence by dissolving the bodies in sulphuric acid. At the Onslow Court Hotel he could take his pick (top).

F. Wilkinson

small for such a body," Haigh went on, "but my experiments showed that as the drum tipped, the body slumped down to the shoulders and the legs disappeared below the surface of the drum."

Having stowed the body neatly in the drum, Haigh poured in the sulphuric acid ("the question of getting the right amount was only learned by experience," he loftily explained) and then added more to make up the correct solution by pumping it in with the stirrup pump. When that was done, he had to wait until, slowly, the acid destroyed every trace of the body.

Tired after his efforts, however, Haigh left the workshop, slipped into his car, and drove to Ye Olde Ancient Priors Restaurant, in Crawley. There he ordered a pot of tea and poached eggs on toast, which he consumed with relish while exchanging good-natured banter with Mr. Outram, the proprietor.

Since this was the beginning of a weekend, during which the small factory would be closed, Haigh left the body in its dreadful bath and returned to the Onslow Court Hotel. There, at breakfast the following morning, Mrs. Durand-Deacon's absence was noticed by some of the other guests —and particularly by a Mrs. Constance Lane who was a close friend of hers.

To Haigh's alarm, it transpired that Mrs. Lane had known of his proposed visit to Crawley with Mrs. Durand-Deacon. While he had been fetching his car, the previous afternoon, the two women had met in the hotel lounge and Mrs. Durand-Deacon had told her friend about her imminent "business trip".

For Haigh it was a devastating piece of information. The masterstroke in his plan had been his expectation that Mrs. Durand-Deacon would want to keep the promising deal over the artificial fingernails a "company secret". Furthermore, at his suggestion, they had met for the start of their journey to Crawley not outside the hotel, but by the entrance to a large London store, some little distance away in Victoria Street. His subtle plan had now been undermined by Mrs. Lane's knowledge, and Haigh knew he would be involved in the questions following Mrs. Durand-Deacon's disappearance.

Little profit

With his nagging fears locked within him, he spent a busy Saturday putting into practice the purpose for which he had murdered the avaricious widow. In the course of a journey which took him to South London, Surrey, and Sussex, he disposed of Mrs. Durand-Deacon's jewellery for around £150. Her Persian lamb coat—which was blood-stained and not yet ready to realize its secondhand purchase price of £50—he left for cleaning at a shop in Reigate. But, since Haigh had pressing debts—including £350 to a bookmaker—which he could no longer avoid paying, his total "gain" was a reduction of his bank overdraft to £78.

Death had brought the blood-drinking criminal little financial profit. By the next day it seemed certain that it would bring him catastrophic personal loss. For Mrs. Lane, now thoroughly disturbed by her friend's failure to return, insisted that she and Haigh should go to the police and make out a missing person report. Haigh had no choice but to agree, attempting outwardly to express a "correct" measure of solicitude and concern.

The report he made, at Chelsea Police Station, appeared plausible enough. He had arrived at the Army and Navy Stores in Victoria Street, on Friday at 2.30, to keep his prearranged appointment with Mrs. Durand-Deacon. When, an hour later, she had failed to arrive he assumed her plans had changed and drove down to Crawley alone. He was thanked for his assistance and returned with Mrs. Lane to the Onslow Court Hotel—still a free man and still not under official suspicion.

But the last grains of sand in his criminal hourglass were flowing fast, and Woman Police-Sergeant Alexandra Maude Lambourne helped to speed them on their

ICI, AP

Daily Mirror

FRI
MAR. 4
1949

ONE PENNY

No. 14,095

Registered at GPO as a Newspaper

FORWARD WITH THE PEOPLE

VAMPIRE— A MAN HELD

THE Vampire Killer will never strike again. He is safely behind bars, powerless to lure victims to a hideous death.

This is the assurance which the *Daily Mirror* can give today. It is the considered conclusion of the finest detective brains in the country.

The full tally of the Vampire's crimes is still not known.

It may take squads of police many weeks yet to piece together full details of the murderer and his ghastly practices.

So far five murders are attributed to him. They are—

Dr. Archibald Henderson; Mrs. Rosalie Mercy Henderson, his wife; Mr. Donald McSwan; Mrs. Amy McSwan, his wife; and Mr. Donald John McSwan, their son.

The police believe that Donald McSwan, junior, was the first of the Vampire's victims—in 1945—followed two months later by his parents.

Dr and Mrs. Henderson are known to have disappeared in February of last year.

Held captive for a month?

Mrs. Rosalie Henderson

Made to sign alibi notes, says brother

AFTER killing Dr. Henderson the Vampire is believed to have kept Mrs. Henderson alive for at least a month writing letters—and signing typewritten letters—to relatives and friends.

When the Vampire thought himself safe Rosalie Mercy Henderson followed her husband to a ghastly death.

Thus theory is held by her brother Mr. Arnold Henry Burlin, 35, hotelier of Arnfield-road, Withington, Manchester.

"I am convinced" he told the *Daily Mirror* last night "that my sister was under duress for at least a month ... she was shot and her body dis...

No. 79—room of horror

In tins, bags and little parcels, detectives bring specimens from the back-basement of 79, Gloucester-road, London, S.W., in which the McSwans are believed to have been slain. Police digging found false teeth in the floor.

3 thirsty Rus... rush the bar...

THREE of the eight Russian repatriation officials broke from the building by American troops ... searchlights. Ignoring calls to halt and the glare of ... tried to start up a car. Ar... hind the building and back into the building.

The officials have ... The authorities to ... said last night.

Gas and water se... off. The phones ha... being allowed in.

One of the Rus... terday asked the guards for ... "We are cut of ... world," he said.

His booby trap tripped the wrong man

The wrong man — a ... motorist—fell into the trap which Alfred Hatcher, 26, admitted he had set one ... for his rival in love ... and a piece ...

According ... radio the ... officer has to ... Supreme will...

He was give... Stars and Str... Army newspa...

way. She was sent to the hotel to gather additional information about the missing widow; but, unlike the elderly guests at Onslow Court, she did not succumb to Haigh's glib tongue and superficial charm. On the contrary, her combination of police experience and feminine intuition aroused a vague but nevertheless persistent feeling of suspicion.

After talking to Haigh she returned to Chelsea Police Station and wrote a report to Divisional Detective-Inspector Shelley Symes in which she said: "Apart from the fact that I do not like the man Haigh, with his mannerisms, I have a sense that he is 'wrong' and that there may be a case behind the whole business."

Symes respected her judgment sufficiently to ask Scotland Yard's Criminal Record Office to check on whether there was, in the British police phrase, "anything known" about John George Haigh. Within a few hours he learned that something *was* "known", and that Haigh had served three prison sentences – two for fraud and one for theft.

Notorious asylum

On Saturday, February 26, the police forced an entry into the storeroom attached to the Crawley factory and found the stirrup pump, carboys of acid, and a rubber apron bearing traces of blood. From a holster they took a .38 Webley revolver which, after being tested by a firearms expert, was shown to have been recently fired.

Haigh was then "invited" back to the police station to answer further questions. However, before many had been put to him, he, himself, asked one which was to set the pattern of subsequent events. "Tell me frankly," he asked his interrogators, "What are the chances of anybody being released from Broadmoor?"

Realizing he hoped to gain "sanctuary" in the notorious asylum for the criminally insane, the detectives refused to answer him. Haigh then drew heavily on the cigarette he was smoking and said dramatically: "If I tell you the truth you would not believe it. It sounds too fantastic."

Having thus set the scene he continued: "I will tell you all about it. Mrs. Durand-Deacon no longer exists. She has disappeared completely and no trace of her can ever be found again. I have destroyed her with acid. You will find the sludge that remains at Leopold Road, Crawley. Every trace has gone. How can you prove murder if there is no body? . . .

"I shot her in the back of the head. Then I went out to the car and fetched a drinking glass and made an incision, I think with a penknife, in the side of the throat and collected a glass of blood which I then drank."

Two days after putting the body into the acid drum Haigh returned to Crawley, he said, "to find the reaction almost complete" with nothing left of the body but a residue composed of the chemically reduced remains of flesh and bone.

"I emptied off the sludge with a bucket and tipped it on to the ground opposite the storeroom," Haigh explained in careful detail. Then he added: "I should have said that after putting her in the tank and pouring in the acid I went round to the Ancient Priors for tea."

Once more the police returned to Crawley and dug up and removed the patch of soil on to which Haigh said he had emptied the "sludge". When this was methodically sifted and examined at Scotland Yard's laboratory, it became clear that Haigh's assertion that no trace of Mrs. Durand-Deacon would ever be found was ill-based.

Among the 28 lbs. of melted body fat, the pathologists found 18 fragments of human bone, partly eroded by acid but still sufficiently preserved to exhibit traces of arthritis—and thus point to the victim having been an elderly person. In addition, a piece of hipbone was positively identified as female. But, most decisive of all, upper and lower dentures were discovered in an undamaged state, and were proved to have been made for Mrs. Durand-Deacon.

Even though Haigh had failed to "completely erase" the widow's body, his work looked like that of someone experienced in acid baths and killings. Indeed, the police soon learned that he had murdered and similarly disposed of five previous victims in recent years. The first was William Donald McSwann, a young amusement arcade operator, killed in 1944, whose mother and father Haigh shortly afterwards also dispatched. The others were a doctor and his wife, Archibald and Rosalie Henderson, done to death and destroyed in February 1948.

Scandalous case

In each case Haigh acquired the money and other property of his victims by highly skilful forgery. Long after their acid-burned remains had been buried, he wrote business and private letters in impeccable facsimiles of their handwriting, successfully staving off inquiries from relatives and friends.

In a letter postmarked Glasgow, Haigh wrote in a forged hand to Mrs. Henderson's housekeeper in London: "Dear Daisy: We are going to South Africa. Mr. John Haigh has the property now and you will hear from my brother, Arnold Burlin. I want to thank you for the splendid help you have always been and I am sure you must have been while we have been away. If you would like to write, our address until we settle down will be c/o the GPO, Durban, South Africa. Shall always be glad to hear from you. Yours sincerely, Rose Henderson."

In recalling the murders Haigh claimed that "in each case I had my glass of blood after I killed them." It soon became evident that his vampirish ritual would play an important part in his trial—on the charge of murdering Mrs. Durand-Deacon—as "proof" of his insanity. He was duly detained on remand at London's Brixton Prison, and it was then that the London *Daily Mirror* told its 15 million readers of Haigh's supposed activities.

On March 4, 1949, the tabloid appeared with the blazoning front page headline: "Vampire—A Man Held." Underneath, the story began: "The Vampire Killer will never strike again. He is safely behind bars, powerless to lure his victims to a hideous death . . ."

Silvester Bolam, the then editor of the *Mirror*, was brought—in the King's Bench Division of the High Court—before Lord Goddard, the Lord Chief Justice, and Judges Humphreys and Birkett and told: "In the long history of this class of case there has, in the opinion of this Court, never been a case approaching such gravity as this one of such a scandalous and wicked character."

Imposing what they described as "Severe punishment", the High Court judges sentenced Mr. Bolam to three months' imprisonment—in another part of that same jail in which Haigh was being held—and fined the newspaper £10,000, plus the costs of the case.

Once this had been settled, the law once again turned its attention to Haigh. On July 18, 1949, he was put on trial at Lewes, in Sussex. The prosecution was led by Sir Hartley Shawcross, the Attorney-General, and the defence by

EXHIBITS—pieces of bone and the decisive dentures—were carried to and from a pre-trial hearing in a syrup box.

Sir David Maxwell Fyfe—two eminent lawyers who had earned high international reputations for their work at the trial of Nazi war criminals in Nuremberg after World War II.

Despite lengthy legal wranglings over the definition of insanity and the alleged blood-drinking rites, Haigh was found guilty after only a 15-minute retirement by the jury, and sentenced to death.

There were no public expressions of pity for the departed John George Haigh, but there were many of curiosity. How was it, people wondered, that an intelligent boy from a good home should have grown up into such a hideous creature? At the age of 12 he had been an angelic-looking choirboy at Wakefield Cathedral, in Yorkshire, and his parents were devoutly religious Plymouth Brethren.

Brand of Satan

While awaiting execution Haigh wrote: "Although my parents were kind and loving, I had none of the joys, or the companionship, which small children usually have. From my earliest years my recollection is of my father saying: 'Do not' or 'Thou shalt not.' Any form of sport or light entertainment was frowned upon and regarded as not edifying. There was only condemnation and prohibition . . .

"It is true to say that I was nurtured on Bible stories but mostly concerned with sacrifice. If by some mischance I did, or said, anything which my father regarded as improper, he would say: 'Do

SMILING inanely rather than insanely, Haigh (below) made great efforts to convince the court that he was a lunatic. Hartley Shawcross (below inset) and Judge Humphreys (right) disagreed. Far right: a crowd gathers outside the jail as execution notices are posted.

Press Association, AP

not grieve the Lord by behaving so.' And if I suggested that I wanted to go somewhere, or meet somebody, he would say: 'It will not please the Lord.'"

According to the same statement, Haigh's father told him that his mother was, literally, "an angel". So that no outside worldly evil might penetrate the sacred home, the couple had built a high wall around the garden of their tiny house in Outwood, Yorkshire. Mr. Haigh, who was a foreman electrician at a nearby colliery, had been struck by a piece of flying coal and, as a result, bore a blue scar on his forehead.

This, the father had explained to the son, was the brand of Satan. "I have sinned and Satan has punished me. If you ever sin, Satan will mark you with a blue pencil likewise." After that, in the night, before sleep came, young John George would pass his fingers, tremulously, across his own forehead to see if he, too, had yet been stamped by Satan's mark.

During his younger days, Haigh asserted, he suffered from dreams in which flowing blood figured prominently. After a car accident in March 1944, in which blood had streamed down his face and into his mouth, the dreams recurred.

"I saw before me," he said, "a forest of crucifixes which gradually turned into trees. At first there appeared to be dew, or rain, dripping from the branches, but as I approached I realized it was blood. Suddenly the whole forest began to writhe and the trees, stark and erect, to ooze blood . . . A man went to each tree catching the blood . . . When the cup was full he approached me. 'Drink,' he said, but I was unable to move."

The dream faded, later to become a waking nightmare for Haigh . . . and to bring eternal sleep to his victims.

THE IMAGINATION of a vampire . . . Haigh's weird, religious background may have turned him into a twisted killer.

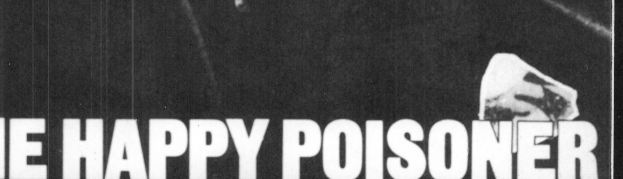

SEEK POISON PLOT IN DEATH OF MICHIGAN MILLIONAIRE AND HIS ... WIFE HERE

AW OF PECKS

Autopsy in Grand Rapids on Body of Mr. Peck, Who Died in Riverside Drive Home of Son-in-Law Shows Arsenic Was Administered Before Death.

WIFE TOO SEEMED WELL THE DAY BEFORE SHE EXPIRED.

Swann's Theory Is Slayer Intended by Third Crime to Gain Half of $1,500,000 Estat... Suspect Und... Watch

THE HAPPY POISONER

Everybody liked the urbane Dr. Waite. Even the jurors giggled and smiled as he told his blood-curdling tale of calculated murder. . . .

Culver

A MAN being tried for double murder might be expected to show a certain degree of strain and anxiety, particularly after having pleaded not guilty. Dr. Arthur Warren Waite, 28-year-old dentist, was exactly the opposite. Throughout the hearing he remained relaxed, urbane and amused. At times during the prosecution case he laughed heartily, and when his own turn came to give evidence he admitted cheerfully—despite his not guilty pleas—that everything the prosecution had said about him was true. Not to put too fine a point on it, he added, he was really even more outrageous and contradictory a character than they had made out.

Yes, he had indeed murdered his mother-in-law, Mrs. John E. Peck, wife of a drug millionaire, when she came to visit her daughter, Clara. Waite had married Clara in September, 1915. Mrs. Peck arrived at their home on fashionable Riverside Drive, New York, just before Christmas of that year. By January 30, 1916, this apparently healthy woman was dead. A doctor certified kidney disease.

But now Waite, with the air of a man relating a diverting story at a cocktail party, was confessing: "I started poisoning her from the very first meal after she arrived. I gave her six assorted tubes of pneumonia, diphtheria and influenza germs in her food. When she finally became ill and took to her bed I ground up 12 five-grain veronal tablets and gave her that, too, last thing at night." And then? "Why, I guess I went back to sleep," he shrugged. "I woke up in the small hours. My mother-in-law was dead. I went back to bed again so that it would be my wife who would discover the body."

Tubes of typhoid

He then went on, in the same bantering manner, to outline his six-week struggle to kill his father-in-law. Mr. Peck came for a visit early in February to cheer himself up after his wife's funeral. By March 12 this sturdy old man of 71 was dead as well.

"I used to insert tubes of typhoid, pneumonia, influenza and diphtheria in his soups and rice puddings," Waite continued gaily. "Once I gave him a nasal spray filled with tuberculosis bacteria. Nothing seemed to affect him, so I used to let off the occasional tube or two of chlorine gas in his bedroom, hoping the gas would weaken his resistance like it did with the soldiers at the front. I used to put some stuff on the electric heater so that if he noticed a funny smell I could say it was something burning.

"Still nothing happened. I tried to give

"FOR THEIR MONEY," said Waite, when asked why he'd killed his in-laws (left), Mr. and Mrs. Peck. Detectives found germ cultures in the suspect's apartment.

him pneumonia by putting water in his Wellingtons [rubbers], damping his sheets, opening his bedroom window and wetting the seat of the automobile before taking him out for a drive. That didn't work either."

Becoming desperate, he had toyed with the idea of faking a car accident. Finally, unable to bring himself to resort to such violence, he had settled for arsenic. However, even after a full 18 grains—far more than the fatal dose—the tough old man was still alive although in a bad way.

"On the night of March 12 he was in great pain," Waite explained, "and he wanted some ammonia and ether. I couldn't find any, but in Clara's medicine chest there was some chloroform, so I gave him that. It did him good, so I gave him a second dose to make sure, and then I held the pillow over his nose and mouth until he was finished."

The jurors, who had regarded Waite with some horror at the start of his recital, had by now become infected with his *bonhomie*. They swopped smiles with him, and some even gave vent to hysterical giggles as Waite went on to reveal that the two murders were only part of the story. He had also tried to kill his wife's aunt, the rich Miss Catherine Peck—despite the fact that he was something of a favourite of hers.

Germs and arsenic

"I gave her repeated doses of germs, then some arsenic, and after that some ground glass," he related. "I also injected live germs into a can of fish before presenting it to her." He had abandoned this attempt at murder, he explained, because Mrs. Peck had come to stay for Christmas, and he couldn't see the point of murdering the aunt when there were much richer pickings to be obtained by murdering his mother-in-law.

Given time, he also confessed, he would almost certainly have murdered his wife, Clara. "She was not my equal in anything," he said. "When I had got rid of her I meant to find a more beautiful wife."

Earlier, the prosecution had filled in the background to Waite's life and the circumstances which led to his arrest. In the fall of 1914 he had returned to his birthplace, Grand Rapids, Michigan, after an absence of several years, during which he had worked as a dentist in South Africa. He had a dental surgeon's degree from Glasgow University in Scotland, a British accent, and a ferocious talent for tennis which soon made him the local champion. In the bank he also had $20,000, a useful sum in those days.

"Waite met and began his courtship of his wife almost immediately," said the prosecution, "and they were married the following September." Waite's charm and slender good looks made an immediate

hit in the New York social circles to which his new wife introduced him. Two people with whom he quickly became intimate friends were Dr. Jacob Cornell, of the Cornell Medical School, and Dr. Cornell's sister, Mrs. Henry Hardwicke.

In addition to setting himself up in dental practice, Waite began to do serious research at the Medical School where later—as the need arose—he was able to lay hands on a plentiful supply of germs to slip into his in-laws' food.

Mrs. Waite told the court of her surprise, after her mother's unexpected death, when Waite said it had been Mrs. Peck's last wish to be cremated. "It was the first I'd heard of it," she said. On the night of March 12 she heard Arthur, who had been sitting up with her father, ring the doctor. Later he came into the bedroom in his robe, looking disturbed, and said: "I don't think Dad's too good."

Already dead

She rushed to her father's room, but he was already dead. Once again she was surprised when Arthur told her: "It was Dad's wish to be cremated." Nevertheless, she accepted his word. The next day Arthur busied himself having the body embalmed and making arrangements for it to be taken, first to Grand Rapids, then to Detroit.

The only time he did not seem his normal charming, helpful, and urbane self was when Dr. Cornell called to pay his respects. Arthur was irritable and offhand with him. In fact, he refused initially to let him see the body of his old friend who, according to the death certificate, had died, like Mrs. Peck, of kidney disease. His behaviour was so uncharacteristically brusque that Dr. Cornell commented upon it that evening to his sister. That comment was to lead to Arthur's undoing.

Arthur and his wife—plus the coffin—set out by train for the Middle West at five o'clock the next morning. The family party waiting at Grand Rapids station included Percy Peck, Clara's elder brother, and Aunt Catherine Peck. Aunt Catherine—unaware at this stage that Arthur had set out at one time to kill her with germs, arsenic and ground glass—was her usual friendly self. But Percy seemed hostile and withdrawn.

Nobody thought that too strange. Percy had lost his father and mother in the space of six weeks. Over and above the natural grief and shock, he and Arthur had never really got on too well. Percy had something else on his mind, however. That morning he had received an anonymous telegram, later discovered to have come from Mrs. Hardwicke, saying: "Don't allow cremation until an autopsy has been carried out."

"Everything's fixed," Arthur announced efficiently. "I've arranged for poor Dad's body to go right on to Detroit to be cremated. I'll go with it and see this sad business finished. Would any of you folks like to come with me?" Percy, however, wanted to do more than that. "Just a minute," he said bluntly. "I guess we aren't in all that hurry to see the last of Father. I'll see to the coffin."

Arthur professed to be puzzled. "I can't understand what that brother of yours is up to," he said to Clara, as they hurried off to see the family lawyer about her father's will. "Why can't he let poor old Dad have his last wish carried out?" Then, as they travelled back to New York later that day, Arthur had recaptured his customary good spirits. Dad had left more than a million dollars, including a bequest of $2000 to Arthur's father "out of regard for his son".

Bombshell news

Back on Riverside Drive, Arthur's high spirits did not last long. First came the bombshell news that Percy had asked for an autopsy. Newspaper reporters descended on Arthur's doorstep. Others were let loose in New York, Michigan, Glasgow, and South Africa. Gradually it emerged that Arthur was by no means the straightforward pillar of respectability that he claimed to be. There was another, and twisted, side to his personality.

As a boy he had been in trouble several times over thefts from his parents, relatives, employers, schoolmates and others. While at the dental college at the University of Michigan, Ann Arbor, he had been expelled from his fraternity for an act of dishonesty. He had used false papers to help him get a quick degree at Glasgow University, so that he could practise in South Africa.

In South Africa itself his attempt to marry an heiress had been foiled by her father on the grounds of Arthur's "unsavoury reputation". As the dossier built up, the New York newspapers suggested pointedly that the $20,000 he had brought home from South Africa could not have been come by honestly. Finally, the Press broke the story that—married less than six months, and in the process of murdering his father-in-law—Arthur had also been carrying on a passionate affair with a married singer named Margaret Horton.

In the middle of this trial by publicity, Arthur, beginning to feel desperate, telephoned Aunt Catherine at her New York apartment. His voice sounded strained. "What is the best thing for a man to do who has been cornered?" he asked. "Do you think suicide would be the right thing?"

Aunt Catherine counselled him against it. But it was the course he decided to take when the news was ultimately released that five grains of arsenic had been found in old Mr. Peck's body after

several days of tests. On March 23 police, who had him under surveillance by now, broke into the Riverside Drive apartment and found Arthur dying from a drug overdose. He was rushed, sobbing "not to be taken to prison", to Bellevue Hospital, where his life was saved.

In the dock Arthur listened good-humouredly—very much the man-of-the-world—as witnesses unfolded this tale. From time to time he gave an amused chuckle. As a dentist, it was explained, he had bought the arsenic quite openly, claiming that he wanted it to "kill a cat". Books about the uses and effects of arsenic had been found in his flat with the pages marked. Initially, however, he had claimed buying the arsenic at Mr. Peck's request.

"He was so wretched about his own life after his wife's death that he implored me to provide him with the means of self-destruction," he explained. "That was all I did. I did not administer the poison to him, nor did I see him take any. But, of course, you won't believe me. I suppose I'll go to the chair."

Arthur, the court learned, had also been caught out in an attempt to bribe two witnesses to keep silent. One was Dora, his Negress maid. He had offered her $1000 not to reveal that she had seen him "putting white powder into Mr. Peck's food". The other was Eugene Kane, an embalmer, who asserted that Arthur had given him $9000 to say there had been arsenic in the embalming fluid injected into Mr. Peck's body.

Small embalmer

The appearance of the small, bespectacled embalmer clearly tickled Arthur's fancy, and he burst out laughing several times during Kane's testimony. Kane explained how Arthur had come out of a telephone booth and "pushed a roll of notes in my pocket".

Prosecution: Did you know what it was for?

Kane: No, I thought it must have been for something I had done.

Prosecution: He told you, though, didn't he?

Kane: He said: "Put some arsenic in that fluid and send it down to the District Attorney."

Prosecution: Were you nervous?

Kane: I certainly was.

Prosecution: Did you count the money when you got home?

Kane: No. I tried to, but I was too

A PASSIONATE AFFAIR with married singer Margaret Horton (far right) was to prove Waite's undoing. Her testimony demolished his hopes of pleading insanity. Was she the "more beautiful wife" that the killer had planned to marry after he had murdered Clara (right)?

A FATEFUL TELEGRAM from Mrs. Hardwicke (top right, with Waite's wife Clara) . . . and brother-in-law Percy (above) demands an autopsy on his father.

nervous. I saw some fifties and some hundreds and that's all.

Prosecution: Any large bills?

Kane: Yes, sir. Two five-hundred-dollar bills. I hid the money in a closet. I tried to count it two or three times. Finally, I went to Long Island and buried it. I went to Greenport, 'way to the east end of the island. I don't remember just how long I stayed. I was too nervous.

Prosecution: Did you deliver a sample of embalming fluid to the District Attorney's office?

Kane: Yes.

It was after this exchange that Arthur himself went into the witness-box. He did not refute any of the testimony given against him. Rather, with the aid of his attorney, he did everything in his power to embellish it and blacken himself still further. After he had confessed to the murder of his in-laws, the start of his attempt to murder Aunt Catherine, and his intention one day to murder his wife, his counsel asked: "Why did you want to kill them?"

"For their money," he answered laconically. "I've always needed lots of money, and it has never worried me how I get hold of it." Into his evidence he dropped various asides about himself and the world around him. He confided that he had always considered himself "attractive and charming". "Everyone liked me," he said disarmingly.

Reincarnation was a topic to which he returned frequently. "I believe," he explained, "that, although my body lives in America, my soul lives in secret in Egypt. It is the man from Egypt who has committed these foul crimes." When the prosecution pressed him for details of his other life by the banks of the Nile, however, there was not much he could recall. He mentioned Caesar, Cleopatra, and the pyramids—to the last of which he applied the improbable adjective "voluptuous".

Streak of piety

The whole purpose of this charade—carried through with unflagging style, laced with wit and laughter—was to implant in the minds of the jury the thought: "Surely such a civilized and intelligent man could not have carried out the crimes to which he has confessed so freely and, at the same time, be sane?" One entire day towards the end of the trial was taken up with a series of witnesses paying tribute to Arthur's impeccable manners and gentle heart.

He had a strong streak of piety in him, some stated, and had attended church regularly while in the process of poisoning his relatives. An alienist told the court that Arthur had informed him: "Miss Peck said that, when she remembered how beautifully I had sung hymns in church while my wife's relations were visiting us, she could not believe that I committed the crimes. It was my real self

that appeared then."

"Whatever they may say of me," he announced on one occasion, "I pride myself on being kind and always giving water to flowers so they will not die. They are beautiful. This is nature."

There were, of course, experts for the defence to say that a man who could murder in such cold blood, and talk about it afterwards in such a carefree manner, could not be sane. And there were prosecution experts to assert that Arthur gave the normal responses and *was* sane. The judge finally ruled in favour of the prosecution. He had, in part, been swayed by his irritation over Arthur's constant smile. But far more vital was the evidence of Margaret Horton.

Between February 22 and March 18, Arthur and the singer had spent many hours together in a studio she rented at the Hotel Plaza in New York. According to her husband, Harry Horton, a 56-year-old dealer in war supplies: "They were brought together by a mutual interest in art and modern languages. She made the kind of mistake any young woman might be guilty of. I personally am ready to forgive her."

It was Mrs. Horton's disclosures that robbed him of any slender chance he might have had of escaping the death sentence. At the time when rumours and innuendos about Arthur were being voiced, she remembered his inviting her

HIS SUICIDE ATTEMPT (below) a failure, Waite lives to face damaging testimony. Among the witnesses is embalmer Kane (far right) who alleges bribery.

to his laboratory—where he showed her various tiny germs wriggling under a microscope.

She had brought everything out into the open by asking: "You didn't really do it, did you, Arthur?"

"Yes," he had answered. "It's true. I did."

After his arrest, Arthur had sent her a letter which she subsequently destroyed on the advice of his attorney. Under pressure, however, she had to admit that she could remember some damning words from it. "If they prove it, I suppose it will mean *la chaise*, but I hope and expect to spend a while in detention as an imbecile, and then I'll be free again to join you . . ."

It was this, more than anything else, that impelled the judge to rule that Arthur was not a moral imbecile but was fit to plead: madmen do not, as a rule, show so calculated a faith in the benefits to be derived from their insanity.

Waite was found guilty in May 1916, and sentenced to die in the electric chair at Sing Sing. The case dragged on, however, until the following spring, pending hearings in the Court of Appeals and before a lunacy commission. In the third week of May 1917, both bodies decided that there were no grounds for interfering with the verdict of the lower court.

The condemned man responded with a gesture matching the performance he had put on in court a year earlier. He sent the following letter to Warden Moyer from the death cell:

"Dear Sir: In one of the newspapers today is the statement: 'A. W. Waite to die next week.' On inquiry I learn that you have power to name the day. I am sure you would not be averse to obliging me if you found it possible and reasonable to do so, and I wonder if we could not arrange for Monday of next week. There really is a reason for asking this, although I will not trouble you with explanations. I would be very grateful indeed for this favour. Yours respectfully, Arthur Warren Waite."

This latest touch of bravado convinced many outsiders that, despite what the experts said, he must surely be abnormal to crave as early a death as possible and show so little fear. They were even more convinced when he walked calmly to the chair on the morning of May 24, 1917, with a boyish smile on his somewhat effeminate lips. He was in full control of himself right to the end, reading the Bible and Keats before he was finally taken to the execution chamber. In his cell was later found the beginning of a poem he had started to write. The first two lines read:

Call us with morning faces,
Eager to labour, eager to be happy . . .

At the autopsy—after Waite had been killed with two shocks of 2000 volts each—doctors found the scars of an old meningitis operation on the right side of the cerebellum. This they thought could be the result of a fall or a blow on the head in childhood. But, they added, they did not think that would affect Waite's sanity. The other discovery they made was that he had an abnormally large heart.

TO THE END Waite (below, in police van) was in complete control of himself. He read Keats and the Bible and wrote poetry as he awaited execution.

THE TRIANGLE FIRE

One of the most horrifying disasters in American history leaves 146 people — most of them young girls, garment workers in a 10th-floor Manhattan factory — trapped and burned to a crisp in the building or crushed and broken on the pavements below. The owners, tried for manslaughter, are lucky not to get lynched. . . .

HISTORY records little about the life of 18-year-old Margaret Schwartz, except that she was one of the teeming mass of young girls who were the mainstay of the burgeoning garment industry in New York in the early years of the twentieth century. But it does chronicle the manner of her death, as one among 146 victims destroyed in a frighteningly swift, devouring fire — for it brought two men to trial and led to reforms that helped to improve the lot of America's working women.

Public anger had rarely shown itself in such a seething form as it did that day, in the autumn of 1911, when Max Blanck and Isaac Harris entered New York's old Criminal Court Building — known as the Tombs — to answer to the charge of the manslaughter of Margaret in the first and second degrees.

Hysterical mobs surrounded the grimly hideous building, constructed in mock Egyptian style, and shrieked abuse at the two ashen-faced men. "Murderers!" they screamed. "We want justice!" It was only by the strong-willed efforts of the police that the two defendants were hustled into the court, unharmed.

Many in the roaring crowd were relatives of girls who, like Margaret, had worked for Blanck and Harris at the men's Triangle Waist Company factory — which had occupied the three top floors of the 10-storey Asch Building at Washington Place and Greene Street in lower Manhattan.

Like human torches

There, at a quarter to five in the afternoon of the last Saturday in March, 1911, 600 workers had been trapped by the inferno which reached its peak within a few short minutes of starting. Many of the victims had died leaping, like human torches, from the blaze on to the sidewalks below. All had been buried in a common grave after a five-hour-long funeral procession, watched by 50,000 silently brooding New Yorkers.

Now they sought vengeance at the trial. The preliminary proceedings had suggested that many, if not most, of the dead might still be alive had it not been for the way Blanck and Harris had operated their factory, and their allegedly inhuman treatment of their workers. The mood of the public was that it would not rest, and no city employer must be allowed to rest, until someone had paid for what had happened to the victims.

District Attorney Charles S. Whitman had assigned the leading of the prosecution's case to his two assistants, Bostwick and Rubin. As soon as Justice Thomas Crain had taken his place on the bench, Mr. Bostwick centred his argument upon one single question: what had happened to the ninth-floor exit door on the Washington Place side of the building?

MAX BLANCK.   MAX STEUER.   ISAAC HARRIS.

Defence Will Probably Be Disclaimer of Responsibility as to Conditions in Washington Place Building, Where 146 Persons Lost Their Lives by Fire.

Isaac Harris and Max Blanck, owners of the Triangle Waist Company, were placed on trial yesterday before Judge Thomas C. T. Crain, in the Court of General Sessions, on a charge of manslaughter growing out of the Washington place fire on March 25 last, when 146 men and women lost their lives. There are six separate indictments against each of the men. The specific charge on which they are now being tried is that they caused the death of Miss Margaret Schwartz, of No. 745 Brook avenue. ... employe in their factory.

building which structurally did not conform to the regulations required by the Building Department.

This is the first case of manslaughter based upon the Factory law. That law requires that lessees of a building used for factory purposes shall keep all exits from their factory open during working hours and that such exits shall open on the outside of the building. Failure to comply with these regulations is a misdemeanor. It is alleged that Messrs. Harris and Blanck kept the doors of their factory locked during working hours and on this account the lives of their employes were destroyed. ...

THE ASHEN-FACED defendants (above), charged with manslaughter, were the target of shrieking abuse from the hysterical mob surrounding the Tombs. Many were relatives (right, identifying the dead) of the victims.

His contention was that the two defendants had insisted on that door, like some others, being kept locked. Because of that Margaret Schwartz and many of her fellow workers had been trapped by the fire. To uphold that contention he called to the stand a 17-year-old girl named Katie Wiener, a shirtwaist worker, who had been lucky enough to escape. Katie appeared in deep mourning, for although she had lived through the appalling fire, her elder sister had died in the blaze.

She made a sad spectacle, yet she told her story to the court with a natural and moving dignity. "I heard some cry 'Fire!' but it seemed a long way off," she said. "In less time than I can tell it all became confusion about the ninth floor. Girls ran about shouting and fighting to get out.

Some crowded about the elevators and others about the Greene Street stairway.

"I rushed to the table where my sister worked and she wasn't there. Then I began to cry, but something told me that would be no good, and then I saw my sister near the window. I started to run towards her, but the smoke was so dense that it choked me, and I could not reach her. I shouted to her, but she didn't hear me, and that was the last I saw of her then. I was at a loss to know what to do for a time, but I saw many girls about the Washington Place door and ran there. Just as soon as I started to the Washington Place door someone said: 'Girls, it's no use. The door is locked and we can't get out!'"

Mr. Bostwick nodded grimly but interrupted the narrative to suggest to judge and jury: "Suppose we allow this girl to illustrate just how she tried to pull that door?" The judge inclined his head in agreement, and, with the members of the jury craning forward for a better view, Katie left the stand and walked across to the door at the side of the bench.

Licking flames

There she grasped the door handle and twisted and pulled at it with all the strength she could muster. Suddenly, it seemed, she was re-living those terrible moments when the flames licked around her and her life was in jeopardy.

Mr. Bostwick let the spine-chilling pantomime speak for itself. Then, with the hint of a bow, he ushered Katie back to the witness-stand and the continuation of her story. Softly, she began to speak

again. "It seemed as though I had been standing at that door for three minutes. Again, I saw the Washington Street elevator come up. Once more I was pushed back by the crowd. All around me I saw flames spreading.

"The elevator car was crowded and was on its way downstairs again. I don't remember just how it all happened, but as the car passed the floor the door was left open and I got hold of the cable and swung myself towards the car. I think I landed on top of the car. My feet were up in the air and my head downward. My ankles were hurt. I must have landed on top of a lot of girls. In that way I made my escape and finally reached the street."

The silence in the court was intense. This palpably honest young girl was making people understand—for the first

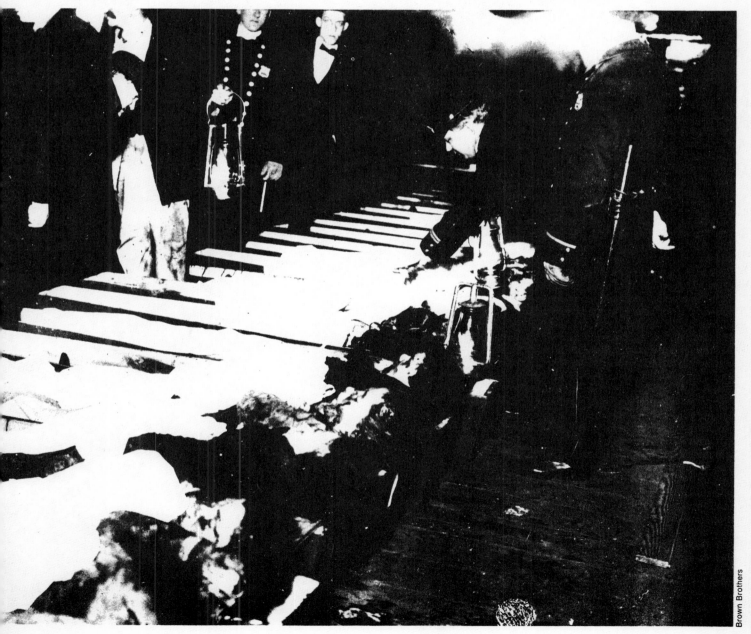

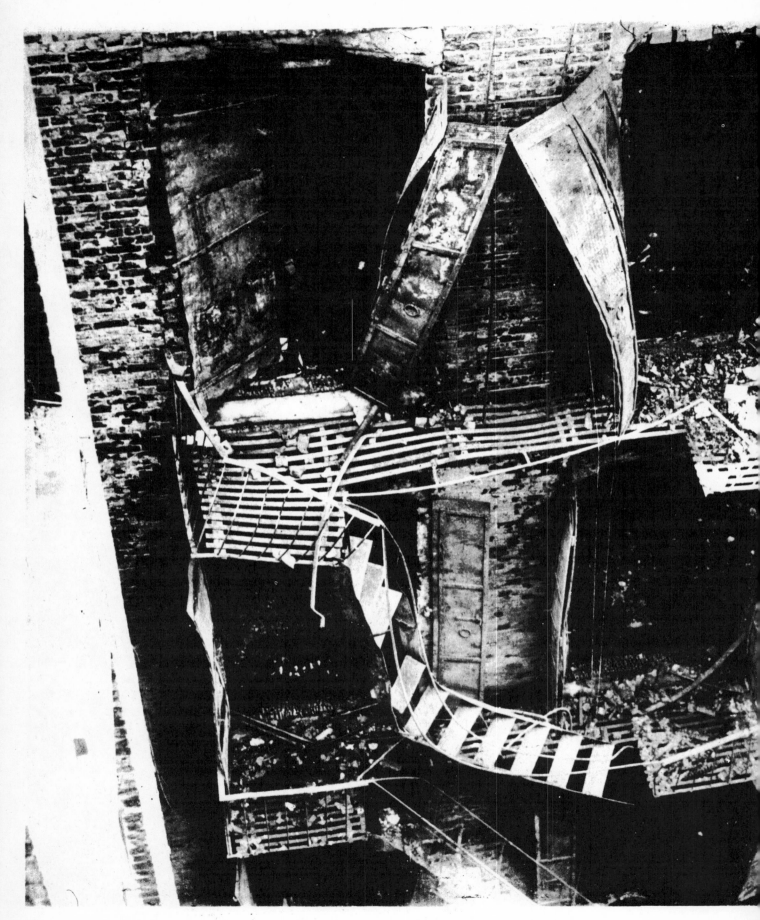

time, and beyond all the previous emotional reactions to the event—just what it meant to confront the bleakly objective face of death. Gently, acutely conscious of the atmosphere in the courtroom, Mr. Bostwick put one final question. "Did you see your sister?" he asked. "Yes," Katie replied. "Yes—but she was dead."

Slowly, Mr. Max D. Steuer, the defence counsel, rose to cross-examine. He was a notable figure of the East Side bar, but, in the atmosphere then reigning in the city, his cause was unpopular. "What was your sister's name?" he asked. "Her name was Rosie," Katie answered and added, "and she was only 18 years old."

Mr. Steuer considered that and then, abruptly, moved his case on to a tack that puzzled many in the courtroom. "Don't you know," he demanded, "that your mother has sued Harris and Blanck for a very large sum of money?" Instantly, Katie responded: "My mother never spoke to me about that."

But it was the locked door that still dominated the prosecution's line of argument. It was locked as a matter of "tradition" in the factory, Mr. Bostwick brought other witnesses to testify, showing that no girl could leave work each evening until she had been searched. Such were the labour relations at the Triangle Company that Mr. Blanck and Mr. Harris acted on the assumption that every employee was intent on stealing the materials on which

Brown Brothers.

"OPEN THE DOOR! Open it! Open it!" But the locks hold as Harris and Blanck's sweatshop goes up in flames like a well-laid bonfire.

they worked—the bits of lawn, lace, muslin and even tissue paper.

Mr. Steuer leapt upon that fact. Was it not a fact, he queried, that some of the women employees habitually came to work carrying suspiciously capacious handbags? Without waiting for an answer, he reached along the lawyers' table and waved aloft such a handbag. Throwing it across to Assistant District Attorney Rubin, he commanded: "Open it and see for yourself how big it is." Mr. Rubin did so and from its interior extracted four silk shirt waists of the kind manufactured at the Triangle factory.

A little dancing

"Oh, yes," said Mr. Bostwick, blandly but somewhat taken aback. "We will concede that the bags carried by the girls were big enough at times to hold shirt-waists such as are shown here to the jury."

However, it was clear that none of this was doing the defence much fundamental good. Mr. Steuer therefore switched his efforts towards showing that the defendants were good employers whose basic decency was being unfairly impugned. He asked another employee, 17-year-old Josie Nicolosi, if she had not known that Mr. Blanck and Mr. Harris had even gone to the extent of installing a phonograph during lunch breaks so that the girls could enjoy a little dancing. But the defence counsel was disconcerted by Josie's answer.

"Oh, yes," she said, "I remember that, but the phonograph only played while there was a strike in the shop. They wanted to treat us very nicely . . . The

AP

moment the strike was over that stopped."

It was apparent to everyone in court that all this was merely a diversion, and that the main road led back to the locked door. The state did its best to keep attention centred on the door, and reserved much of its effort for the appearance of another ninth-floor employee, Kate Alterman, who had been with Margaret Schwartz at the end.

For the drama and clarity with which she told her story, in answer to Mr. Bostwick, she was as impressive as young Katie Wiener had been. She had been in a dressing-room with Margaret when the alarm was given, and she vividly recalled what had happened then:

"We ran out together and saw a great crowd near the door on the Washington Place side. I saw Mr. Bernstein, a brother of the superintendent, trying to open that door, but he couldn't budge it. I ran over to the windows, but there was nothing but flames around them.

Her hair was loose

"I saw Margaret once more—trying to open the door I had just turned away from. I pushed her aside and tried the door myself, but I couldn't open it. It was locked. Margaret was kneeling at the door when I noticed her again, a moment later. Her hair was loose and the hem of her dress was on fire. She was using all her strength to turn the knob. She was tearing at it. Then she screamed: 'The door is locked! I am lost! Open the door! Open it!'"

Kate paused and Mr. Bostwick let the silence make its impression upon the court. Then, finally, he asked, quietly: "And then what became of Margaret?" Kate lowered her eyes and all in the courtroom strained to hear her answer. "That was the last I saw of her," she said.

She continued with the story of what had then happened to herself: "I ran to the sink and wet my hair. I saw Mr. Bernstein flying around like a wildcat, putting his head out of the windows and pulling it back again. Then I took my fur coat, turned it inside and put it on that way. I picked up some unfinished dresses from a table that had not yet caught fire, wet them and wrapped them about my head.

"Purple flames were following me along the floor. My pocketbook, which I had in my hand, caught fire, and I pressed it to my breast to put out the flames. I ran then for the door and the Greene Street side of the building. Flames were all around me, and finally my dress began to burn.

"A girl caught me around the waist as I ran. I begged her to let me go, but she wouldn't. I knew I couldn't save myself if I had to drag her along with me. I struck her, I hit her, I kicked her away from me. I don't know what became of her, but I reached the stairs and I was safe."

When Mr. Steuer opened his cross-examination, everyone waited, tensed, to hear how he would deal with this crucial witness. His approach was surprising. Ignoring, for the most part, the details of the girl's evidence, he concentrated on the suggestion that her story was, as he put it, "so pat" that she must have been carefully rehearsed in it by the prosecution. He made her relate her story over again and hammered at the fact, which he seemed to find so suspicious, that she retold in words almost identical with those she had previously used.

Mr. Steuer worried at the issue like a frustrated terrier vainly seeking to claw a rat from its hole. "Can you," he asked, almost in desperation, "tell that story in other words than those you have told it in?" Kate looked at him with innocent bewilderment. "Tell it in any other words?" she repeated. "I remember it this way, just exactly how it was done."

There were many others who remembered how it was done, such as Fire Chief Worth, who found that the extension ladders of his fire-trucks reached only to the sixth storey, and who ordered a jumping net to be spread. To his horror, three girls leapt together from the ninth floor so that when they struck the net they had gained a velocity which produced an impact equivalent to 16 tons.

"Nobody could hold a net when those girls from the ninth floor came down," the fire officer told the court. "There were so many bodies hitting the ground that it was impossible to see them. You just did not see them. You heard the impact of the bodies hitting the ground." But he and others did see one heart-tearing spectacle: a man and a girl, sheathed in flames, jumping to their deaths while tightly embraced in each other's arms.

The court was told how it was on the Washington Place side of the building. There an elevator—weighted beyond all possible limits by the frenzied girls who had packed into it and jumped onto its roof—gave way and plummeted to the foot of the shaft, shattering the bodies of many of the would-be escapers.

Shrieking down the shaft

The jury heard how one elevator man had rushed from the building in panic, and his place had at once been taken by a man passing by in the street. This gallant helper operated the elevator on a series of trips, bringing around 30 girls a time to safety, until the fire finally made any further ascent impossible. When that happened, he said, desperate girls still caught in the blaze fell shrieking down the shaft.

Beyond all else the tragedy was made poignant by the fact that, as witnesses testified, work at the Triangle factory was just finishing for the day as the blaze began. Its source, too, was known. It had

THE IMPACT of bodies hitting the ground adds to the fearful din. Relatives (below) are lucky to get $75 compensation. Most get none at all.

broad and strong, and at the top of the
flight was a large door which was easily
opened by those who went in that direction.

Theoretically the employes, well posted
through frequent fire drills, should have
used these methods of escape. In practice
the most of them staggered over machines
and chairs, cut off from flight by the flames
which were converting the stairs into a
very flue. Some there were who were
rigid where they sat at their machines or
were flung suffocated to the floor, to be
trodden upon by panic-stricken fellow
workers.

Women and girls, terror maddened,
faced the windows seeking air and aid,
most of them were roaring Tophet, before,
whose death in the brick walled abyss.
Some made the choice, others were instinctively hurled off the window ledges
by the crazed and stifling throngs at their
backs, clamoring for air. In twos and
threes the women and girls dropped from
the sills, hurtled through the air and fell
to the pavements, where they lay shattered messes of riven flesh and protruding
bones.

The sound of the fearful impacts which
came like hail of death, caused men to
hide faces and women operators to sink
to their knees on the flags and moan over
the calamity.

The response to the first alarm had
been prompt and efficient and soon the
street was gorged with engines, trucks and
towers, which followed each other with
precision to the fourth alarm. The firemen shouted and gesticulated and climbed
ladders with them not to leap. In twos and
threes of the Fire Department would reach
out to the seventh floor, and before the
firemen could get even that far scores
had gone to their deaths on the flagging
of the street. It was the carnage of battle
which killed those short blocks in Washington place and Greep street.

Perish by Twos and Threes

The women employes hurled themselves
by twos and threes to their doom, descend-
ing with hair and clothing ablaze. Here
in the valley of the shadow of death
they had been a mass of humdrum trade,
the ashes of the victims were blackened,
which contrasted with the pallor of their
faces. There was no time to perform the
offices of the dead, for uncovered they lay
and their faces to the sky. In one window
of disaster were counted fifty-three
dead.

Three young women, fully dressed for
leaving the factory, with the exception of
putting on their hats, met death locked
arm in arm. They were employed in the
Triangle Shirt Waist factory, and evidently were close friends in the work.

The first crowd that gathered in the
street below saw them standing on the
ledge of a window imploring for help for
one to come to their assistance. They
were seen to converse with each other,
and, as if they were advising the best
course to pursue. One of them looked

then to remove the bodies of the dead
that were strewn all over the street. Part
of the water played on the building was
dashed back upon the bodies in the street,
and the gutters were crimson. When
coffins were rushed to the scene the bodies
were picked up and placed in them, and
a card attached with a number for the
purpose of identification.

Firemen and ambulance surgeons who
assisted in this work were horrified on
finding two girls alive at the bottom of
the heap of victims killed when the fire
net proved inadequate. One of the girls
was found to be breathing as she was
lifted up and the other gave evidence of
life just as she was laid in a coffin. The
two girls had been left beneath the bodies
of their dead companions for twenty min-

Dr. Keefe, of St. Vincent's Hospital,
hailed a passing taxicab and the two
girls were hurried to the hospital. One
tried to narrate her harrowing experience.
Soon afterward she lapsed into unconsciousness, and both of them died within
an hour after they entered the hospital.
Their bodies were not identified.

DOCTOR HUNTER ATTENDING FRED.
RUTT, AN INJURED FIREMEN.

BODIES COVERED WITH
CANVAS ON SIDEWALK.

MISS CLOTILDE
TERRANOVA

TAGGING BODIES ON PIER, FOOT OF EAST TWENTY-
SIXTH STREET, WHICH WAS USED AS A MORGUE.

SCORES SAVED BY ELEVATOR RUNNERS

**Joseph Zito and Joseph Gaspary De-
scribe Scenes of Panic in the
Burning Building.**

Two elevator operators, their clothing
burning and their faces and hands
scorched by flames, staggered out of the
building twenty minutes after the fire
started. The conduct of each was last
night acclaimed as heroic, and the police
reports gave them credit for rescuing
more than a hundred young women from
certain death. They were Joseph Zito,
twenty-three years old, and Joseph Gaspary, twenty-five, both foreign born.

To this modest list of two names, others
will be added to-day and to-morrow when
more details of yesterday's disaster become known.

Zito and Gaspary were standing in their
respective elevator cars, resting at the
ground floor of the building, when at a
quarter before four o'clock
both heard shouts of "fire" and a shower
of splintered glass rained down upon them
from the shaft doors leading from the
upper three stories of the building.

"The building's on fire!" shouted one of
them, and a few seconds later they were
at the eighth floor, where a swaying and
struggling crowd of young women
fought to gain entrance to the elevators
and be carried to the street and safety
below. Each operator made four or five
trips, and ceased in their work of rescue
only when the mechanism of the elevators
became disordered.

Elevator Hero Describes Panic.

"At the first alarm of fire," said Zito
last night, "Gaspary and myself ran our
elevators up to the eighth floor, where
in front of the door were hundreds of
young women. Mr. Max Blanck, one of
the owners of the Triangle Waist Company, was standing there, holding the
young women in check as best he could.
Mr. Blancke shouted to me to run the
elevator until she came, and then I heard
him yell, 'Let the women go down first.'

"When I opened the elevator door
leading to the eighth floor all I could
see were the girls and men and behind
them great flames and clouds of smoke.
Fully twenty women crowded into my
elevator on the first trip and as many
more came down with me on the second
trip. When I went to the floor the third
time I could see some of the girls standing on the window sills surrounded by
fire, but they seemed so terror stricken
that they didn't hear the shouts of Mr.
Blancke and other men on the floor who
called to them not to jump.

"After the third car load had been
taken to the street I started up the
fourth time and, hearing screams and
shouts from the ninth floor, I ran my
elevator there. The girls were more
frightened there than were those on
the eighth floor. Gaspary also made a
trip to the ninth floor, but after the
fourth trip I could not go by the
eighth floor as the girls would jump
on my elevator and I was afraid, to
cause the door was open, that they
would fall into the shaft.

"Perhaps both of us made more than
five trips, but I can't say for sure."

Hundreds Escaped by Stairs.

Zito said that several hundred persons
escaped by way of the stairs, which
were adjacent to the elevator shaft on
both the Washington place and Greene
street sides of the building. Also the
elevator operators, who ran the freight
elevators on the Greene street side,
made several trips to the burning floors
and carried scores of women to the
street. The freight elevators were not
so swift, however, as those on the
Washington place side.

When the mechanism of the elevators
became disordered there were fully three
hundred young women and men still
trapped on the eighth, ninth and tenth
floors. Among these was Mr. Blanck, who
had left his wife and two daughters in
the firm's office on the tenth floor, hurry-
ing, at the first alarm of fire, to the operating room on the eighth floor. Caught
in the struggling crowd which blocked the
stairway between the eighth and ninth
floors, Mr. Blanck found it impossible to
the office. De-
scribing his experience late, Mr.
Blanck said that he rushed to the seventh
floor, believing that perhaps his wife and

building had gone safe-
ly. Unable to find them
had given them up as lost
Among the workers
were a number who had
to escape by way of the
stairs rushed to the roof of
their way to the windows
where later they were
bodies were found in the

Half Down Elev

Half crazed with frigh
uninjured. Human
was cut off by No. 62 Pav
a cutter employed by
Company, was found
elevator shaft about the
last shaft. For four
clinging to the drum
water up to his waist,
the exit from the
escape by the windows
off. He told his
eight hundred persons,
girls, on the tenth floor

He was taken to St.
where an examination
had been applied, he re-
to tell a fairly coheren
comings on the tenth
of fire spread through
was found by Battalion
five men who were safe
floor. Hearing feeble
the cellar, they ladd
through a door on the
side and reached below
with ladders and gave
prise of their lives nov
able to walk. For hour
were carrying the dead
all parts of the building
reached the street he be
"I was working on
eight hundred other per
the cry of fire," said M
seen more than a few
heard it that the flame
from the windows. The
coming from the shaft
who were among the fir
doors were driving bac
Women screamed and
humping and then they
are who would jump in
windows to the street

"As I recall it now
half a dozen trips and
many women as we co
men in my vicinity als
whom the elevator faile
was a case of each one
could describe the frenz
the tenth floor.

"It seems as if I hav
place for weeks listenin
As a last resort I ju
elevator shaft and crept
to the bottom. When
pouring down on the f
being drowned, and if th
ened me they would have
The water was too muc
have clung to the drum
lot of people jumped
shaft and their bodies fa
top of it, I thought I
for a dozen hours."

Mcabell's hands were to
the cable.

Girl Slides to

A miraculous escape
related by Miss Cecilia
waist with company.
Stanton street. She is
jured in St. Vincent's I
recover.

The young woman wa
floor of the building who
get into an elevator
hers ceased running an
young woman leaped to
companion, she said, fo
fell. Of her own tori
top of the elevator car
below, she remembered
Pathetic scenes were
the Mercer street police
the catastrophe. The pl
of relatives and friends
ployed in the Triangle
were sent to police
to send inquirers to the
injured. Housie Horowit
street, living at No. 98
street, walked into the
for her brother, Maur
placed as a shipper. He
the first to escape by
from the eighth floor.
While she pleaded wit
sought their assistance
tered the police station,
the crowd lining the
roof.

Runs Frantic Thro

While the fire was
young girl, with hair di
clothing almost torn fro
through Broadway, sc
more and gave to her
for the first intimation of
from the scenes of disas
which she had escaped,
out between street cars
the crowd lining the str
"Don't let them hurt n
hurt me."

She was taken to a dru
she was quieted she sai
Dougherty, of No. 28 Ea
She said:
"We were all ready to
having finished our work
most of us had on our
called 'Fire!' and the cre
the room was filled with
knew which way to turn
fire of girls running to
room, where I knew the
located. I followed. The
ahead of me and knew t
to get out that way. I f
the elevator, when I hea
out, 'My God, they sav
up again.'

Rescued by Ope

"I grew weak and c
on the floor when little
office boy, took hold of m
past me, saying, 'Come
that's the only way.' I
found no way along, but
two other girls who had t
stairway leading to the r
prayer when I saw the ce
and fell on my knees.
"I had only been there
another girl turned back
me to come on. I arose
There were about twent
the Cohen boy, in the r
for the roof of another b
arms. I understood all
lower college students th
University Law School.
Through fear I clung to
the irony of it and tho
girls left behind would r
Miss Dougherty was a fri
in a textile factory and

---

other bills of five and ten dollar
values. Surmising that other bills
were hidden and possibly the woman's
pay, and as the search is examined
more closely and along the shoes
stockings, resulting in discovery of
Up to a late hour last night no
identified the woman.

Miss Terranova, one of the dead, was
daughter of Calogero Terranova, of
President street, Brooklyn. Her
father seriously ill and it is feared that
shock of his daughter's death will result fatally. She was expected home early
yesterday because of her father's illness.

START INQUIRY TO-DAY TO
LEARN CAUSE OF FIRE

**Man Who Escapes Tells of Terror
When Cry of "Fire!" Rings Out
in Factory.**

To determine the exact cause of the
fire it had not been ascertained late
last night by several firemen working
under special orders of Fire Chief Croker,
an exhaustive inquiry will be instituted
to-day, when women and men who escaped from the building will be questioned.

The Triangle Waist Company occupied
the three upper floors of the structure, a
newly completed ten story fireproof loft
building. From all accounts gathered
the employes of the firm the blaze started on the eighth floor in a corner of the
loft room nearest the elevators and
stairway on the Greene street side. This
part of the factory was given over entirely to the shirt waist operators and cutters. There were about five hundred persons at work on the eighth floor when the
fire started.

Rothen, of No. 92 Washington
street, the Bronx, a cutter, furnished
police with the most accurate description of the start of the blaze.
"With sixty other cutters I was at
work over long benches and tables
which were placed on the Greene street
side of the room," said Rothen. "The
cutters had the places nearest the windows because of the necessity for light.
To the best of my knowledge every man

OFFICES
SHOW ROOMS
AND
SHIPPING DEPARTMENTS

MACHINE
OPERATORS

WHERE
FIRE
STARTED

BUILDING AT NORTHWEST CORNER OF EAST
WASHINGTON PLACE AND GREENE STREET, THE
THREE TOP FLOORS IN WHICH LOSS OF LIFE
OCCURRED, WERE COMPLETELY DESTROYED.

space for an area three a
square feet in area three a
required and for some ad
stairways. Furthermore,
stairways were required for
exceeding the 10,000 square

Might Have Saved

If that code had been ad-
garded as almost certain the
escapes would have been re-
Washington place building.
fire escapes would have been
all buildings, of more than
in height.

In the building code in e
entirely with the Departmen
to order such fire escapes a
factory building safe. The
under the jurisdiction of
Ahern, President of Manha
who appointed the present
of the bureau, Rudolph P.

Section 103 of the code pro
buildings occupied by three
lies, and including factorie
and other structures, 'shal
with such good and sufficie
capes, stairways or other m
in case of fire as shall be re
Department of Buildings; an
ment shall have full and exc
and authority within the cit
escapes and other means of
provided upon or within su
It is further provided that a
must be kept free from encu
a fine is prescribed for pla
tions on a fire escape. An
ment is that 'all such buil
equipped with stationary iron
ing to a suitable opening to t
Cyrus W. Miller, pres
Borough of the Bronx, was
Washington place disaster
of it by a Herald reporter.
When told that there was
escape for the entire ten stor
said he could not understand
condition was allowed to exi

"One fire escape certainly
vide sufficient egress for a bu
size," he said, "and I am su
have been some other means
well. The law provides tha
ings shall have fire escapes
rear and the enforcement o
is within the province of the
ment. The fact that there
and stairways was enough to
tion.

"I recall that not long ago
owner a building about six st
the Bronx was ordered to
ment to place a fire es
front. There were are alread
and the owner of the building
was enough, so he came
whether I couldn't get the or

The Dead and the Injured

body burned off wore
on left hand. Body

woman, about twenty-
height five feet seven
face, black hair,
coat, black trousers.
Body

women, twenty-four
ve feet two
air, white head ear-
waist and skirt, black
on left hand bear-
Body No. 11 at

woman, twenty-five
feet three inches in
button shoes; most of
off. Body No. 34 at

woman, twenty-seven
aist, black stockings
shoes, imitation gold
inch in height; red
on shoes, black stock-
so at Morgue.
woman, fifteen years old,
ned off except black
ck laced shoes; body
Body No. 2 at the

woman, thirty years
clothing burned off;
on left hand; appar-
body No. 26 at the

woman, about twenty-
ve feet six inches in
air, eyes and coat
12 at the Morgue.

INJURED.

A.
boys, twenty-one years
home street; shock,

B.
twenty years old,
opher street; cut by
oken home.

F.
Fannie, twenty-one
waist maker, No. 354
Brooklyn; fell down
and internal in-
me. Will recover.

G.

Disastrous Fires and Lives Lost

Victims' Friends Besiege M

AP

THE SURVIVORS attend memorial ceremonies 50 years later. Among them: Josie Nicolosi (second from right), who testified at the trial that her employers' one good deed was forced by a strike.

broken out in a rag bin between two cutting tables, and the most likely explanation was a carelessly discarded cigarette butt. Waste was stacked knee-deep in the factory so that the whole building resembled a perfectly prepared bonfire.

It was this monstrous fire hazard that made the question of exit from the factory so important. Mr. Steuer called a series of witnesses to testify to the claim that even if the ninth-floor door had been locked, it could quickly have been opened—since a key, secured by a piece of string, was kept permanently in the lock.

Commissioner John Williams, of the Department of Labour, told the court that a factory inspection of the premises, just before the fire, had been satisfactory. But although some additional safety recommendations had been made, these were passed to a telephone operator and not directly to Blanck and Harris themselves.

Other evidence then came out which did not do any credit to the two accused men and their sweatshop. It was said that labour relations at the factory had continually been bad. When workers had turned to strike action as their only effective means of protest, the company had hired thugs to beat up pickets, and prostitutes to harass and intimidate women employees with street-corner abuse. Heavy fines, it was said, were levied against workers for material they allegedly damaged, and girls had even been charged for the needles with which they sewed.

The prosecution also contended that some "damaging witnesses" who would have been called had been blackmailed by the company by the sudden offer of pay rises. The factory superintendent, it was said, had even personally threatened some of the employees at the time of the earlier grand jury hearing.

In his summing-up Judge Crain reminded the jury that the charge was manslaughter in either the first or second degree. But, to give that substance, it had positively to be shown that culpable negligence on the defendants' part led directly to Margaret Schwartz's death. On the central issue of the locked door the judge emphasized that the jury needed to be satisfied that it was, in fact, locked. And, moreover, that it was locked with the full knowledge of the defendants.

"It was murder!"

This was the first time that the essence of the law had intruded into what had otherwise been an emotional occasion. From their expressions, it seemed that some members of the jury had only suddenly realized the extent of the responsibility they carried. They trooped thoughtfully out, and returned an hour and 40 minutes later to deliver their verdict. It came as a shock to most of the spectators, if not to some of the lawyers. Blanck and Harris, the jury declared, were not guilty.

Outside the court building the unofficial "jury" of the mob was waiting to make its own verdict known. "Not guilty! Not guilty!" the crowd shrieked in a new wave of incredulity and rage. "It was murder, murder!" Little Katie Wiener's brother, David, collapsed with hysterics and was taken to hospital.

The howling for "justice" was heard by the two terrified Triangle company owners. The fear of a lynching was clearly etched on their faces. Accordingly, the police smuggled Blanck and Harris out through a back entrance of the court building and off to safety.

So far as the criminal law went, the Triangle fire case was over—later, the families of 23 girl victims each collected $75 in full settlement of all claims. But at least it gave rise, indirectly, to measures intended to avoid future repetitions of the sweatshop conditions.

A state commission was set up to investigate factory operations. As a result of this, radical new controls over buildings and fire hazards were introduced.

Limitations on women's hours of work came into force, and—learning from the experience of its members involved in the Triangle tragedy—the recently formed International Ladies Garment Workers' Union commenced the growth and development that was to make it one of America's foremost labour unions.

For years the Richardson brothers and their gang of vicious hoodlums terrorized all south London with their remorseless violence. For the sake of "security" they beat and mutilated all potential informers—calmly munching fish and chips as their victims bled and writhed in agony. Any juror would have been brave indeed to vote for conviction. . . .

THE FRATERNITY OF TORTURE

THE most notable factor about the appearance of 32-year-old Charles William Richardson in the prisoner's dock of London's Central Criminal Court was that it ever happened at all. Many people —especially senior officers of Scotland Yard—had long thought it the proper place for Richardson to be. But most had suffered the frustrating belief that he would never be seen there—and Charles William Richardson himself had held it, as a matter of faith, that he would never cross the Old Bailey's threshold.

Not only was he among the most vicious of London's criminal thugs, but he was one of a select underworld band who had taken almost total security measures to ensure that no witness would dare to point a finger at them and say: "These men are evil—and I can prove them to be so."

In Richardson's case the "security measures" involved torture to "persuade" the would-be informers to maintain their silence. So it was that Richardson was as much surprised as the authorities, that

TORTURE CHAMBER and "office", this seedy warehouse in a remote south London suburb was often the end of the line for victims of the Richardson gang who were recruited in the Astor Club (below).

April day in 1967, when he found himself arraigned for trial.

With seven of his henchmen—the "Richardson Gang"—he stood charged with the violence and intimidation with which he had built, over several years, a criminal empire in the densely packed tenement and high-rise housing estate areas of London that stretch south from the Thames.

On the charge sheet he was described as a "company director". But, as the evidence was to show, his "company" consisted of a motley collection of executives who made their profits from shady deals, and whose "labour relations" were based upon the theory that dissident employees or business associates were best kept in line by being stripped naked and given electric shock treatment.

Latter-day Capone

Richardson moved in a criminal world that was a scaled-down replica of the Prohibition era of Chicago and its mobs, and he liked to think of himself as a kind of latter-day Al Capone. As he stepped into the dock in his £50 suit there was an air of arrogance on his chubby features. This was reinforced by the deliberately careless manner in which he bore his stocky, boxerlike frame. When the charges of violence were put to him he snapped out: "Not guilty."

The Crown had decided to concentrate on the torture and other forms of violence, and not upon the actual criminal activities of the Richardson gang. Mr. Sebag Shaw, leading the prosecution, made that clear to the jury in the first few moments of his opening speech. Charles Richardson, he told the 11 men and one woman in the jurybox, was the dominant leader of a "somewhat disreputable business fraternity" who operated through a number of phoney companies.

"But," he said, with a wave of his arm, "this case is not about dishonesty or fraud; it is about violence and threats of violence. Not, let me say, casual acts of violence, committed in sudden anger—but vicious and brutal violence systematically inflicted, deliberately and cold-bloodedly and with utter and callous ruthlessness."

Beatings and torture of people who upset Richardson—or who were even suspected of jeopardizing his "business" career—ensured that no one ever complained to the authorities about south London gangsterism. Such methods had succeeded for years until, finally, some of the sufferers had told their disgruntled stories to the police.

The first of the alleged victims to be seen by the jury was Jack Duval, born in Russia in 1919, and a one-time French legionnaire. He acknowledged that he had come to the Old Bailey that day from prison, where he was serving a three-year sentence for an airline tickets fraud.

Duval was asked to recall a day in 1960, and did so in tones that suggested it was the unluckiest day of his life. That was the day on which he was first introduced to Richardson—in the Astor Club, off London's Berkeley Square. Very soon he was serving his apprenticeship as European representative for one of the gang's "companies"—whose main purpose was to import Italian-made nylon stockings on credit and then omit to pay the bills. His efforts were not of a high standard, and he was recalled to London.

He duly reported to the Richardson headquarters in south London's Camberwell, where he was greeted by Edward Richardson, the gang leader's younger brother, who "punched me in the face. Then, when I fell down, I was beaten with golf clubs. When I asked what I had done to deserve that, Edward Richardson said, 'You just do as Charlie tells you.'"

Later, still serving as a loyal employee, he was sent to Germany to order goods on credit for the Common Market Merchants Ltd.—another of the Richardsons' concerns.

"I was in Germany for about eight weeks," said Duval wistfully. Then, once again, his return to "head office" turned out to be a far from festive occasion. The greeting he received from Charles Richardson was in the traditional gang fashion. "As I entered the Camberwell office," said Duval, "Mr. Richardson hit me with his fist, and I still have the mark on the side of my nose from his ring."

Relating his ordeal

Members of the jury peered at Duval to see the scar. But, in the excitement of relating his ordeal, he was moving his head too rapidly from side to side. "When I came to," he recalled, "I found I had been relieved of my watch, ring and wallet containing 200 dollars. Mr. Richardson was sitting behind his big desk with chairs all around, like a court."

But "Mr. Richardson" was far from behaving with the decorum of a judge. He was, in fact, selecting knives from a canteen of cutlery, and throwing them in the direction of a Mr. Alfred Blore—the manager of Common Market Merchants. The knives, some of which were striking Blore in the arm, were intended to draw Blore's attention to his business failings.

According to Duval, Richardson "kept saying to Blore: 'I'm the boss and if I tell you what to do you will do it.' Mr. Blore asked, 'What have I done, Charlie?' Naturally, I was quiet; sitting in my corner. Mr. Blore was screaming: 'Don't do it to me!'" The crux of the matter, Duval explained to the jury, was that "Mr. Blore came in as a director of Common Market Merchants and he did not want to run the company under the orders of Mr. Charles Richardson."

Other cronies of Richardson, minor "executives" of the company, had been lurking on the fringes of the bizarre Camberwell office-cum-courtroom, and two were ordered to go to Common Market Merchants' office in Cannon Street (in the square-mile business section of London called "the City") "and collect the stock and books and make it look as if there had been a robbery". The reason for that, Duval drily testified, was that by then Mr. Blore "was covered in blood", and if any questions were asked it would be said that he had been attacked during the supposed robbery.

Mr. Geoffrey Crispin, defending Richardson, suggested that it was Duval, and *not* Charles Richardson, who was the real gang leader. Duval agreed that he had lived a life of fraud, involving large sums of money. But he denied that in the fraudulent companies run by the gang he was, as Mr. Crispin put it, "the guvnor".

A guest of Her Majesty

Sharply, Duval told the lawyer: "I have never been the boss. I have worked for Charles Richardson because I had to." But, continued Mr. Crispin, Duval was hoping to receive a large sum of money by selling his life story to the newspapers. Duval had a swift answer to that. "I am," he said, haughtily, "at present a guest of Her Majesty and cannot indulge in any business activities while I am in prison."

Duval was followed into the witness box by a nervous, 38-year-old Polish-born businessman, Bernard Wajcenberg, whose dealings with Richardson and his "firm" had also been of an unhappy nature. He, it appeared, had sought business "references" about Richardson from the police—a move which had met with Richardson's disapproval. At a meeting in the notorious Camberwell office—at which Wajcenberg was "so paralyzed with fear I could not speak"—Richardson told him: "You have ratted by making inquiries about me from the police. If you don't pay £5000 you will not get out of this office alive."

To add weight to his threat, Richardson showed Wajcenberg a cupboard stocked with knives, axes, and a shotgun. Hoarsely, the witness told the jury: "Richardson grabbed me by the lapels and said, 'When I go berserk you know what happens.'" Wajcenberg did know and took swift steps to borrow £3000, which Richardson accepted in settlement.

ARROGANCE characterized the tough appearance of Charles Richardson (left), which was reinforced by the careless way he carried himself. Charles was sentenced to 25 years, his brother Edward, who was already in prison, 10.

Derek John Lucien Harris, another business associate of Richardson's, was not so fortunate as Wajcenberg. He had been selected as victim for the most sophisticated form of torture employed by the "firm"—torture by electric shock. Harris testified that this had happened in June, 1964, when he was negotiating the sale of a company to Richardson, and called at the Camberwell office to collect money owing to him.

Since Richardson was in the habit of receiving, rather than paying, money, this was an unwise approach by Harris—who was taken by some of the gang's gorillas to a nearby warehouse. There Richardson greeted him with the pained comment: "I like you, Lucien, and I don't want to hurt you." Then, aided by another member of the gang, he proceeded to beat Harris up. On tiring of that, the gang boss muttered orders to a couple of his men, who left and returned a few minutes later. One carried a parcel of scampi; the other a hand-operated electric generator of the type used for testing car spark-plugs.

Bound and gagged

"Everyone," Harris recalled, "began eating. After he had finished, Charles Richardson screwed his thumbs in my eyes. It was very painful, and I could not see for some moments. On Richardson's instructions my shoes were removed, and my toes were wired up to the generator. Roy Hall [another member of the gang] turned the handle, and the shock caused me to jump out of my chair, and I fell to the floor.

"After that I was stripped except for my shirt, and the shock treatment was repeated. As I rolled on the floor Richardson said the generator wasn't working very well and orange squash was poured over my feet. Then I was bound and gagged and given further electric shocks to various parts of my body. Finally, Richardson said I was to be taken to the marshes where I gathered I would be killed and dumped under a pile of refuse."

As he was dressing after the "treatment", Harris said, Richardson pinned his left foot to the floor with a knife. On the instructions of the judge, Mr. Justice Lawton, Harris then removed the shoe and sock from his left foot and rested the foot on a chair in the witness box. For the next 10 minutes the attention in the courtroom was wholly concentrated on the Harris foot. First the judge came down from his bench to examine it, then the members of the jury filed past it, in pairs. Finally, it was surrounded by the barristers on both sides of the trial, Crown and defence.

Two scars were visible on the foot, and Harris pointed to each during the inspections and repeated, again and again: "The knife went in there and came out here."

TORTUR
CHAIR

Counsel tel
pattern of vi

'.. WHEN ANYONE INCURRED
OF CHARLES WILLIAM RIC

Evening News rep
Stephen Claypole, John
Aldo Nicolott

THE 17 ACCUSED

THE accused are:

Charles William Richardson, aged 32, company director, of Acland Crescent, Denmark Hill.
His wife, Mrs. Jean Richardson.
Roy Hall, aged 25, metal sorter of Rangefield Road, Bromley, Kent.
Derek Brian Mottram, aged 32, caterer, of Somers Road, Balham.
Albert John Longman, aged 40, director of no settled address.
Thomas Clarke, aged 33, unemployed, of Fulham Road, Fulham.
James Henry Kensitt, aged 51, salesman, of Homer Road, Croydon.
James Thomas Fraser, aged 24, porter, of Midwell Street, Walworth.
Robert Geoffrey St. Leger, aged 44, dealer, of Broomhill

Altogether, he said, his session in the warehouse torture chamber lasted for six hours—at the end of which the mercurial Richardson "apologized and then gave me £150".

Next another victim of the shock treatment, a man named Benjamin Coulston, told the court that he, too, had undergone a six-hour torture ordeal. He was stripped naked, some of his teeth were torn out with a pair of pliers, lighted cigars were stubbed out on his arms and legs, and he was "toasted" on face and body by a closely held electric heater. As an endpiece to the session he was bundled into a tarpaulin sheet, along with two 14-lb. weights, and from inside the shroud he heard Richardson say: "Get rid of him."

Coulston stared at the jury with saddened eyes. "I thought I was going to be dumped in the river," he said. "And all the time this was happening Richardson and the others were drinking, laughing, smoking and enjoying the fun." But, luckily for him, Richardson wearied of the episode once the victim's terror had been savoured and ordered him to be released. "He gave me a new shirt," said Coulston, "and his brother, Edward, drove me home."

Other victims came to the witness box to recount similar experiences in the firm's office and warehouse. One man—who had been beaten and burned and had his toes broken—heard the screams of another sufferer as he lay in a hole,

34

woman

don

E IN ELECTRIC

E-CROWN

FIRST WITH THE NEWS RING FLEET ST 6000

ROCKS
ITY

of

ence

'PLEASURE
DSON'

by and

'I won't be at talks' —Kaunda snub for Wilson

By MAURICE ROMILLY

MR. WILSON was snubbed today by President Kaunda of Zambia, who let it be known that he is staying away from next week's Commonwealth

TOWN HALL

URGENT STAFF VACANCIES

Gus

" I could put in four hours' clerical work every week-end until I'd worked off my rates."

John Frost

Epoque

LAUGHING, drinking, smoking and enjoying the fun . . . while the victim suffered the agony of shock treatment and "toasting" with an electric heater. Then Charles (right) would give the victim a new shirt, and brother Edward would drive him home.

beneath a trap door, into which he had been thrown when his torturers had finished with him.

The highlight of the trial came on the morning on which Richardson himself finally entered the box to tell his own story. Tough and self-assured, his defence was based on the simple line that all the evidence against him was perjured. Duval's story was an example, and he blandly told the jury: "It is something out of a storybook and never happened at any time. It is a ridiculous allegation that I should beat him up just to do what I told him to."

Had he ever attacked anyone? he was asked. He looked around the courtroom with the smile of a man who would endeavour, patiently, to answer all nonsensical questions. Of course he had never attacked anyone. "Never had a cross word," he declared. "They are a lot of clever fraudsmen, putting these allegations and getting out of their own frauds by blaming me for these incidents."

On a table in the well of the court stood the electric generator said to have been the principal torture machine. But Richardson eyed it as though it were some totally mysterious piece of equipment. "That's the only one of those I've ever seen," he insisted. "I have never owned one, and I don't know anyone who has." He looked at the machine again. "It's a conspiracy," he said. "It's a tissue of lies. These people have ganged up against me."

Alive and well

One moment of humour came when prosecuting counsel, seeking information about a potential witness whom the police had been unable to trace, asked Richardson: "Is this man alive and well?" With mock exasperation, Richardson retorted: "You keep asking me all the time if people are alive and well, and I object to it. It has a very serious inference!"

Richardson was followed into the stand by his henchman Roy Hall, who was alleged to have operated the electric generator. But, like his boss, he firmly declared that he had never before seen such a machine. What was more, he added, he had never seen the two victims, Harris and Coulston, "never in my life before I saw them in the magistrate's court. I am an innocent, hard-working man. Prosecution witnesses have tried to frame me."

The jury witnessed a parade of other gang members alleged to have acted as assistants to the chief torturer. One was the man said to have attempted to draw a victim's teeth with pliers, and who succeeded only in tearing the man's gums. Again, he had done nothing, seen nothing, knew nobody. On the day that the loudest screams were being enjoyed by the scampi-eating gang—and the electric generator was emitting its agonizing stream of current—he was busy putting flowers on the grave of his wife's father.

For the Crown, Mr. Sebag Shaw summed up this, and similar defence evidence, as "poppycock produced in the hope of creating a smokescreen through which you, the members of the jury, would not be able to see. But this trial is concerned with matters of the gravest import to society. If the charges made out are well founded, it reveals a canker in our midst which, if unchecked, would undermine the civilized society in which we live." Of Richardson, he said: "He was the man of power who could get things done and who could succeed by his methods where other methods had failed."

But it was on the 38th day of the trial—the longest trial so far in British criminal history—that an important and significant announcement came from the judge. He had been informed, he said, that threats had been made to members of the jury that "there had better be a disagreement in the Richardson case." One threat had been hastily whispered to a juryman's 75-year-old mother as she waited at a bus stop. Similar "warnings" had been given to other jurymen by telephone.

Mr. Justice Lawton, careful to preserve the fair-trial rights of the prisoners, told the jury: "Whatever has happened must have been done without the co-operation of the defendants, most of whom have been in custody since last July.

"But, unfortunately, whenever there is a trial of this kind it attracts publicity, and there are busybodies, evil-wishers, misguided acquaintances and friends who will interfere. When they do interfere there is a danger that a jury might take the view that what did happen came about as the result of the intervention of the defendants. Now that I have pointed out the position to you I am confident that no such view will be taken by you."

All the same, the judge went on, a special police telephone post had been set up with a secret number for jurymen to ring immediately, at any hour, if they were approached again. "A police patrol car will be on the scene within minutes," Mr. Lawton added.

New trial threat

The judge repeated his concern over the issue in his detailed summing up of the trial. There was "not a scrap of evidence," he warned, that Richardson and his fellow defendants had been parties to the jury threats, and the jurors must put the matter out of their minds in reaching their verdicts. He reminded the jury of the importance of a unanimous decision. "If you cannot agree, there will have to be a new trial," he told them. "Just think what that will mean."

Mr. Justice Lawton spent three days on his summing up—one of the longest addresses ever made from the bench—and on June 7 the jurors retired for nine hours and 26 minutes. As they finally filed back into court, many of them showing signs of fatigue, the eight men in the dock stared anxiously at them. The list of charges was long, and it took time for the foreman to deliver the several verdicts. Richardson and five other gang members were found guilty of some—although not all—of the charges against them.

Richardson, pronounced guilty on nine counts, told the judge, "I am completely innocent of these charges." But he and the rest still had to wait before hearing their sentences. Mr. Justice Lawton said he would hand down verdicts the following day. Meanwhile he discharged the jury "from your long, wearisome and worrying time" but added: "You are not concerned with sentencing, but having regard to your long connection with the case you might like to be in court to-morrow."

The jury accepted his invitation and were back at the Old Bailey the next morning to hear the judge sentence Charles Richardson to 25 years' imprisonment. Mr. Justice Lawton told him: "I have come to the conclusion that no known penal system will cure you but time. The only thing that will cure you is the passing of the years."

Sadistic disgrace

"I am satisfied that over a period of years you were the leader of a large, disciplined, well led, well organized gang, and that for purposes of your own material interests, and on occasions for purposes of your criminal desires, you terrorized those who crossed your path, terrorized them in a way that was vicious, sadistic and a disgrace to society.

"When I remember some of the evidence of your brutality I am ashamed to think that one lives in a society that contains men like you. It must be clear to all those who set themselves up as gang leaders that they will be struck down by the law as you are struck down."

Richardson stared, tight-lipped, at the judge as the sentence was delivered. Then, as three police officers formed a guard around him to take him to the cells below the courtroom, he turned to the jury and snarled: "Thank you—very much!" Sentences ranging from eight to ten years were given to the other guilty defendants. Edward Richardson, the gang boss's brother, collected one of the 10-year sentences, which was to follow the five years he was currently serving for other offences.

It was the end of the notorious Richardson gang, and it had been achieved through the concentrated efforts of a team of 100 policemen. As his last duty in the trial the judge called before him the dozen senior detectives of the team—including young, blonde Woman Police-Constable Gillian Hoptroff.

Mr. Justice Lawton told the police team: "I want to thank all of you on behalf of the court—and I think I am speaking on behalf of every law-abiding citizen in this country—for the work you have done in breaking up one of the most dangerous gangs I have ever heard of."

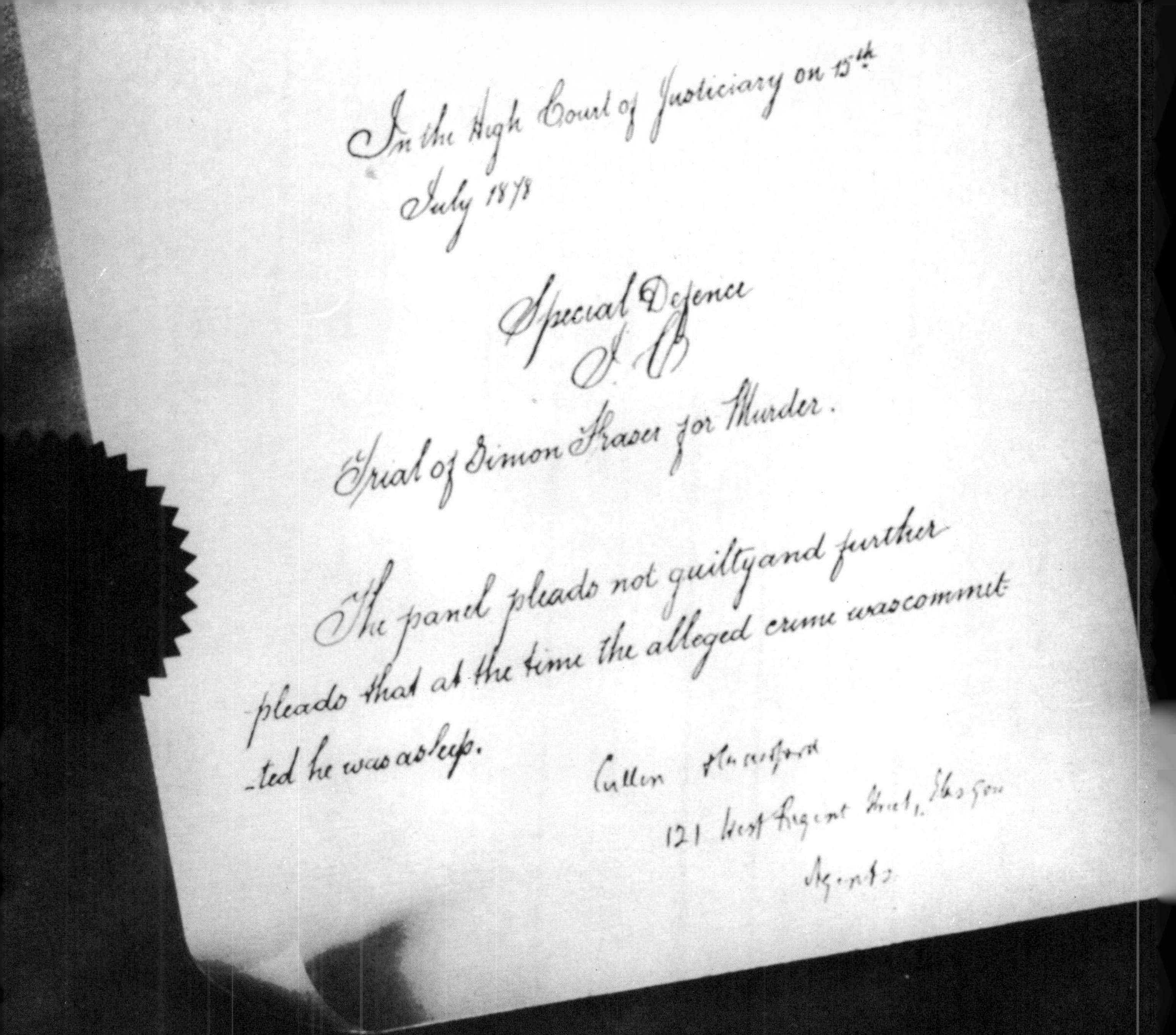

In the High Court of Justiciary on 15th
July 1878

Special Defence
J. B

Trial of Simon Fraser for Murder.

The panel pleads not guilty and further
pleads that at the time the alleged crime was commit-
-ted he was asleep.

Cullen + Beresford
121 West Regent Street, Glasgow

Agents

THE BEAST IN THE BEDROOM

It was a monster that killed baby Simon. Its eyes glowed with a hideous green light and its mouth foamed with steaming saliva. The child's father saw it . . . and expert witnesses backed up his story.

High Court.

—

INDICTMENT

AGAINST

SIMON FRASER.

—

Murder.

Trial, Monday, 15th July.

The Declaration and
medical certificate are
produced

Mr C. S. Dickson.

NO FATHER could have been more loving or gentle than 27-year-old Simon Fraser, it was stated at his trial. Sometimes his wife used to protest laughingly that he might be spoiling their 18-month-old son. But that did not stop him pampering the boy . . . buying him expensive presents . . . taking such a delight in showing him off to friends and relatives.

Then one night, in a frenzy of violence, he battered the child to death—to save himself from a savage beast which did not exist. Fraser made no secret of it. He ran to fetch neighbours to the blood-spattered room. He told a doctor how he had picked up the peacefully-sleeping infant and smashed his head against a wall. He made a frank and detailed statement to the police. But he considered himself completely innocent. "You see, I was fast asleep at the time," he explained.

That night of savagery, in April 1878, was the bizarre climax to thirteen years of terror for the Fraser family. For the quiet man, the easy-going, home-loving man, who lived in the little terraced house in Lime Street, Glasgow, Scotland, was a sleep-walking psychopath. Evil forces trespassed through his sleep and goaded him to violence. And his son was not his first victim.

Wicked and felonous

On July 15 Fraser was locked in a cell below the High Court of the Justiciary in Edinburgh. As the early routine cases of the day were heard—and the sentences relayed along the warders' grape-vine—his chances of winning leniency seemed hopelessly remote.

"The old man's really hitting them up there today," said one warder. And it certainly did seem as if "the old man"—Lord Moncrieff, the Lord Justice-Clerk—was in a harsh mood. A man called Reynolds admitted having stolen three watch-chains whilst he was drunk. Seven years' penal servitude. Another called Goodwin pleaded guilty to having taken some old iron from a ship. Seven years' penal servitude. Fraser's fears grew as he heard of these sentences. These men's crimes seemed so trivial compared with what he had done.

Then it was his turn. He stared impassively ahead from the dock, not taking his eyes from Lord Moncrieff's face, as the charge was read aloud: ". . . did wickedly and felonously attack Simon Fraser junior, a child of eighteen months, did seize him violently and did

THE NIGHT brought searing episodes of endless terror to the terraced street where the Frasers lived. Evil forces trespassed in the sleeping family's home, bringing horrific fire, flood . . . and a roaring, violent, psychopathic frenzy.

throw or push him several times against the door or floor or walls of the house and thereby did fracture his skull and lacerate his brain so that he was mortally injured and was thus murdered by the prisoner . . ."

Fraser's voice, flat and drained of emotion, was so low that his answer to the charge could not be heard at the back of the crowded courtroom. People towards the front, who had been queueing since dawn for the best seats, whispered his words back to those behind. "I am not guilty. I am guilty in my sleep but not in my senses."

The prosecution's first witness was Mrs. Janet McEwen, a capable and motherly woman, who lived near the Frasers in Lime Street. At one o'clock on the morning of April 10 she had been awakened by Fraser pounding on her door.

Seized hold of it

"He was wringing his hands and seemed to be in great distress of mind," she said. "He asked me to go and see his bairn. I went with him to his house and saw his wife who was screaming with the child unconscious on her knee. Mr. Fraser was terribly excited and kept calling the child 'my dear' and 'my dear little son'. He wasn't pretending at all. He seemed quite sincere in his distress. I asked him who had done this awful thing and he said: 'It was me that did it, mistress. I did it through my sleep.'"

The Public Prosecutor repeated the key words for the benefit of the jury: "'It was me that did it, mistress.' Now tell me, Mrs. McEwen, did you, at that time, put any further question to the prisoner?"

Janet McEwen nodded. "Aye, that I did. I asked him if he was in the habit of pacing in his sleep. He said he used to do it when he was a boy. Then he told me he thought he'd been dreaming and that he'd thought he'd seen a beast running through the room. It leaped into the bed and he seized hold of it."

She had then ordered Fraser to get a doctor while she stayed to comfort his wife. It seemed there was little she could do to help the baby. Her view was confirmed by Dr. Alexander Jamieson of Main Street, Gorbals, Glasgow, who had been roused by Fraser. "He told me he thought he had killed his child," said Dr. Jamieson. "I found the child Simon in convulsions and he was dying. There was a severe injury on his forehead, such as would be caused by the head being driven against the wall or floor. Fraser told me that, in his nightmare, he had thought the baby was a wild beast. He also said he had been violent before whilst sleep-walking—that he had used violence against his half-sister and his wife."

The baby died at 3.00 a.m. and, once

again, Fraser had rushed from the house to share his burden of grief and fear. This time he had run to near-by Rutherglen Road to wake a man called John Pritchard who worked with him at the local saw-mill. Once again he poured out the same story: "Wee Simon is dead and it is me that is the cause of it."

What sort of father then was Fraser? Pritchard, called to the box, said: "I can tell you the answer to that question without any doubt. We used to go visiting at his house quite a lot and I could see he was very fond of his child—none more so."

This opinion was endorsed by Fraser's father—yet another Simon Fraser—who told the jury: "He is of a kindly disposition and he was extra fond of his wife and child." Mr. Fraser, a big and ungainly man, was uncomfortably aware that he was helping to parade his family's secret shame before the eager public. He shuffled uneasily as he gave evidence on behalf of the prosecution. The prisoner was the child of his first marriage and had been quite well educated, not having left school until he was twelve or thirteen.

"But ever since he was a little one there has been a dullness and stupidity about him," he added. "He could not learn his lessons at school. It was a common thing for him to rise during the night and go through capers."

"Capers?" repeated the Prosecutor. "Could you be a little more specific, Mr. Fraser?"

"How d'you mean?"

"These capers—what form did they take?"

Monstrous hooves

"Well, all sorts, really. Sometimes he supposed the house was on fire and sometimes he was fighting with dogs and horses. They weren't there, if you follow me, but he was fighting with them. When he was in this condition his eyes were open but, having seen him so often in this state, I knew that he was not awake. He spoke but what he said was nonsense."

Then Mr. Fraser described the first time he had been injured by his son. Fraser, at about the age of fourteen, had a vivid nightmare in which a white stallion was stampeding through the house. It was so real, so horrifyingly real. Steaming saliva was dripping from the creature's jaws. Its eyes glowed with hideous green light and its monstrous hooves were shattering the furniture and crushing the unprotected family. Young Fraser, in an agony of desperation, had sprung from his bed to fight the beast. Seconds later, Mr. Fraser woke with blood streaming over his pillow—his demented sleeping son on top of him, punching and clawing at his face. "When he had come to his senses he used always to be ashamed of what he had done." said Mr. Fraser.

But there was always another night, another nightmare, another explosion of violence. "We lived in Norway for a while with my present wife and my daughter Elspeth—she's my daughter by this second marriage. I was over there as the manager of a sawmill. There was one night, I remember, when he went wandering from the house and into the sea in his sleep. It seemed he'd been having this nightmare about her drowning and he was trying to save her."

On another occasion Elspeth woke to find him trying to strangle her—in the belief that she was some wild monster. "He left the marks of his nails on her neck," stated Mr. Fraser.

Tortured mind

So the stories, which had never been told before by the Frasers to protect their family pride, now began to flow. Like how Fraser, in his somnambulistic state, had grabbed his wife by the legs and pulled her out of bed—convinced he was saving her from a fire which was blazing only in his tortured mind..

The Public Prosecutor then put a question which was already intriguing many people in the court. "Tell me, Mr. Fraser, did your son ever harm himself on these occasions?"

"Just once," came the reply. "That was when he was jumping over a bed and broke his toe."

But the pain, apparently, had not woken him. The only explanation seemed to be that Fraser's brain, if it registered the pain at all, translated it as being part of the nightmare. This could have made it even more imperative for him to use all the brute strength he could muster to kill whatever monster was haunting him on that particular night.

Still more evidence of Fraser's sleep-walking habits came from his step-mother, Mrs. Elspeth Fraser. She was a woman who had always treated him with great affection and understanding. Even after his attacks on her daughter she had tried to comfort him and help him. "I tried to cure him of his habit by putting tubs of water by his bedside so that when he stepped into them he might wake up."

This was not always effective. There were also times when Fraser jumped over the tubs. "On April 9, just a few hours before that . . . that thing . . . happened, he and his wife and baby came to see me," she continued. "He was quite steady and all right at that time. He is a man who can take a dram, but I've never seen him the worse for drink."

The next time she saw him was in the early hours of the following morning. He had run to fetch her after getting the doctor. All the witnesses so far—although called by the prosecution to help prove the case of murder—had shown some sympathy for Fraser. The next witness, however, did not try to disguise her loathing for Fraser. She was his mother-in-law, Mrs. Elizabeth Parker of Dundee, and she could not forgive the horror he had unwittingly brought to her daughter. She had loved her grandson, and this grotesque man in the dock had killed him.

She had stayed at the Frasers' house in Glasgow for just one night—and, during that night, Fraser had slept through one of his bouts of violence. He had thought there was a mad dog in the house and he had shrieked aloud as he had tried to kill it. "I was so frightened that I left the next day." Mrs. Parker stated.

The Prosecutor looked keenly at her. "Do you consider him to be a stupid man?" he asked.

Mrs. Parker glanced at Fraser and then picked her words with elaborate care: "Perhaps it was his want of education that made him seem a little droll."

Controversial stage

At this stage the foreman of the jury rose to say that he and his colleagues felt there was little point in hearing any more evidence. They were all agreed that Fraser was not responsible for what he had done. Lord Moncrieff considered the suggestion for a moment before replying: "I quite agree with you but I think the testimony of one or two medical men would be desirable."

It was then clear to the prosecution that they were not going to secure a conviction for murder. So the Public Prosecutor, after a hurried discussion with his advocate-deputy, decided to concentrate on a slightly different aspect.

INSANE OR NOT? If a man's whole life seems to be hypnotized by an endless kaleidoscope of nightmares, should he be judged as mad? Should he be locked up in the great grey castle of lunacy that serves as the local asylum? The evidence confounded superintendent Dr. Yellowlees.

Declaration of Simon Fraser 10th April 1878

At Glasgow the tenth day of April eighteen hundred and seventy eight years In presence of Alexander Erskine Murray Esquire Advocate, Sheriff Substitute of Lanarkshire Compeared a prisoner and the charge against him having been read over and explained to him and he having been judicially admonished and examined, Declares and says. My name is Simon Fraser, I am a native of Aberdeen 28 years of age a Saw Sharper and I reside at 44 Lime Street Glasgow. ~~I have been subject to rising in my sleep~~ since I was ten years old. Last night I, my wife and my child / S Fraser

A Erskine Murray

child, Simon Fraser — now deceased an infant not quite 18 months old were in bed, in my said house. I think that I saw a white beast flying through the floor and round to the back of the bed where the child was. ~~I tried to catch at the said beast, and I caught something which I believed to be~~ the beast and I got out of the bed and dashed it on the floor, or against the door. I woke up in consequence of my wife crying and then I found that it was the child I had had in my hands, instead of a beast, and that the child was very severely injured.

S Fraser

A Erskine Murray

And the trial moved into its most controversial stage.

Should a man who acts violently while in the grip of a nightmare be considered medically insane—and therefore be locked away in a lunatic asylum? That was the proposition now being put before the court. The Public Prosecutor was determined that—one way or another—Fraser would never again be free. It was a question that could only be answered by an expert—Dr. Yellowlees, the superintendent of a local asylum.

The doctor, stoop-shouldered and scholarly, told the court that he had examined Fraser. He then waited to answer the prosecution's questions.

"What do you consider to be the nature of the case from a medical point of view?"

"I think somnambulism is a state of unhealthy brain activity coming on during sleep of very varying intensity—sometimes little more than restless sleep, sometimes developing into delusions and violence and amounting really to insanity. This man labours under somnambulism in its most aggravated form."

Bluntly aggressive

"Do you attribute his condition to a mental disorder?"

"To the abnormal condition of the brain. That is the case in every instance of delusion, even where there is no insanity."

The Public Prosecutor paused before putting the next question. He wanted to get the phrasing exactly right. "I suppose," he said, "I suppose there is no doubt that a person in such a state as this is as unconscious of the actuality of the thing which he is doing as a person who is insane?"

He shouted the final, crucial word. The doctor, aware of the line of attack, did not disappoint him. "Quite as unconscious," he responded. "The word 'insane' describes his condition or nature."

Mr. C. S. Dickson, defending Fraser, was clearly concerned by the evidence. During a spirited session of cross-examination he tried to force the doctor to change his mind about the accuracy of the word "insane" in the context, and eventually won the grudging admission: "I thought him below average intelligence certainly, but he was practically sane when I examined him."

That, for Dickson, was a step in the right direction. But it was not nearly a big enough step. If he could not get Yellowlees to retract completely the damaging word, he had no alternative but to try to discredit Yellowlees himself. Was the doctor an authority on somnambulism? he wanted to know.

Yellowlees looked uncomfortable and made no reply. Let the question be put again. It was a very simple one. Was the doctor an authority on somnambulism—or was he not?

"I have no experience of somnambulism," confessed Yellowlees grudgingly. "That is to say I have not seen a man in his condition."

Dickson was satisfied. He was confident that he could now persuade the jury to discount the so-called "expert opinion". The next doctor called by the prosecution, however, was a far more dominant personality. Alex Robertson—physician and surgeon at Glasgow's City Poorhouse and at the City Parochial Asylum—was a squat and bluntly aggressive man, supremely confident in his own infallibility. His voice was loud and firm as he opened with a categorical statement which threatened to prove vital in any consideration of Fraser's future:

"I have had considerable experience of abnormal conditions of the brain. I know the facts of this case and I am of the opinion that the prisoner was insane when he committed this act."

He was equally adamant throughout his examination by the Public Prosecutor. Could he put the prisoner's condition in the category of a disease?

"Certainly. It most nearly approaches mania. The fact that he roared, that he was violent and dangerous, that he had extravagant delusions under excitement—along with the unconsciousness of the act—in my opinion constitutes insanity." Then, to ensure that the jury completely understood his viewpoint, he added: "It is my opinion that this somnambulism was just short fits of insanity that came on during sleep. In medical parlance there is no name for this particular kind of delusion. It is altogether exceptional."

Contrasted starkly

It began to look more and more certain that Dr. Robertson's Parochial Asylum would soon have one additional inmate. "Thank you, doctor," said the Public Prosecutor. "Now would you please tell the court in what respect does somnambulism differ from a dream—except in degree?"

"A dreamer fancies he sees and feels objects, but this man really *did* see and feel."

"What do you mean by 'really did see'? Do you mean that he saw a thing that was not in existence?"

"He saw and felt a child in reality and mistook it for a beast."

Robertson was too tough to be shaken by the defence. He stuck to his opinion. Fraser was a victim of insanity. So that was the case for the prosecution. Only one witness was to be called for the defence—a Dr. Clouston of Morningside, Edinburgh. He contrasted starkly with Robertson. He was a slight, anxious man who coughed nervously as he took the oath, and who glanced at his notes as he addressed the court.

"I had an interview with the prisoner for an hour yesterday and for ten minutes today," he said. "I have heard the history of the case and I could not detect any symptoms of unsoundness of mind or insanity. However, I consider that the prisoner was the subject, while asleep, of somnambulism. Intellectually I found him to be a man of fair judgment for his education. His memory is not good but he seemed a particularly affectionate man."

Clouston consulted his notes. "One thing struck me very much in my conversations with him. I asked him if he felt very much over the death of his child and he said that he had but, as his wife had felt it so much more, he had concealed his own feelings and appeared calm for her sake."

Normal, loving man

This was seized upon by the defence as an indication of the intrinsic good in Fraser. Even in his own agony of mind, he was still concerned for the feelings of those he loved. Did this sound like a man who was tainted by insanity? Or did it sound like the generous and protective response of a normal, loving man? And that time he had plunged into the sea to save the sister he had genuinely believed to be drowning—did that give the same picture of a man who was basically caring and sane? Anyway, was the case *really* so unusual? Had not other people reacted in an uncharacteristic style while under the domination of a nightmare—without being labelled as insane?

Clouston reassured the jury that Fraser was not such an exception as they might have been tempted to think. "I once had a case similar to this one," he said. "It was the case of a missionary connected with the church in Yorkshire. He was a most respectable man in every way. He had been in ill-health and on one occasion in a town whither he had gone for a change he went to see a wax-works display which made a great impression on his imagination.

"He was especially struck by the figure of some murdered person. He went home and went early to bed that night. His wife came into the room about an hour afterwards and he started up, thinking she was a robber coming to rob his house. He would have throttled her if a neighbour had not come to the rescue."

The Public Prosecutor was now eager to start his cross-examination, eager to steer Clouston towards considering the possibility of Fraser's insanity. "Why may a man not be insane although the fit only comes on him while he is asleep?" he asked.

"I should say that the condition is

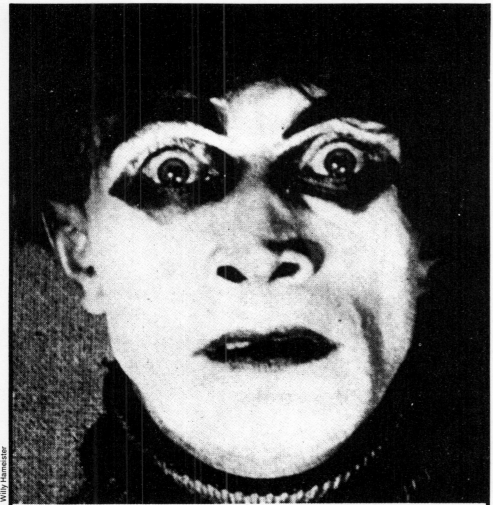

Willy Hameister

CESARE'S DEADLY DAWN

ON A mild October evening in 1913 the young Czech writer, Hans Janowitz, was strolling through a fair in Hamburg looking for a girl who had previously appealed to him. He thought he heard her laughing in some shrubbery, investigated, but only caught a glimpse of what he later called "the shadowy figure of an average bourgeois". The next day he read in the local paper of the TERRIBLE SEX CRIME AT THE FAIR—LOCAL GIRL MURDERED. Six years later—together with a young German story-editor, Carl Mayer —he used his experience as the basis for the classic film dealing with a sleepwalking slayer, *The Cabinet of Dr. Caligari*.

The film—which was a sensation in Europe, Great Britain, and North America—tells of a mysterious fairground barker, Dr. Caligari, and the somnambulist he manages, Cesare—played by Conrad Veidt. Awakened daily from his trance, Cesare predicts the time of death of anyone who asks him. Standing in an upright coffinlike box he tells one young student that he will only live "until tomorrow's dawn". Sure enough, the student is found dead early the following morning, and Caligari and Cesare—who is dominated by his master's hypnotic power—are suspected of the crime.

Seizing the girlfriend of the dead student, Cesare seeks refuge in the local lunatic asylum (the film is set in a fictitious North German town), and it is in the asylum that the story comes to a shocking, but weirdly logical, ending. Intended as an attack upon the "upside down" Germany of the years after World War One, *Caligari* is one of the few horror films to pose the question: can people kill in their sleep?

Its answer is blunted by psychiatry, the revelation of the true "madman", and a statement by the Director of the Asylum: "At last I understand the nature of his madness . . . Now I see how he can be brought to sanity again."

physiological, during which the brain rests. Hitherto the medical profession has not called anything occurring during sleep 'insanity'."

"Is there not ground for holding that the delusions of a man in a state of insanity should not fall within the category of insanity?"

Clouston coughed again and the court awaited his reply. He dabbed a handkerchief at his mouth. "It may at some future time," he said. "It has not been so reckoned yet. There is merely an abnormal condition of the brain producing delusion and violence."

"Is that not just the same as insanity?" the Public Prosecutor pursued.

The defending counsel, angered by this pressure on his witness, rose to protest but, before he could speak, the doctor was already replying: "We do not regard it as such. A sane man may have delusions during sleep which, while sleep lasts, he believes are true. In that state he is not morally responsible when that develops into action because he is not conscious of the true nature of what he is doing."

Labouring under delusion

Lord Moncrieff felt that the court had now heard quite enough. He told the jury he supposed they had "not the slightest doubt that when this unhappy and lamentable event took place, the prisoner—who is certainly to be pitied—was totally unconscious of the act". He went on: "There seems to be not the slightest doubt that when he was labouring under this delusion he was in a state of somnambulism and acting under the belief that he was trying to kill a beast.

"It is a matter of some consequence to the prisoner whether he is considered to be insane or simply as not responsible. His future might be, to a great extent, dependent on the verdict you might return on the question of whether the state of somnambulism, such as this, is considered a state of insanity or not."

There, finally, was the core of the matter. Was Fraser to be allowed to go free? Or was he to be committed to an asylum for the insane? The decision rested with the jury. Lord Moncrieff, for their guidance, suggested the verdict:

"The jury unanimously find that the prisoner killed his child when he was unconscious of the act by reason of a condition of somnambulism, and that the prisoner was not responsible for his act at the time."

The jury did not retire and, after less than a minute of whispering among themselves, their foreman announced that they were prepared to accept the terms of the verdict without any reservation. Not a word about insanity. Not a chance of Fraser going to an asylum.

Mr. EVANS, Inns of Court, gained the Armourers' Prize ; and the winner of the Rifle Oaks is Sergeant-Major TAIT, 3rd Renfrew, with 34 points—Private CALDWELL, 1st Renfrew, being third in the competition with 33 points.

In the High Court of Justiciary yesterday, SIMON FRASER was tried for having, in his house at Lime Street, South Side, Glasgow, murdered his child by striking it against the floor or walls of the house. The contention of the defence was that accused, at the time he committed the act, was in a somnambulistic fit, and imagined that he was destroying a wild beast which had come into the room and attacked him. The jury, by direction of the LORD JUSTICE-CLERK, returned a verdict finding FRASER guilty, but not responsible, and sentence was deferred.

The show of the Royal Agricultural Society of England at Bristol closed yesterday. The aggregate attendance has been 121,851, as against 163,145 at Birmingham, and 138,031 at Liverpool.

For the first time in the trial, Fraser showed signs of emotion. Through all the evidence and the legal wrangling he had been almost expressionless. Staring straight ahead most of the time as though he were somehow detached from everything around him. Now came just the hint of a smile, and he rubbed his left eye with the back of his hand. The courtroom ordeal was over. In just a few minutes he would again be a free man.

But it was not to be quite so simple. The Public Prosecutor had the attention of the court—and he was asking for the case to be adjourned, for Fraser to be kept in custody. Fraser heard him say:

"In consequence of the verdict it seems to me that the most advisable course would be to adjourn the case for a short time so that possibly some arrangement can be come to with those who are responsible for the prisoner to see that the public are kept safe."

Lord Moncrieff agreed. When the hearing was resumed two days later he an-

nounced that the Public Prosecutor had come to "a special arrangement with the prisoner and his family which might have the effect of guarding against any possible repetition of such a disaster." He then acquitted Fraser and told him: "It is right to impress upon you that you are bound to take every possible means of curing yourself of this unfortunate and involuntary habit which has already landed you in so much misery."

And what was the special "arrange-

AN HISTORICALLY BIZARRE murder case, beasts and all, is summarily recorded for posterity in the grey type between a shooting match and a livestock show.

ment"? The lawyers refused to reveal it. So did Fraser and his family. But neighbours in Lime Street were later confident that they knew. For the rest of his life Simon Fraser was a free man by day. But he slept alone—in a room locked from the outside. His wife kept the key.

44

THE BEDROOM KILLER

He slaughtered whole families while they slept. Sometimes he even lingered at the scene of the crime . . . to gloat. What was it that stimulated Peter Manuel's loathsome appetite for human suffering?

cannot name. About halfway along this road I pulled her into a field gate. She struggled and ran away, and I chased her across a field and over a ditch. When I caught up to her I dragged her into a wood. In the wood she started screaming and I hit her over the head with a piece of iron I picked up. After I had killed her I ran down a country lane

WILLIAM WATT, master-baker, of Burnside, a comfortable suburb of the Scottish city of Glasgow, was looking forward to forgetting about the cares of his chain of bakery shops for a couple of weeks and taking a holiday around Loch Lomond and on to Lochgilphead, 90 miles away, near Argyll. There he proposed to indulge in nothing more taxing than some quiet, contemplative fishing.

On the afternoon of September 9, 1956, he packed his suitcase, fishing gear and black Labrador bitch, Queenie, into his car and gave his 45-year-old wife, Marion, a goodbye kiss. He was a little concerned about Marion. She had suffered for some time from a heart condition, and although a recent operation had brought an improvement in her health, she was still very frail. However, she had agreed that her husband deserved a short break from his business.

During his absence her sister Margaret — Mrs. George Brown — would be staying with her, and the Watts' 16-year-old daughter, Vivienne, would also be at home. There was therefore no question of Mrs. Watt being lonely.

Later that crisp, fall evening Mr. Watt arrived at Lochgilphead's Cairnbaan Hotel and immediately put through a telephone call to his wife to report on his safe journey and inquire if all was well at home. All was indeed well, Mrs. Watt confirmed, and told her husband not to worry about her but to be sure to enjoy his fishing. He promised to do so but said he would still keep in contact by phone.

46

"COVERED WITH BLOOD!" gasped the daily help, at the horror scene in William Watt's suburban Glasgow home. Dead were (from left) Watt's sister-in-law Margaret, daughter Vivienne, and wife Marion . . . shot in the head at close range.

Life settled down smoothly and peacefully for the next week in the Watts' bungalow home in Burnside's Fennsbank Avenue, and the evening of September 16 was particularly convivial. Marion Watt and her sister were deeply engaged in women's chatter and there was much noisy giggling from the kitchen, where Vivienne and her girl friend were exchanging teenage gossip.

By midnight the household of three was in bed. Some 20 minutes before that Vivienne had seen her friend off from the front door and called out the parting comment, "I'll see you in the morning." Tragically, she was wrong. She would not see her friend again; she would see no one ever again; and when next she, and her mother and her aunt were seen by others all three would be dead.

At 8.45 the following morning Mrs. Helen Collison, the Watts' daily help, arrived at the bungalow and was surprised to find it still locked and the window curtains closed. Mrs. Collison wandered around the house, rapping on window panes and calling Mrs. Watt's name, but there was no reply. Then, when she came to the front door — it was her last point of call since she normally entered through the kitchen door — she began to grow distinctly uneasy.

Struggling for breath

The door had glass panels and one, set just above the lock, had been smashed. Mrs. Collison's natural and immediate instinct was to fear that the house had been burgled. Anxious for help, she went next door to the home of Vivienne's friend, Deanne Valente. With Deanne and her mother, Mrs. Collison returned to the bungalow, and as the three stood around debating what to do, Mr. Peter Collier, the postman, arrived on the scene.

After listening to the women's story, Mr. Collier suggested that they had better explore further. Slipping his hand through the broken glass panel, he opened the door. Mrs. Collison pushed past him and went at once into the first room on the left. In only a second or two she appeared again at the front door, ashen-faced, clutching at the door jamb for support. She was struggling for breath and for speech. Then, as the alarmed little group gaped at her, she gasped: "They are — they are covered with blood!"

Without waiting to question her, the postman hurried into the room. In the half-light, he saw a bed, dark with blood, and in it Mrs. Watt and her sister, Margaret, dead from bullet wounds in the head. Even at a quick glance it was clear to a layman that they had been shot at close range.

Meanwhile, Mrs. Collison, bravely overcoming her own sense of shock, thought at once of Vivienne and went into her room. From the doorway she could see blood on the bedclothes and a covered form lying in the bed. As she made to move towards it, the form gave out a most terrifying noise, clearly heard by the postman out in the hall. It sounded, he said afterwards, like the growling of a large dog, the sort of sound he would have expected from the Watts' Labrador, Queenie. It was, in fact, the final and dreadful death agony of Vivienne Watt.

By soon after 11 a.m. the murder bungalow was swarming with police, who quickly established that the two women and the girl had been killed by bullets from a .38 revolver. In the circumstances it was understandable that senior officers, puzzling over the fact that robbery was apparently not the motive for the killings, since the rest of the house was in good order, should have paid little attention to the fact that there had been a break-in at another bungalow in the same street during the past night.

Dark eyes and oily hair

But an officer sent to investigate, returned with some important information. There were certain characteristics about the newly discovered burglary, he said, that clearly pointed to the handiwork of a local villain who was, by that time, well known to the police. The suspect's name was New York-born Peter Thomas Anthony Manuel, aged 30, whose family had returned from America to Britain in 1932. He was currently on bail awaiting a court hearing on charges of an attempted break-in at a colliery canteen.

He was already "known" for a series of offences that had first begun when he was 12 years old, and which included shop-breaking, housebreaking, various forms of larceny, unlawful wounding, robbery with violence and indecent assault. The police at once hurried around to Manuel's home — where he lived with his parents, and which was only a short distance from Fennsbank Avenue — and searched it. The search was totally unrewarding.

While the policemen went about their work at his home, Manuel, a strongly built man, with dark eyes and oily hair, slicked down, sat and watched them with a faint smirk on his face. His hatred for the police ran deep, and he fancied himself as something of an amateur lawyer who could outwit authority with his cunning mind. He refused completely to account for his movements on the night of the murders or to answer any questions. Frustrated, the police went away.

Questionable beginnings

A few weeks later Peter Manuel was in jail, serving an 18 months' sentence for the colliery break-in, but by that time the Watt murder inquiries had taken a new and dramatic turn. Suspicion had centred on Mr. Watt, the master-baker, and it had done so for a number of curious reasons. One of these reasons was that the police had been in touch with a river Clyde ferry-master who thought he had ferried Mr. Watt, his car and his dog across the river in the early hours of the murder day.

From such questionable beginnings the police had convinced themselves that Mr. Watt had slipped out of his Lochgilphead hotel soon after midnight on September 16, driven the 90 miles back to his home in Burnside, broken in and murdered his wife, daughter and sister-in-law. Then, they suspected, he had raced in his car back to Lochgilphead, had arrived at the hotel in time to eat a large breakfast, and given the impression that he had spent an undisturbed night. On that theory he was held in Glasgow's Barlinnie Prison, where a fellow inmate was Peter Manuel.

On October 8, Mr. Lawrence Dowdall, the lawyer acting for Mr. Watt, received a very odd letter, from Barlinnie Prison: "Dear Sir," it said. "Last Tuesday, October 2, I was sentenced to 18 months' imprisonment in Hamilton Sheriff Court. To-day I lodged an appeal and decided I should like you to represent me. I wish to obtain bail during the period as an appellant and desire to have this accomplished with all urgency. I would like you to come and see me on Wednesday. The proposals I have outlined are to our mutual advantage, mainly due to the fact that I have some information for you concerning a recently acquired client of yours who has been described as 'an all-round athlete'." The letter was signed "P. Manuel".

A rambling story

Mr. Dowdall kept the appointment, and Manuel told him a lengthy and rambling story—the main points of which were that he knew the man who had committed the Watt murders, and, as confirmation of that, the man had described the inside of the Watts' home in considerable and specific detail. Manuel refused to name the man.

His suspicions aroused, Mr. Dowdall asked why Manuel did not tell his story to the police, but Manuel insisted that he had no intention of co-operating with any policeman. Then, pointedly, Dowdall declared: "Look, Manuel, information such as you have and the suggestion that the man who committed these murders would start and tell you piffling information about the furniture leads me to one

conclusion: that you were there." But, instantly, Manuel protested. "Oh, no!" he said. "No, I wasn't there."

On December 3, Mr. William Watt, who had spent 67 gruelling days in prison was freed. The police action had saddled him, as an innocent man, with the lifelong burden of having been accused of killing those closest to him. He had not even had the extra benefit of a trial and a positive acquittal. His innocence would, in due course, be proved beyond all question. For the moment, however, he had to resume his life and bear such gossip as inevitably must circulate.

Precisely a year later to the day of his release, Mr. Watt met Peter Manuel. Having served his own sentence, Manuel had asked Mr. Dowdall to arrange the meeting, and, at whatever painful cost to Mr. Watt, he repeated his tortuous story.

ALL THE MORE NAUSEATING was the matter-of-fact style in which Manuel told the story of his nocturnal prowling, like a man anxious to boast of great feats. A number of young girls out alone at night ended up buried in remote country spots ...

GLASGOW

MOUNT VERNON ✗ BAILLIESTON

COATBRIDGE ●

ISABELLE COOKE, 16, MISSING SINCE DEC. 31st.

MOIRA ANDERSON VANISHED FEB. 19.

RUTHERGLEN ○

CAMBUSLANG ○

○

UDDINGSTON ○

BELLSHILL

○

FRANCES CASSIDY, 16, ATTACKED HERE, DEC. 31st. ✗ BURNBANK

ANNE KNEILANDS, 17, KILLED JAN. 4th. 1956.

BLANTYRE ○

● EAST KILBRIDE

○ HAMILTON

Topix. Syndication International

Once again he described the details of the Watt household, as told to him by "the man", and finally Mr. Watt was moved to shout: "Now look, you know far too much about the house not to have been there!" Manuel vehemently denied this.

Immediately after his interview with Mr. Watt, Manuel made a brief excursion out of Scotland and travelled to Newcastle-upon-Tyne, the English industrial city to which he had previously paid an occasional visit in the course of his criminal career. At 4.30 on the morning of December 7, 1957, he appeared at the city's railway station and hired a taxi, owned and driven by 36-year-old Sydney Dunn. It was a dark night of lashing rain and a gale-force wind screaming through the deserted streets.

The following day, a police constable, cycling along a lonely moorland road near Edmundbyers, 20 miles from Newcastle, saw an abandoned car in a roadside gully. There was what appeared to the con-

stable to be blood on the steering wheel, but no sign of any driver or passengers.

Accordingly the policeman cycled to summon assistance. He returned with colleagues, and 140 yards from the car they found the body of the owner, taximan Sydney Dunn. He had been shot and killed with a .38 bullet, and his throat had been gashed. Nearby was Dunn's wallet containing £5 in notes.

The story of mysterious deaths and disappearances continued. On December 28, 17-year-old Isabelle Cooke set off from her home in the Glasgow suburb of North Mount Vernon to meet her boy friend and go with him to a dance at nearby Uddingston. The boy friend waited at the bus stop where they had arranged to meet, but she did not turn up; and when, by nine o'clock the following morning, she had not returned home her father reported to the police that he feared she was missing.

That day, and the next, various possessions, including panties, an underslip,

a cosmetics bag and a raincoat, were found by police scattered around the area. One by one these pathetically mute witnesses to disaster were shown to Mr. and Mrs. Cooke, who identified them as belonging to their daughter. But of Isabelle herself there was no trace.

In a bungalow in Uddingston, the venue of the dance to which Isabelle should have gone, lived 45-year-old Peter Smart, Glasgow manager of a firm of civil engineering contractors, with his wife, Doris, and their 10-year-old son, Michael. On New Year's Eve, 1957, they had avoided the usually boisterous celebrations of the famous festival that Scots call Hogmanay, not because they were unsociable, but simply because they had planned to drive the 70 miles to Ancrum, near Jedburgh, the home of Mrs. Smart's parents.

At 1.30 a.m., neighbours completing the rounds of first-footing, that Scottish custom of friends and relatives calling upon each other to wish good luck for the newly arrived year, noticed that the Smarts' lights had been extinguished and the family had obviously retired to bed, ready for their early New Year's morning start.

Everyone might have assumed that the Smarts had left for their visiting. However, in the days immediately following their neighbours began to notice strange things about the family's bungalow. It seemed that, at one moment, window curtains were closed and, at the next, were open again. Gradually a sense of unease spread among the adjoining homes. It was intensified at around 5.45 on the morning of January 4, when two local residents, a Mr. and Mrs. John McMunn, awoke in time to see a leering face peering around their bedroom door.

With great presence of mind Mr. McMunn cried out: "Who is it? Where's the gun?" Mrs. McMunn, astutely accepting her cue, answered. "Here it is", at which the intruder fled. When the McMunn story was heard, thoughts turned again to the mysterious movements of the window curtains at the Smart home.

When Mr. Smart failed to return to his work on January 6, and his car was found abandoned in a Glasgow street, the police were alerted and a sergeant and a constable were sent to the bungalow. The sergeant forced open the back door and began a cautious exploration of the house.

The sergeant went first to the main bedroom and, since the curtains there were drawn, even though it was eleven in the morning, he switched on the light. The scene that met his eyes was barbarous and sickening. Beneath their heavily blood-soaked bedclothes Mr. and Mrs. Smart lay dead from gunshot wounds. The officer turned at once to the smaller bedroom, fearful of what he would find there and shaken when his fears were justified. Young Michael lay between his covers, the tell-tale gore around him, also destroyed by shooting.

By this time fear was spreading through the suburban fringes of Glasgow. It seemed that anyone might fall victim to the rash of apparently senseless killings, and the police were baffled by the absence of any clearly discernible motives. But then events began to assume their final, decisive shape.

Information reached senior officers that the usually hard-up Peter Manuel had been seen in bars spending money with surprising abandon. Fortunately, some of the notes he had used were recovered and proved to be part of a newly printed batch. The bank had the serial numbers and reported that one group of notes, in number sequence, had been paid over to Mr. Smart when he cashed a cheque for holiday spending money.

Moving swiftly now, the police swooped upon Manuel and put him into an identification parade. Witnesses from the bar, where he had placed lavish orders, were able to testify that he had tendered crisp new blue Commercial Bank of Scotland notes. Some of these notes had not yet been passed on from the bar, and their serial numbers tallied with the sequence handed over by the bank to Mr. Smart.

Peter Manuel was cornered. On January 13, 1958, he was arrested and, for his own dark reasons, was ready to let his tongue wag. From that tongue came not merely an admission of the Smart family murders, but a confession of the killing of the Watts and Isabelle Cooke, and also of a 17-year-old girl named Anne Knielands — whose body with its brutally smashed skull had been found near the fifth fairway of the golf course at East Kilbride, another Glasgow suburb. The area in which all these people had died was within Manuel's home territory.

There was still the case of the Newcastle taximan, Sydney Dunn, and although Manuel did not include his murder in the confession, there was no doubt in the minds of the authorities that he was the killer. A jury, concluding its hearings after his arrest, cited him as responsible.

All the vicious details

Like a man anxious to boast of great feats which had satisfactorily baffled authority, Manuel poured out the details of his vicious crimes. Much of his narrative was made all the more nauseating by the matter-of-fact style in which he dictated it to the police. Of the heart-rending end of the Watt family, he said:

"There were two people in the bed. I went into the other room and there was a girl in the bed. She woke up and sat up. I hit her on the chin and knocked her out. I tied her hands and went back into the other room. I shot the two people in this room and then heard someone making a noise in the other room. I went back in and the girl had got loose. We struggled around for a while and then I flung her on the bed and shot her, too."

He recounted the end of poor, young Isabelle Cooke, who had left her home with such happy expectations of a pleasant evening at a local dance:

"I met the girl walking . . . When we got near the dog track she started to scream. I tore off her clothes and tied something round her neck and choked her. I then carried her up a lane into a field and dug a hole with a shovel. While I was digging a man passed along the lane on a bike. So I carried her again over a path beside a brick works into another field. I dug a hole next to a part of a field that was ploughed and put her into it."

Even though that murder, like the others, had taken place under the shroud of night, Manuel took the police unerringly to the burial spot. The officers were astonished at his total lack of sensitivity as, leading them across the ploughed field, he stopped suddenly and said, with the air of a craftsman who knows what he is about: "This is it! This is the place. In fact, I think I'm standing on her now." The police dug and, indeed, he was right.

Peter Manuel had confessed to killing eight people. At his trial he was found guilty of killing seven since, on the judge's direction, he was acquitted of Anne Knielands' murder for lack of the corroboration

A SICKENING SCENE met the eyes of police at the Uddingston bungalow (below) where the Smart family died at the hands of Peter Manuel (leaving trial, right).

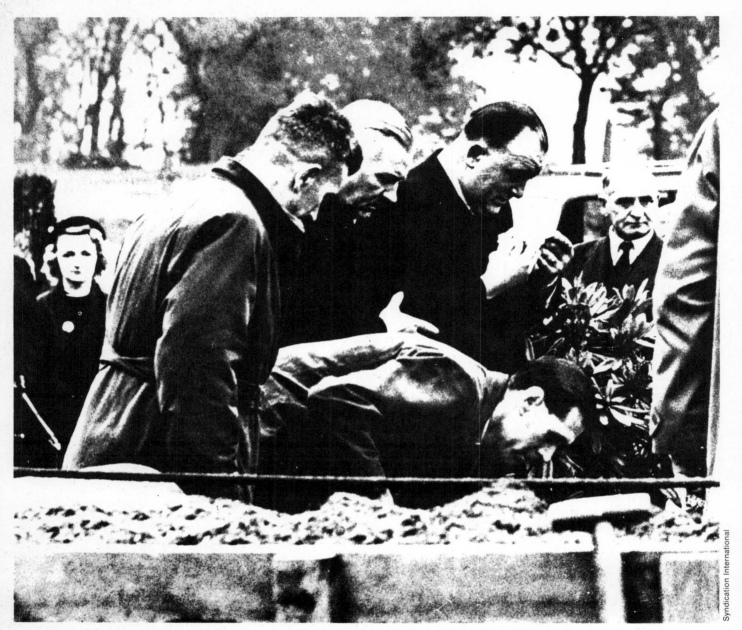

of his confession required by Scottish law. He was not tried for the murder of Sydney Dunn, the taximan, for that had been committed outside the jurisdiction of Scotland. But there is no possible doubt at all that this mass murderer took the lives of nine people.

No one could positively decide what stimulated his loathsome appetite for inflicting so much human suffering. But it seemed likely that, somehow, he gained some dark, partly sexual satisfaction from selecting innocent victims at random and destroying them in their moment of most complete defencelessness.

The mysterious movements of the window curtains at the Smart home quite certainly indicated that Manuel had returned to the house several times after the killings, no doubt to gloat over the gratifying sight of the slaughtered family.

Undoubtedly the two luckiest people were Mr. and Mrs. McMunn, who had awoken to find an intruder in their bedroom and scared him away by their quick thinking—for that intruder was Manuel.

Afterwards it was seen that there had been many earlier, ominously portending moments in Manuel's criminal life, including a night when he had struck down and raped a young housewife while her three-year-old daughter looked on.

If he was mad, it was not a form of madness such as would spare him in the eyes of the law. His trial judge, Lord Cameron, commented: "A man may be very bad without being mad." And since Manuel conducted his own defence with remarkable wiliness, there was evidence of a mind that could be coldly rational when its possessor's survival was in danger.

On July 11, 1958, Peter Thomas

A TRAGIC OCCASION — William Watt (pictured holding handkerchief) at the funeral of his wife, daughter and sister-in-law. He was held for 67 gruelling days in prison on a mere shred of evidence.

Anthony Manuel—named after some of the great saints—met the end to which he had so mercilessly brought others. However, he was shown greater compassion than his victims had received, for he was allowed to hear Mass and take Holy Communion.

When the hangman entered his cell in Barlinnie Prison, he asked simply if the time had come. Told that it had, he muttered that he was ready. In the areas around Burnside, where the mass murderer had stalked, there was overwhelming relief that he had "talked" his way to the gallows.

DOCTOR DEATH

The ex-mayor of Villeneuve-sur-Yonne seemed a respectable doctor who had worked against the Gestapo. But his house reeked of burning flesh . . .!

THE TRIAL of Dr. Marcel Petiot which began on March 18, 1946, was, next to the liberation, the greatest event in post-war France People had been starved of excitement during the German occupation, and their appetite was whetted by lurid stories of Petiot's activities. All the papers carried horrific details of the discoveries at 21 rue Lesueur, which helped to create a sensational atmosphere.

When Petiot's well-groomed figure appeared at the Seine Assize Court he was greeted like a film star. Crowds pushed and fought to catch a glimpse of him and the press cameras clicked and flashed. Marcel Petiot was news and he enjoyed every minute of it, adjusting his tie and smiling for the photographers.

Foul smoke

The indictment against him contained the names of the 27 persons whose bodies had been found at Petiot's "death house", 21 rue Lesueur. The discovery had been made two years earlier, when a badly smoking chimney directed attention to the house. With the revelation that the smoke resulted from the burning of flesh, the story quickly became headline news.

On Saturday, March 11, 1944, the foul-smelling smoke belched all day from the chimney of No. 21 rue Lesueur, a side street in the fashionable Etoile district. Mme Marçais, the occupier of No. 22, was annoyed by the stench, and the greasy smuts which settled on her furniture even with the windows closed. The smoke did not lessen and by early evening her husband, fearing that the chimney might catch fire, rang the bell at No. 21. There was no reply so he telephoned the police.

Gendarmes soon arrived and they found out that the tenant of No. 21 was a Dr. Marcel Petiot who lived nearby. The doctor was contacted. He said he would come at once with the keys.

After kicking their heels for half an hour the police could wait no longer. They called the fire brigade who quickly forced an entry to the house. Guided by the appalling smell, the firemen reached the basement where they found the source of the offensive smoke—a boiler fuelled with human corpses.

The floor around the boiler was littered with bits of bodies: arms and legs, some with the flesh stripped from them, and corpses in every state of dismemberment. While the police stood about open-mouthed with shock, Dr. Petiot arrived at the house. He did not reveal his identity. Rapidly assessing the situation and gesturing towards the basement, he said to one of the gendarmes, "What you see there are Germans and traitors."

He declared that he was a member of the Resistance and was in fear of the Gestapo. The mere mention of the dreaded

Gestapo made the policeman flinch and he let Petiot go without question.

A thorough search of the premises revealed an outhouse containing a heap of lime-covered corpses. Inside the house was a medical consulting room joined by a passage to a mysterious, triangular-shaped room. This had thick, soundproof walls, a false door and a spyhole. Its purpose in the death house could be imagined —but Dr. Petiot was not available to answer for it.

While Petiot was being hunted, the gruesome remains at the house were examined by doctors. They had 34 recognizable limbs to work on, a number of scalps, some with hair attached, bone fragments and 33 lbs. of charred remains.

The experts were unable to state either the time or the manner of death, but the technique for dismemberment had been the same in every case. The collar bone, shoulder bone, and arm had been removed in one piece—indisputably the work of a skilled dissector.

Petiot was not found until November 1944. It had not been difficult to lie low during the turmoil of the last days of the occupation and the liberation of France. The doctor helped the detectives by revealing himself. He wrote a letter to the paper, *Résistance,* refuting a claim that he had been a pro-Nazi collaborator. His patriotic motives led to his arrest and he was charged with 27 counts or murder.

The list of victims—which included names like Jo the Boxer, François the Corsican, and Paulette the Chinese—had

GENERAL EXECUTIONER . . . Dr. Petiot's medical practice looked harmless enough (below) but, as police discovered (left), his home was a chamber of horrors.

a ring of fantasy to it. The evidence which followed, coupled with Petiot's conduct, was equally fantastic.

Clutching a large dossier and cocksure of mood, the doctor admitted responsibility for killing 19 of those named. They were, he alleged, all traitors and German collaborators. He denied murdering the other eight, but for good measure, confessed to killing another 44 people, also traitors. He was then the self-confessed killer of 63 persons.

Mental hospital

Following French trial procedure, the President of the Court began by giving an account of the previous history of the extraordinary man standing in the dock. It was hardly a character reference. Marcel Petiot, born at Auxerre in 1897, had always sailed close to the wind. When serving in the army in 1917 he had been court-martialled for stealing drugs. The charge was dismissed but he was sent for psychiatric treatment.

In 1921, Petiot qualified as a doctor. At the time he was, incredibly, still being treated in a mental hospital. Three years later, he set up in practice at Villeneuve-sur-Yonne. He was energetic and politically active and in 1927 was elected mayor. He later married and had a son.

There followed a catalogue of skirmishes with the law. He was questioned about the disappearance of his housekeeper and faced charges of stealing, drug peddling, and murder. Asked about his relationship with his housekeeper, Petiot gave a flippant reply which was to mark his contemptuous attitude to the court. "She told everyone she was having sexual intercourse with me. In fact, I declined the honour." This brought howls of laughter from the public gallery—this was what they had come for.

In 1930, Petiot was accused of murdering a patient, a Mme Debauve, and he was also linked with the death of the chief witness, also a patient. But Petiot had the gift of avoiding trouble and he managed to slip out of these charges.

Considerable fortune

He moved to Paris in 1936, and in no time at all was caught stealing from a bookshop. Again, he balked the authorities. On this occasion the charge was dismissed provided he undertook psychiatric treatment.

Despite his unprofessional, not to say criminal, conduct, Petiot was never struck off the medical register. When he started his practice at 66 rue Caumartin, he had printed an exotic prospectus advertising the medical services he could provide. This was not illegal in France—it was a matter of conscience. The President of the Court scathingly referred to "these prospectuses of a quack". Petiot replied,

"Thank you for the advertisement."

The medical practice was such a success that Petiot soon had 3000 patients and managed to amass a considerable fortune. He used part of this in 1941 to buy the 15-roomed house at 21 rue Lesueur—near to his apartment in rue Caumartin. He had various alterations made to the interior of the house and raised the height of the wall surrounding the courtyard.

With his life history made public Petiot now faced his accusers. Advocate-General Dupin prosecuted and a number of lawyers representing relatives of the rue Lesueur victims had the right to put questions. The President of the Court conducted a great deal of the examination himself. It was a powerful array, and apart from his own aggressive conduct, Petiot was defended by Maître Floriot, an acknowledged lawyer of brilliance.

Argentine letters

The prosecution argued that Petiot had contrived a scheme to grow rich by finding wealthy Jews who wished to escape from occupied France. He lured them to 21 rue Lesueur telling them to bring as much money and valuables as they could find. There they were disposed of and their disappearance went unnoticed—for stealthy escape from France was their avowed intention. It was a situation which played right into the hands of Petiot. His victims escaped not to the free world but to oblivion. The Advocate-General decided to test Petiot on the eight victims he denied killing. To show that the doctor had murdered just one of them would send him to the guillotine.

Joachim Guschinow, a furrier, had gone to Petiot for help to escape the Germans. He took with him a suitcase containing jewellery, watches, money, and fur coats. These were intended to set him up in the Argentine. "I sent him to Robert Marinetti . . . the great expert at 'passing' along the route to the Spanish frontier," explained Petiot. He added that Guschinow had reached the Argentine, from where he had written letters to his wife.

The police had checked these letters but could find no trace of Guschinow at the hotel address given. "Of course not," snapped Petiot sarcastically. "Don't forget that the Argentine was almost a German colony. He wouldn't, in the circumstances, register under his own name."

"Why did you instruct Guschinow to remove his initials from his linen?" asked the Advocate-General. "That was elementary," replied Petiot, affecting a

PETIOT'S PIT . . . It was there that the deadly doctor kept the iron stove which he used to burn his victims. Telltale traces of lime were also found, as well as (inset) numerous human bones.

weary expression. "However little you worked with the Resistance . . ." He was cut off by the Advocate-General, "I know the Resistance better than you do." "Yes," retorted Petiot to the delight of the public, "but not at the same end of the pipe."

Petiot's tactics were a mixture of bluster and abuse. He passed off the fact that Guschinow's furs had been found in his apartment by explaining that they had been given him out of gratitude. Mme Guschinow's lawyer asked about injections given at 21 rue Lesueur.

"If you are one of those who think I administered injections to my presumed victims you have been reading the newspapers," replied Petiot. The lawyer was not easily put off. "But Mme Guschinow has said that her husband was nervous about the injections." Petiot's brief reply was, "She is lying."

Unique document

Among the exhibits in court were 47 suitcases. These had been found by the police in a private house near Villeneuve after several witnesses had testified that a large number of suitcases had been removed from 21 rue Lesueur in June 1943. Mme Marçais, who had raised the alarm about the smoking chimney, had seen the cases loaded onto a truck driven by Petiot's brother.

When the police opened the bags they found an incredible assortment of clothes. There were 1691 articles in all, including 29 men's suits, 79 women's dresses, and five fur coats, few of which bore any identification marks. The police inventory alone was a unique document of 140 pages listing item by item the garments and luggage of the death house victims.

One of the cases contained a hat and a shirt which Mme Braunberger claimed belonged to her husband Paul, one of the eight murders denied by Petiot. If the prosecution could prove beyond doubt that the clothing belonged to the dead man, Petiot's case would be severely weakened.

But hard as they tried, the prosecution could not effectively lay Braunberger's death at Petiot's door. This was partly due to the brilliant argument about sweat bands and sizes of shirt cuffs put up by Maître Floriot. He routed the opposition, revealed the shortcomings of the police and destroyed Mme Braunberger's validity as a witness by pointing out that she was almost blind.

As the roll call of witnesses continued it was clear that the prosecution was failing to drive home the nails. There was circumstantial evidence in abundance—but Petiot, as he had done all his life, slipped the net at the last moment. The Advocate-General, however, was also aware that he had plenty of tricks up his sleeve. He

had only to prove that Petiot killed one of the eight he denied, or show that any one of the 19 he admitted was not a German collaborator.

Yvan Dreyfus had been a potential escapee. Petiot had been asked to "pass" him and admitted being responsible for his death. Maître Floriot was not disposed to waste much time on him ". . . there is a German dossier," he said, "which shows that Dreyfus was a Gestapo informer." His voice trembling, and in a great state of emotion, Petiot interrupted, "He was four times a traitor. A traitor to his people, his religion, his fatherland and . . ." His outburst was only stopped short by the President of the Court who thundered at him to be quiet.

Perhaps Petiot sensed that his fortunes were beginning to change, for reliable evidence was called which showed Dreyfus to be a patriot. His bold front also foundered in the next case, that of Kurt and Greta Kneller and their small son René. They were among the group he denied killing.

The story was that Kneller, despite owing money to the doctor, was offered help by Petiot to escape from the Germans. "I provided them with false papers," explained Petiot, "which showed they were not married." "But they had a child," pointed out the President of the Court. "Yes," replied Petiot conversationally. "He was a nice little boy."

Petiot argued that the Knellers did escape, and he claimed to have received a postcard from them indicating that all

THE TRIAL . . . Petiot (below) listens to the evidence and (facing page) looks confident as he poses for photograph. The courtroom (inset) was always crowded.

had gone well. "How do you explain the presence of the boy's pyjamas in one of the cases?" inquired the President of the Court. "They were the pyjamas the boy slept in on the last night. There was no point in their taking dirty linen with them," answered the doctor.

On various occasions Petiot claimed to have been sent letters from people he helped to escape. These were examined by handwriting experts who without hesitation concluded that the writers were under nervous strain if not actually under physical duress. But they were not able to say that Petiot had actually written them.

It was in the matter of the letters that Petiot made a bad mistake. He had shown some of the letters to a patient saying that they came from two escapees who had got safely away to South America. But later on the doctor admitted killing the two men in Paris. Clearly they could not have sent the letters—but Petiot solved the contradiction by admitting to writing them himself.

Resistance group

Petiot's defence was quite simply that he was a member of the Resistance and acted under orders to eliminate traitors and collaborators. If he could show that he killed only the enemies of France he would be acquitted and most likely hailed as a patriot.

But throughout the trial he steadfastly refused to give the names of any of the Resistance people he had worked with. The Advocate-General assured him that any who came forward would go free if they had only been responsible for killing Gestapo agents. "I know that tune all right," shouted Petiot. "You won't arrest them, but your pals will!"

He was, however, prepared to name the group to which he had belonged—it was called Fly-Tox and he was known as Dr. Eugène. As a result of a German collaborator infiltrating the group, Petiot said that he was arrested by the Gestapo in May 1943. He was interrogated in a brutal fashion but revealed nothing.

A fellow prisoner at the time, Richard Lhéritier, was questioned in court. He stated that he had heard about Fly-Tox from Petiot with whom he had shared a cell. He spoke highly of the doctor and especially of the way he raised the morale of the prisoners by being hostile to the Germans. Lhéritier concluded, "Whatever the result of this trial, I shall always be grateful for having Dr. Petiot as a cell companion."

Petiot was visibly moved by this and Maître Floriot was quick to point out that this proved "Petiot did not invent Dr. Eugène and Fly-Tox for his defence at this trial."

At this stage in the trial Petiot lapsed

into moody behaviour. At times he would sit quietly, doodling in the margins of his papers, at others he would throw out shafts of wit. It was a highly eccentric performance even in a French court.

He clashed several times with prosecuting lawyer Maître Véron and during questioning about his Resistance activities he shouted at Véron, "Shut up, you advocate of Jews." To which the lawyer replied, "I won't allow you to soil the Resistance purely so that you may defend yourself." Purple with anger, Petiot screamed, "You're a double agent!"

Special weapon

The Advocate-General asked Petiot for more information about his Resistance activities. "It would be quicker to ask me what I have *not* done," was his modest reply. He went on to say that he planted explosives in German vehicles, provided false papers, gathered military intelligence, and invented a special weapon. "What was this weapon?" asked Maître Véron. "Do you think I will reveal something that could be harmful to Frenchmen?" retorted Petiot.

But Maître Véron persisted: "You have boasted of having experimented with plastic explosive . . . tell us something about it; how, for example, it is used." Petiot gave a rambling answer that carried no conviction at all. Pressing the attack, Véron said, "Petiot says that it takes half an hour for plastic to explode — in fact, it takes seven seconds." Enraged, Petiot could only shout abuse. But telling points were being scored by the prosecution.

Now the President of the Court took up the questioning. "Tell us about your escape organization. Who, for example, supplied the false papers?" Putting his hands to his head, Petiot thought for a while, then said, "I think he was on the staff of the Argentine Embassy." Pressed to give names, he could only reply, "There was a man called Robert . . . at Orléans there was a man with a black beard." For the first time he seemed to be floundering.

Maître Floriot came to the rescue by trying to play down the Resistance. He argued that if Petiot, in the course of carrying out "private resistance", had killed from motives of patriotism, no one would reproach him. But even the brilliance of Floriot could not divert attention from Petiot's claim to have worked for the Resistance: it was vital to his case.

When he was released by the Germans in January 1944 Petiot said he retired to Auxerre for a while to recuperate, and because he knew he was being followed. After a while he thought it safe to reappear in Paris and he went to 21 rue Lesueur. He was shocked to find a number of partially decomposed bodies covered with quicklime. He at once wrote to his brother asking for four hundredweight of quicklime and some disinfectant.

He concluded that while he had been in prison, members of his group had carried on business as usual. His group denied this and it was assumed to be the work of another group. At any rate they agreed to clean up the mess. As it was not feasible to transport the bodies away from the house, they lit the central heating boiler, cut up the rotting corpses, and began burning them.

Challenged to give the names of those who had carried out this grisly operation, Petiot refused, saying that it was against the principles of the Resistance. This was arguable, but it was open for any one of the group to come forward and give testimony on his behalf. But none did.

Triangular room

Early on in the proceedings, the President of the Court, Counsel, and the jury visited the death house at 21 rue Lesueur — when great interest was shown in the triangular room. Petiot said it was intended to house radio therapy equipment, hence the thick walls and observation hole. A medical expert dismissed this as ridiculous on the grounds that the room was not large enough to contain both

STAR EXIT . . . The flamboyant doctor clearly enjoyed the trial and used it as a vehicle to entertain his public. Leaving the court (below) he appears at ease even though surrounded by police and spectators. It was V.I.P. treatment.

Keystone

patient and equipment. The sinister room, the boiler in the basement, and knowledge of what was in the 47 suitcases created a vivid image of evil-doing in the minds of the jury.

Hoots of laughter

As the trial drew to its close, psychiatric evidence was called to show that Petiot was considered sane and responsible for his actions. Counsel for the relatives of the victims addressed the jury and asked for the death penalty. One of these lawyers confounded everyone by launching into a complete review of the case. The President of the Court seemed unable to stop him, but Petiot lent a helping hand by shouting, "I'd like to point out that I haven't paid this advocate." After hoots of laughter, order was restored.

The Advocate-General in his closing speech drew the irresistible conclusion that Petiot had organized an escape route which began and ended at 21 rue Lesueur. It was a sure way of making money. Petiot's profits were estimated at over £1 million. But the suitcases full of clothes — what could be said of them? Perhaps Petiot anticipated a market for them in post-war France.

Maître Floriot pleaded strongly for Petiot. Many thought it the most brilliant defence speech heard in a French court for half a century. But in the end the sheer weight of circumstantial evidence crushed Petiot's reliance on showing that he worked for the Resistance. His answers — and the lack of them — damned him in most people's eyes.

Addressing the prisoner, the President of the Court said, "Petiot, have you anything to add to your defence?" Petiot replied, "Nothing. You are Frenchmen. You know I have destroyed members of the Gestapo. You know what you have to do."

The jury found Petiot guilty of 24 of the 27 murders. Amid uproar, the President of the Court pronounced the death sentence. Petiot did not hear at first, so great was the hubbub. When it became clear he resisted the guards and shouted to his wife, "You must avenge me!"

Relieve himself

Marcel Petiot waited in the Santé Prison in Paris for the result of his appeal. Both the appeal and a plea for presidential clemency failed. On May 26, 1946, he was escorted to the guillotine. He rejected the services of a priest, and smoked the traditional cigarette. It was said that he asked to relieve himself but was refused permission. He shrugged and replied, "When one sets out on a voyage, one takes all one's luggage with one."

Then, in the name of justice, the knife crashed down and severed Marcel Petiot's head from his body.

DOCTOR CRIPPEN

A PATHETIC man . . . hen-pecked and humiliated by a wife who preferred her lovers to her husband. But Crippen turned into an unrepenting poisoner. He fled the country with his mistress — disguised as his son. But when they landed in Canada, the police were waiting . . .

Mary Evans

EVERYONE aboard the S.S. *Montrose* considered them to be a most considerate and devoted couple—the father and son who were travelling to start a new life in Canada. Mr. and Master Robinson—to use the names they gave to the purser—were never seen apart, and although they were polite and agreeable they spoke to no one unless they had to.

During the day they sat together on deck, chatting quietly about the sea, the weather, and the marvels of the recently installed Marconi wireless aerial which crackled above their heads sending messages both ways across the Atlantic.

At meal-times their concern for each other was even more marked. Mr. Robinson made an inordinate fuss of the boy—a shy, delicately-built youth who appeared to be in his mid-teens.

Mr. Robinson was quick to crack nuts for his son, to help him cut up his meat, and to give him half of his own helping of salad. Master Robinson thanked his father in a low gentle voice, and ate his food in a fastidious, almost ladylike way.

But as the voyage continued, one person on the ship found the Robinsons a little too loving to be true. Captain Kendall's suspicions were first aroused when he noticed that Master Robinson's trousers were too large for his slender body, and were held in place by means of a large safety-pin.

Long wavy hair

Added to that, there was the slouch hat which sat somewhat incongruously on top of the boy's long brown hair—the locks so soft they could be a girl's.

But what really set the captain thinking was the regularity with which Mr. Robinson kept on fondling his son, squeezing his hand and kissing him tenderly on the cheek.

Captain Kendall was an avid newspaper reader and knew that the *Daily Mail* was offering a reward of £100 for information concerning the whereabouts of the suspected wife-killer, Dr. Hawley Harvey Crippen. Crippen was said to be on the run with his mistress, Ethel Le Neve, and Scotland Yard detectives were on their trail.

According to the press, American-born Dr. Crippen—who stood at only 5 feet 4 inches—could be identified by his sandy moustache, balding hair, gold-rimmed glasses and false teeth.

Except for the teeth—which Captain

THE VICTIM . . . Cora Crippen (left) was left mutilated and buried in a cellar while her husband and his mistress, Ethel Le Neve (insets, left) fled to Canada on the S.S. *Montrose* (right). But Captain Kendall (inset right) became suspicious. And, for the first time, radio caught a killer . . .

Kendall had not been able to examine—this was a perfect description of the man calling himself John Philip Robinson. On the second night out from Antwerp, the captain made a point of inviting the Robinsons to dine at his table.

The ship's master was at his best, cracking jokes, telling humorous naval stories, making Mr. Robinson open his mouth and throw his head back in laughter. Under cover of the merriment, the captain looked closely at his guest's undeniably false teeth.

When the joviality had died down, and the meal was over, Captain Kendall excused himself, hurried to the wireless room, and sent an urgent radio message to the authorities in London:

Criminal history

"Have reason to believe Dr. Crippen and Miss Le Neve are travelling as passengers on my ship. They are posing as father and son and should reach Quebec on July 31. Await instructions. Kendall."

The year was 1910, and it was the first time in criminal history that such a message had been sent by wireless. It was sufficient to make Chief Inspector Walter Dew of Scotland Yard book a passage on the *Laurentic*, a faster vessel than the *Montrose* and one which would reach Canada before her.

For the rest of the voyage, the captain kept the suspect couple under close surveillance. If Crippen knew he was being watched he gave no outward sign of it, and nor did he look the kind of man who was soon to appear at the Old Bailey accused of murdering and mutilating his buxom American wife, Cora.

The marital problems of Hawley Harvey Crippen began some while after he and his wife left New York, where he

practised as a doctor, and came to live at 39 Hilldrop Crescent, Camden Town, in North London.

At the time Crippen was employed as the manager of an American patent medicine company with an office in London's Shaftesbury Avenue. By 1907—seven years after their arrival—the 45-year-old physician found that his boisterous, full-bosomed wife was beginning to irritate him, in two deadly ways.

First of all there were constant and steadily increasing sexual demands, which took more out of him than he was willing to give. Then, and even worse, there was her grandiose ambition to become an opera star.

As a classical singer Cora—or Belle Elmore as she called herself professionally—made a fairly indifferent chorus-girl. Her voice matched that of her personality, and was loud, vulgar, unsubtle and lacking in feminine charm.

This obvious dearth of talent, however, did not prevent her joining and becoming treasurer of the Music Hall Ladies' Guild, and filling her three-storied terrace-house with a collection of so-called artistes—mainly low comedians and third-rate vocalists like herself.

Flamboyant characters

In comparison to these flamboyant but shallow characters, Dr. Crippen seemed even more mild-mannered, self-effacing and meek. His place in Cora's bed was taken by an American entertainer Bruce Miller, and he found himself reduced to the status of unpaid domestic servant.

To pay for her costumes, stage attire, and blonde wigs, Cora took in a succession of theatrical lodgers. Too lazy to look after these boarders herself—and too mean to employ a maid—she forced

THE HUNTERS . . . Detective Sergeant Mitchell and wardresses Miss Stone (left) and Miss Foster set off for Canada to arrest Crippen and Le Neve.

her husband to rise each morning at dawn.

Outwardly uncomplaining, Crippen went down to the kitchen where he blacked the grate, cleaned-out and set the fire, made the tea and polished the "paying guests'" boots.

These tasks done, he left the house, went to his office, and consoled himself with the modest, undemanding love offered to him by Ethel Le Neve, whom he had recently engaged as a book-keeper and secretary.

Ethel, aged twenty-four and unmarried,

was everything Cora was not—demure, understanding, sympathetic and genteel. She cared for Crippen in a way that made him feel a man again and not a flunkey. Most important of all, she was the one person with whom he could discuss his shameful and humiliating home life.

Three years passed in this way—with Crippen and Ethel meeting and consummating their love in cheap hotel rooms in London. Apace with this, Cora's conceit reached almost manic proportions, and resulted in her being booed off the stage at her one professional appearance at the Bedford Music Hall in Camden Town.

By 1910 it was clear that things could not continue as they were. To satisfy Cora's sexual appetite, Crippen was still

expected to act as a stand-in whenever she was without an admirer, and he took to staying her passion with hyoscine—a poisonous drug used as a nerve-depressant and hypnotic.

On January 17, he bought five grains of the narcotic from a chemist and two weeks later invited two of Cora's music hall friends, Mr. and Mrs. Paul Martinetti to dinner. The meal broke up at 1.30 on the morning of February 1st. The Martinettis bade a genial goodnight to Cora who had been in typical form all evening—flattering her guests and speaking angrily to her husband.

Although they didn't know it, the Martinettis were not to exchange theatrical gossip with Cora again. A month afterwards Crippen pawned some of his wife's jewellery for £80, and wrote to the Ladies' Guild explaining that she could no longer attend their meetings as she had gone to stay with a sick relative in America.

At the time nothing was thought of this, although plucked eyebrows were raised when Ethel Le Neve moved into 39 Hilldrop Crescent and was seen in the district wearing clothes and furs belonging to the absent Cora.

In fact, Mrs. Crippen was not far away. Her fleshly remains were buried in the cellar, wrapped in a man's pyjama jacket containing quicklime, while her bones had been filleted from her body and burnt in the grate which her husband had spent so many hours cleaning on his hands and knees.

The death notice

On March 26, Crippen inserted a notice of his wife's death in the *Era* magazine. "She passed on of pneumonia," he told sympathisers, "up in the high mountains of California."

This story was accepted, and Crippen might well have been left to marry his Ethel and live lovingly ever afterwards. What happened next, however, is beyond rational explanation—unless his actions are viewed as an unconscious Freudian desire to draw attention to his crime and be caught.

He took Ethel to a ball given by the Music Hall Ladies' Guild at which she prominently displayed a diamond clip which had last been seen decorating Cora's ample chest. Reports of this "tastelessness" were passed on to Scotland Yard, and in July Chief Inspector Dew visited Crippen at his home.

The quietly-spoken doctor then confessed that Cora was not lying in a grave on the west coast of America. She had,

THE GUESTS . . . Paul Martinetti and his wife were the last people—apart from Crippen—to see Cora alive. They were guests of the Crippens at Hilldrop Crescent (large picture).

Syndication International

IN DISGUISE . . . Ethel Le Neve (left) dressed as Crippen's son. But she was really his mistress. An eagle-eyed captain spotted her wavy hair and soon police were sailing out to take Crippen to face trial (above).

he claimed, run away with her old flame, Bruce Miller. The couple were living somewhere in America, and only pride had stopped him from publicly admitting this.

This seemed a reasonable explanation, but even so the inspector insisted on searching the house from cellar to attic. Apart from her gaudy clothes no physical trace of Cora was found and the detective went away satisfied.

Crippen was not under any definite suspicion, and could have remained where he was without further interference from the police. He could not, however, believe that the inspector really accepted his story.

He felt he would be arrested at any moment and charged with the crime he had so painstakingly committed. To avoid this possibility, he obtained a boy's outfit for Ethel, and fled with her to Rotterdam. On July 11, while they were still in Holland, Inspector Dew returned to Hill-

drop Crescent to check a date in the account of Cora's alleged desertion.

To his surprise, he found that the house was empty and learnt that Crippen and his "housekeeper" were not expected back. Dew immediately sensed that the building had at least one occupant — Cora, or whatever was discovered to be left of her.

Pieces of flesh

This time Dew's investigation included the digging up of the cellar and the uncovering of a man's pyjama jacket, parts of a human buttock, pieces of skin and bits of muscle, and chest and stomach organs. Although the remains were sexless, old scar tissue showed that the subject had undergone an abdominal operation.

This tallied with what little was known of Cora, and on July 16th, a warrant was issued for the arrest of Crippen and Miss Le Neve. Four days after this — without knowing that the search for them was on — they boarded the *Montrose* at Antwerp and began their extraordinary but unsuccessful deception as father and son.

After Captain Kendall had sent his first radio message, he kept abreast of the

ON TRIAL . . . Crippen and his mistress in the dock (top) facing murder charges. Some of Mrs. Crippen's friends (above) were called as witnesses and the deadly doctor was sentenced to death. But Ethel Le Neve went free . . .

developments as Inspector Dew and his sergeant sailed from Liverpool. Their ship forged ahead of the *Montrose* at the entrance to the St. Lawrence River.

The *Montrose* arrived in Canadian waters early in the morning of July 31. At 8.30 a.m. the pilot boat came alongside, and Dew and Sergeant Mitchell boarded the liner. They were accompanied by a chief inspector of the Canadian police, and posed as river navigators.

They were taken straight to Captain Kendall's cabin, and there brought face to face with the self-styled John Philip Robinson. Dew wasted no time in bothering with questions of identity of disguise.

Wife mutilated

"Good morning, Dr. Crippen," he said briskly. "I am Chief Inspector Dew of Scotland Yard. I believe you know me."

Crippen blanched, but found the voice to say: "Good morning, Mr. Dew."

The detective gazed down at the small, clerkish-looking fugitive and told him: "I am arresting you for the murder and mutilation of your wife Cora Crippen in London on or about February 2 last."

Crippen made no reply, and Dew went out to find and charge Ethel. The run-

away lovers were then taken on to Quebec and a month later brought back to England, London, and the Old Bailey.

The doctor was the first of the two to be put before a jury, and his five-day trial opened on October 18, 1910. From the start it was clear that he had no chance of being acquitted. He seemed indifferent to his own fate, and his main concern was for Ethel, whom he swore knew nothing of Cora's murder.

After duly being pronounced guilty,

WIFE-KILLER Crippen, his life in ruins, was only too happy to leave a world where he had known only the briefest moments of happiness.

he waited feverishly to hear how Ethel had fared on a charge of being an accessory. As it turned out, he had nothing to fear.

Her trial four days later was almost a formality for her defence counsel, the brilliant and foxy F. E. Smith. He chal-

lenged the prosecution to prove that she was anything other than innocent. The case against her failed, and she was found not guilty and discharged.

For Crippen there was little to live for—even if his neck had been spared. Without Ethel—who disappeared without trace from the public eye—he wished only to die, and to do so quickly.

He was hanged on November 23, and his last request was that a photograph of her be buried with him.

THE BLACK DAHLIA

From the top of her raven-tressed head to the tip of her black patent shoes, her sombre sexiness was indelibly blazoned on the soul of any man who knew her. Miss Elizabeth Short knew a lot of men. At least one man too many.

ON the chill, blustery morning of January 15, 1947, a sobbing, hysterical woman frantically flagged down a passing police patrol car in a suburb of Los Angeles, California, and screeched out an incoherent stream of words. When the patrol car crew had managed to calm her a little she pointed with shaking fingers to a nearby, garbage-strewn vacant lot. The police car leapt forward, turned on to the lot, and there the officers immediately understood the woman's behaviour.

What she had seen, and what the policemen now saw for themselves, were the nude halves of the corpse of a young woman. The body had been crudely cut in two at the waist, and each half tied with ropes. Deep into one thigh the killer had carved the initials "BD".

It was a sickening sight, but the repulsion which the hardened police officers felt was deepened when pathologists examined the body in detail and found that it had been revoltingly mutilated. What was even more hideous was the fact that most of the injuries had been

A SICKENING SIGHT met the horrified gaze of the police: Elizabeth Short's hideously mutilated body. Her injuries had obviously been inflicted while she was still alive. Her mother (below) had often been unable to cope with her young family. . . .

inflicted before death—probably while the victim was suspended, head down, by ropes or wires. She might, indeed, have been still living when her murderer began the incisions to sever her body.

It was clear that the girl had not been long dead when the passing woman came across the dismembered corpse. The immediate theory was that she had been killed somewhere nearby, and the remains tipped on to the lot from a car. The police were puzzled by the incised initials "BD", and there were no obvious clues to identification. But, as a matter of routine, the police took fingerprints from the few fingers that had escaped mutilation. These were sent to the Federal Bureau of Investigation in Washington, D.C., for checking against the millions on file.

The Los Angeles police knew only too well that the print check was an outside chance. To their satisfaction, a message came back from the F.B.I. within hours stating that the prints matched those on file for 22-year-old Elizabeth Short, born in the small town of Medford, Massachusetts, who had a police record as a juvenile delinquent.

Her mother, Mrs. Phoebe Short—who was separated from her husband—was then traced. She had the task of trying to identify the body. So thoroughly had the killer carried out his work that she was

THE TIDE TURNED in Elizabeth Short's life when she met Army Air Force Major Matt M. Gordon Jr. (above). But he was killed in action . . . and the Black Dahlia was born. Many men felt driven to confess to the spectacular murder; one, Joseph Dumais (bottom far right), was arrested, but released to a psychiatrist.

unable positively to say that what she looked upon had once been her daughter. But she *was* able to produce a letter which Elizabeth had written to her a few weeks before from San Diego. Detectives went immediately to the address and learnt that Elizabeth Short had left there six days before the discovery of her body. Since she had taken no luggage with her, it seemed as though she had intended to return, and had gone to Los Angeles for no more than a brief visit.

Slowly the police built up a picture of Elizabeth Short, her life and her background. One fact was beyond any doubt and dominated all others: she had been tall, graceful, and exceedingly beautiful, with milk-white skin and a mass of raven hair. She was the kind of girl upon whom all men's eyes focused when she walked into a room; if ever any girl was instantly desirable, that girl was Elizabeth.

Great Depression

However, there was little of beauty in her background. She had grown up in an unhappy home and was only six when, in 1931, her parents separated and her father moved to California. He took one child of the family with him, and left his wife to look after Elizabeth and their other three children.

It was the period of the Great Depression, and Phoebe Short often found herself unequal to both making a living and bringing up the youngsters.

Often alone and miserable, without much close contact with her mother, Elizabeth's one main ambition began to grow into an obsession: the moment she was old enough she would leave home

and make a new and independent life for herself.

The opportunity came in 1942, when she was not yet 17. With the United States engulfed by world war there were plenty of job opportunities for young women. Elizabeth decided to seize one of those opportunities for herself—but as far away and as different from Medford as she could make it. She chose Miami.

It seemed to her that the "sun city" was tailor-made for her ambitions. She was already well aware of her physical appeal; there was an air base near Miami, and at week-ends there was no shortage of young servicemen enjoying their brief leaves on the Florida beaches.

The only information the police could obtain about her life in Miami was sketchy—but it was enough to show that it had finally added to her unhappiness and loneliness. She had taken a job as a waitress. For a time it seemed that she had found her hoped-for young lover. But the romance languished when the man went off to the war. Then, while she worked and counted the days to his return, he died on a distant battlefield.

It was a blow from which Elizabeth Short did not recover. She took to drink, and she took to men—any men. She became so promiscuous that word of her

readiness to go to bed with anyone who would buy her drinks and a meal swiftly spread around the Miami bars.

Eventually, almost inevitably, the police caught up with her, and, found drinking with soldiers in a café, she was arrested as a juvenile delinquent. The authorities decided that, since she was in need of care and protection, she should be sent home to her mother. They gave her a rail ticket to Medford and a small amount of subsistence money and put her on a train.

She stayed aboard the train as far as Santa Barbara, and there she got off and found herself another job as a waitress. In the distraction of war no one had checked to see if she had reached home and the custody of her mother, and Elizabeth stayed in Santa Barbara until 1944. But once more, as though she were singled out to be one of nature's chosen victims, the fates were unmerciful to her.

Having got over her first sad love affair, she formed an attachment for an Army Air Force major. It seemed like the turning of the disastrous tide of her life, and, as though to confirm her own good intentions, she returned, in 1944, to her mother in Medford, to await the major's homecoming from the Far East and the marriage which was to follow.

Home was no happier than it had been in the past, but this time, at least, she could look forward to settling down to a new life with a husband to whom she could devote herself. On the morning of August 22, 1946, when it seemed so certain that her major would soon be back from the war, the front-door bell rang and Elizabeth answered it. A taciturn postal messenger handed her a telegram addressed to herself. Excitedly she tore it open. The message inside was from the mother of the major. Cryptically, it said: "Have received notification from War Department my son, Matt, killed in air crash."

Zombie-like trance

In a zombie-like trance, Elizabeth screwed the telegram into a tight-knit ball of paper, tossed it aside and went straight to the nearest bar. There she drank until her lovely grey-green eyes were cloudy with alcohol and her tall, elegant frame sagged over the edge of the bar. The barman became embarrassed by her tipsy monologue in which she declared: "Some people have a hex on them, y'know what I mean? Some people can't never get the breaks, and nuthin' they can do will give 'em the breaks. Y'listenin' me, now? Why'd things happen to me, this way?"

The next day she decided that there was nothing to keep her in Medford any longer, and she set out for California, this time to the place for which her

poise and stunning looks seemed to be so perfectly fitted: Hollywood. The major studios had not yet been overtaken by the TV revolution, and the feeling in the movie capital was that business would be as it always had been, booming. Every day there were calls for "extras", and Elizabeth Short joined the casting lines successfully. For her there was regular and reasonably well-paid work.

She had heard that there were producers and casting directors who were prepared to give a photogenic girl a chance in pictures, for "a consideration". Elizabeth was only too ready to oblige, especially when she was sufficiently anaesthetized with liquor, and she devoted her spare time to going to bed with almost all men who invited her, even though most had no more than tenuous associations with the studios.

Black stockings

She had learned that in Hollywood it was as well to establish some kind of particular identity. Her method was to match her raven hair by dressing totally in black: black sheath dresses, black stockings and underwear, black shoes, even a jet black ring. In its own strange way the ploy worked, and someone named her the "Black Dahlia". The title stuck, she used it herself, and few men who passed in and out of her life were unaware of it.

She took, and discarded, lovers the way most women accept and discard clothing fashions. Some of them she lived with for brief periods. With one man she formed something more than a passing attachment, for in the few effects found after her death was a note addressed to her which read: "I might be gone before you arrive. You say in your letter that you want us to be good friends. But from your wire you seemed to want more than that. Are you really sure what you want? Why not pause and consider just what your

coming out here would amount to? You've got to be more practical these days."

No one would ever discover where "out here" was, and certainly one thing that the Black Dahlia seemed incapable of achieving was practical behaviour. In any case, as the Hollywood movie empire declined into an era of uncertainty it was clear that stardom was not waiting around the corner for Elizabeth Short, and, no longer earning anything like a regular income, she drifted south to San Diego and resumed her career as a waitress.

Her drinking continued unabated, and men pursued her as readily as ever. One man with whom she established a brief liaison was tall and red-haired and reported as having been seen with the Black Dahlia in a San Diego bus station a few days before her dismembered body was discovered. The man was traced by the police and admitted that he had been with the girl. He declared that he went on a drunken binge with her, took her afterwards to a motel and then drove her to the Biltmore Hotel in Los Angeles.

"She said she was going to meet her sister at the hotel," the man told detectives. "I left her there. That was the last time I saw her, and I have no idea what happened to her afterwards or where she went." The police accepted his story; in any case, the man was able to prove that, at the time when the Black Dahlia must have been murdered, he and his wife were visiting friends.

For the authorities the trail set by Elizabeth Short ended at the front entrance to the Biltmore Hotel. She had become lost in the city sprawl; somewhere she met the man who was to so brutally slay her. Her clothing had totally disappeared, and extensive searches — including examinations of drains and sewers — failed to produce any garment that could be traced to her.

From the moment that the news of the severed corpse discovery appeared in the newspapers the police were overwhelmed by supposed "confessions" and reports of suspects. The anxiety of so many men to "confess" to such a deed said a great deal about individual mental states, but told the police nothing that was relevant to their inquiries. One man, at least, had an unusual motive for presenting himself as the killer. His wife, he said, had deserted him. He hoped that if he could make himself notorious, and have his picture in the papers, she might return.

Hysterical cases

One person sent the police a message, composed of pasted-up letters cut from a magazine, offering to meet them and provide them with information. He signed himself "Black Dahlia Avenger". Detectives waited at the proposed rendezvous but no one turned up. One woman walked into a police station and announced: "The Black Dahlia stole my man, so I killed her and cut her up."

Tired-eyed but patient officers chatted to the eager woman, and discreetly mentioned one or two facts about the murdered girl's corpse that could only have been known to the killer. From the woman's response, it was clear that she was no more than another hysterical case.

In the midst of such confessions there was one curious and baffling event. A Los Angeles newspaper received a note which read: "Here are Dahlia's belongings. Letter will follow." Enclosed with the note were Elizabeth Short's birth certificate, address book, and social security card. No letter followed and fingerprints, clearly visible on the envelope and note, were forwarded to the F.B.I. — but they matched none on file. Detectives spent long days searching out men named in the address book, but none of the interviews produced a positive murder lead.

Calls promising information were made to the Los Angeles police from all parts of the United States, and some of the

CURIOUS AND BAFFLING, this note (and the package with it) was never followed up. The killer had made a gesture and turned away — perhaps to new victims.

UPI

callers were asked to appear in person. But officers discovered nothing of value.

One development, however, looked promising. U.S. army investigators arrested a 29-year-old corporal, just back from 42 days' leave, who had talked loudly and convincingly about having known the Black Dahlia, and having been with her a few days before her body was found. There were bloodstains on his clothing and, in his locker, newspaper clippings about the murder. He seemed to possess a lot of circumstantial evidence about some of the injuries to the body, and he insisted: "When I get drunk I get rough with women." However, on closer examination, he, too, was found to be an unbalanced personality and recommended for psychiatric treatment.

The gory facts

Despite all the time and energy that the police spent on such confessions, they were helped by one important factor in the case: some of the mutilations of the body were so foul that no newspaper had written about them in any detail. This served in eliminating false confessions, since it was clear that none of the would-be "murderers" knew the full, gory facts.

As a variation on the theme of most of the confessions, one man later came forward and announced that, although he

THE MYSTERY surrounding her death has helped keep alive the memory of the Black Dahlia: this beautiful young victim who seemed so destined for suffering.

had not murdered the girl, he *had* helped to dismember her body. The murderer, he said, was a friend of his. He did not, or could not, identify him—and, as in other offers of "information", his statements did not conform to the facts known only to the police.

Almost certainly someone, somewhere in Los Angeles, knew the identity of the killer. The police considered it hardly credible that he could have committed such an atrocious crime without leaving some clues behind. The killing and mutilation might have taken place in a deserted warehouse, or some remote building— and yet there was no evidence of the girl being seen with a man just before her death. It seemed unlikely that she might have gone to meet her end, in a place conveniently designed for it, without even being observed by a passer by.

In fact two bartenders reported having served her with drinks, two or three days before her death, when she was in the company of a woman. These reports gave rise to rumours that she had been murdered by a lesbian acquaintance. But there was neither direct evidence nor

even remote indications to suggest that she was homosexual.

Then there were those who claimed that the murder was the work of a madman driven by motives similar to those of Jack the Ripper—the unidentified nineteenth-century killer who disposed of prostitutes in the East End of London. Perhaps, they argued, the Black Dahlia murder was a case of a man wishing to rid the world of a woman of easy virtue.

The bald fact was that the killer was never found, and his motives, therefore, remain undisclosed. For some time the police inquiries continued and—for a long time after—the "confessions" flowed in.

These—and the nickname she was given—have kept alive the memory of the young victim who seemed so destined for suffering. The most important is that her murderer knew her, and had probably been out with her several times before.

From the address book, sent anonymously to the local newspaper, one page was missing. It had apparently been removed because it contained the name and address of the Black Dahlia's "friend", who turned out to be her murderer. Was the person who posted that book to the newspaper the killer himself? The odds are that it was. And that, having made his "gesture", he turned his attention to other women—and perhaps other victims.

A POISONER IN THE FAMILY

When Mary Ann Cotton was arrested on a
charge of poisoning her stepson, it looked like an ordinary
cut-and-dried case of murder — until the true facts began to emerge . . .

so many people wanted to be at the trial that admission was by ticket only. Even then the demand was so great that special arrangements were made for the gentry of the county and their womenfolk to sit on the bench alongside the judge. On the surface, the case did not seem to warrant so much excitement.

Mary Ann Cotton, a 40-year-old widow, had been committed for trial on a charge of murdering her seven-year-old stepson, Charles Edward Cotton, with arsenic. She had acted, it was alleged, from two motives. There was about £8 to come from the Prudential Insurance Company on the boy's death. Charles Edward was also an impediment to her marriage to an Excise Officer named Quick-Manning, by whom she was already pregnant.

But everyone in the packed Durham Assizes courtroom in the north of England knew that the charge was just the tip of the iceberg. They had read the black headlines in the local newspaper, THE GREAT POISONING CASE AT WEST AUCKLAND – HORRIBLE REVELATIONS, and the story that went with them.

The story, written at a time, the 1870s, when British newspapers were not inhibited by the strict modern libel and contempt of court laws, alleged that Mary Ann might be the greatest mass murderer in the history of British crime.

Soap mixture

Nobody could be certain then, and nobody is certain now, exactly how many people died at her hand. But the candidates include her own mother; two of her three husbands; one bigamous husband; 10 of her 12 children; five other children; one lover; and one of her best friends.

The entire courtroom craned forward for a closer look as the warders escorted her into the dock a few minutes before ten o'clock on the morning of Wednesday, March 5, 1873. She had fine eyes, but she looked pale under her black bonnet, worn with a long black dress and black-and-white shawl.

Despite the setting up of a defence fund, she had not had enough money to pay the full fees of an advocate to represent her. Two days earlier the judge had asked Thomas Campbell Foster, a Leeds lawyer, to act on her behalf. Now she chatted with him for a moment before taking the seat provided for her in the dock. When the charge was read, she rose to plead in a firm, but quiet, voice: "Not guilty."

Charles Russell, Q.C. – later to be known as the greatest advocate of his time, to be appointed Lord Chief Justice and raised to the peerage – opened the case for the prosecution. The basis of his argument was that Mary Ann – who had once been a nurse at nearby Sunderland

Mary Evans

PROSECUTION COUNSEL was Sir Charles Russell (above), one of the great British advocates. Opposite: Mary Ann Cotton's last house in West Auckland.

Infirmary and was therefore familiar with poisons – had murdered her stepson with arsenic because "she was badly off and Charles Edward was a tie and burden to her". Then came the witnesses to relate the events which preceded the child's death on July 12, 1872, and Mary Ann's arrest six days later.

Mary Ann Dodds, a former neighbour, told the court how she had gone to a chemist's in West Auckland – the village where the prisoner lived – the previous May to buy a mixture of soft soap and arsenic. "The mixture," said Mrs. Dodds, "was needed to remove bugs from a bed in Mary Ann's home. I rubbed most of it into the joints of the bed and the iron crosspieces underneath." John Townend, the chemist who sold the mixture, explained that it would contain somewhere between half-an-ounce to an ounce (240-480 grains) of arsenic. Three grains,

according to medical evidence, would be enough to kill an adult. Townend also made the point that his was not the nearest chemist's shop to Mary Ann's three-roomed stone cottage at 13 Front Street.

One of the key witnesses was Thomas Riley, a public relief official. He described how, on July 6 – six days before he was to die – Mary Ann had asked if a place could be found for her stepson in a workhouse. "It is hard to keep him when he is not my own," she explained, "and he is stopping me from taking in a respectable lodger." Riley had asked jokingly if the lodger might be the Excise Officer the village gossips said she was going to marry.

Pauper's grave

"It might be so," said Mary Ann, "but the boy is in the way." The following Friday, about 6 a.m., he was passing Mary Ann's house when he saw her standing at the door, looking upset. He went over to her. "My boy's dead," she told him.

"I was immediately suspicious," said

Riley. "The boy had seemed a perfectly healthy little chap when I saw him only six days earlier. I went straight to see the police and Dr. Kilburn, the village doctor." Dr. Kilburn, too, was surprised to hear of Charles Edward's death, although the boy had been ill—with gastro-enteritis, he thought—since the previous Sunday. His assistant, Dr. Chalmers, had called three times during the week, and Dr. Kilburn himself had seen the child twice only the previous day.

"In the circumstances," he said, "I decided to withhold a death certificate and asked for permission to carry out a post-mortem examination." The coroner, on hearing that the doctor had refused to issue a death certificate, ordered an inquest to be held the following afternoon in the Rose and Crown public house, next door to Mary Ann's home.

The pressures of caring for the living prevented the two doctors from starting their post-mortem—on Mary Ann's kitchen table—until an hour before the time fixed for the start of the inquest. As a result, Dr. Kilburn, the chief witness, was ill-prepared when the time came for him to give evidence. He was forced to admit: "I have found nothing to suggest poisoning. Death could have been from natural causes, possibly gastro-enteritis." His words left the jury with no choice but to return a verdict of natural death.

Charles Edward was buried in a pauper's grave. But Dr. Kilburn was not yet finished with his tests. He had bottled

PHYSICALLY she was attractive enough to acquire a new husband whenever she needed one . . . Right: the pharmacy where Mrs. Dodds bought the arsenic and soap.

George Backhouse

contents of the boy's stomach, and the following Wednesday he subjected them for the first time to a proper chemical examination. "I found distinct traces of arsenic," he told the court, "and went to the police at once." The next day Mary Ann was arrested and charged with her stepson's murder. The boy's coffin was dug up, and examination by Dr. Thomas Scattergood, lecturer in forensic medicine and toxicology at Leeds School of Medicine, disclosed arsenic in the stomach, bowels, liver, lungs, heart and kidneys.

It was not merely the suddenness of the little boy's death that had aroused Riley's suspicions. Four other people close to Mary Ann had died in similar circumstances in the two years since she had come to Johnson Terrace, West Auckland.

The Cotton household consisted of Mary Ann; her bigamous husband, coal miner Frederick Cotton (her third husband, a Sunderland shipwright named James Robinson, was still alive); Cotton's two children by a previous marriage, Frederick and Charles Edward; and Robert, her baby by Cotton. Her "husband" was the first to die, on September 19, 1871, two days after their first "wedding" anniversary. He was 39 and had

been suffering from severe stomach pains. The doctor certified the cause of death as gastric fever.

Mary Ann spent a quiet winter, but after becoming the mistress of Quick-Manning—the Excise Officer who lived nearby and called her in to nurse him through a bout of smallpox—she wasted no time when she resumed her murderous career in the spring.

Her next three killings, designed to clear the way for marriage, took place in the space of three weeks. Cotton's son Frederick, aged 10, died on March 10, 1872; her son Robert, aged 14 months, died on March 27; and an old lover, Joseph Nattrass, who had moved in with her again, died on April 1. Gastric fever and, in the case of the baby, teething convulsions were given as the causes of death.

Green wallpaper

One of the most contentious aspects of the trial—long to be argued about in legal circles afterwards—was whether evidence should be allowed about these earlier deaths when, at this particular time, Mary Ann was merely being tried for the murder of Charles Edward.

In the weeks after Mary Ann's arrest,

the bodies of three more of her victims—Joseph Nattrass, 10-year-old Frederick Cotton, and her baby Robert—had been dug up and examined by Dr. Scattergood. In each case he had found evidence of arsenic poisoning. In a letter to the Home Office about Nattrass he wrote:

"There is no doubt that Nattrass was poisoned by arsenic. I find there is a considerable quantity in the stomach and bowels, between four and five grains of it being still in the state of undissolved powder. Arsenic is in all the viscera."

Campbell Foster—whose main line of defence had been that some green floral wallpaper, heavily impregnated with arsenic, was the accidental source of the poison which killed Charles Edward—argued that to allow evidence about the earlier deaths would prejudice a fair trial. The judge, Sir Thomas Archibald, ruled against him, however, relying chiefly on the case of the Queen v Geering.

That case had been heard at Lewes, Sussex, in 1849. Mary Ann Geering was charged with poisoning her husband with arsenic, and in order to prove that death was not accidental, evidence was admitted that she had subsequently poisoned her three sons, two of whom died.

From that point the outcome of the case was virtually a foregone conclusion. Campbell Foster did not call any witnesses on her behalf, and, after retiring at 5.50 p.m. on the third day of the trial, the jury took only an hour to bring in a verdict of guilty. Said the judge, donning his black cap: "Mary Ann Cotton, you have been convicted, after a careful and patient trial, of the awful crime of murder . . .

Indelible record

"You seem to have given way to that most awful of all delusions, which sometimes takes possession of persons wanting in proper moral and religious sense, that you could carry out your wicked designs without detection. But, while murder by poison is the most detestable of all crimes, and one at which human nature shudders, it is one the nature of which, in the order of God's providence, always leaves behind it complete and incontestable traces of guilt. Poisoning, as it were, in the very act of crime writes an indelible record of guilt.

"In these last words I shall address to you, I would earnestly urge you to seek for your soul that only refuge which is left for you, in the mercy of God through the atonement of our Lord, Jesus Christ. It only remains for me to pass upon you the sentence of the law . . ."

A MERE FORMALITY . . . The Home Secretary is duly informed of the impending execution (right). Mary was arrested by the local sergeant (left).

14514

County Gaol. Durham
7th March 1873

Sir,

I beg to inform you that at the Assizes holden in Durham on Friday the 7th day of March 1873. Mary Ann Cotton was convicted of Wilful Murder and sentenced to be hanged. Consequently in accordance with the Rules laid down in your Order dated 13th August 1868. Mary Ann Cotton will be executed on Monday the 24th Inst. at 8 o'clock A.m.

I have the honor, to be,
Sir.
Your most Obedt Servant
Armstrong
Lt Colonel
Governor

The Right Hon. H. A. Bruce
Secretary of State
Home Department
Whitehall
London

Mary Ann paled as she heard the words of the death sentence. Then, semi-conscious, she was half-carried out of the dock and taken to Durham County Gaol to await her execution 17 days later. Meantime, the newspapers had pieced together the bizarre story of a woman—supposedly kindly and good-natured—who spread death wherever she went.

She was born Mary Ann Robson in the Durham pit village of Low Moorsley in 1832, daughter of a pitman still in his teens, and brought up as a devout Methodist. At the age of 20 she married a labourer named William Mowbray, and, shortly afterwards, they moved to Devon. There four of the five children born to them died. They returned to the north-east, where she constantly changed addresses—South Hetton, Hendon, Sunderland, Pallion, Seaham, Monkwearmouth, North Walbottle and, finally, West Auckland. She and Mowbray had three more children. They died. Mowbray himself died.

Mary Ann married again. Her new husband was George Ward, a Sunderland engineer. In October, 1866, 14 months after the wedding, he died. A month later, Mary Ann moved in as housekeeper to James Robinson, a widower and shipwright, and quickly found herself pregnant by him. He was to become her third husband.

Meantime, within weeks of Mary Ann moving in as housekeeper, Robinson's 10-month-old son John had died. Worse was yet to come. Within the space of 12 days in the spring of 1867, three more children in the Robinson household died—Robinson's son James, aged six, on April 21; Robinson's daughter Elizabeth, aged eight, on April 26; and, on May 2, Mary Ann's daughter Isabella, aged nine, the only survivor of her marriage to Mowbray.

Conventional dosage

Incredibly enough, the catalogue of death did not stop there. Mary Ann went to visit her 54-year-old mother, fearing, she said, that this apparently healthy woman "might be about to die". Nine days later she did—and Mary Ann promptly departed with clothing and bed linen. Mary Ann then made a friend, Margaret Cotton, who introduced her to her brother, Frederick, later to be one of the West Auckland victims. When Mary Ann, finding herself pregnant yet again, decided to become Frederick's bigamous wife, she saw Margaret as an impediment. Margaret also had £60, a sizeable sum in those days, in the bank. She died.

Altogether, Mary Ann bore 12 children of her own. Only two survived her. One was a second daughter—the first died within days of birth—born of her marriage to Robinson: Mary Ann had given her to

AN UNREMARKABLE WOMAN . . . and yet she has gone down in history as Britain's greatest mass murderer. Her motives remain a mystery to all.

a friend to care for when the marriage broke up. The second child to live was Quick-Manning's daughter, born in Durham Gaol and named Margaret Edith Quick-Manning Cotton. Robinson himself is believed to have escaped the conventional dosage of arsenic in his soup and tea because, despite Mary Ann's entreaties, he refused to have his life insured.

In all, 21 people close to Mary Ann met their death in less than 20 years. How many of them did she actually murder? The number is usually put at 14 or 15. Records don't show, for instance, exactly how the children who died in Devon met their end. In nearly all the other cases the death certificate gave the cause as "gastric fever". It was a common ailment in an unsanitary age, with symptoms similar to those caused by arsenic poisoning.

Her motive was to collect insurance or burial money, or to clear the way for marriage with someone new who did not want to be burdened with other men's children, or sometimes a combination of both. A number of factors helped her to escape detection for so long—the state of medical knowledge, the ease with which arsenic could be bought, the trust she created by once having been a nurse, the fact that she always called in a doctor to care for her victims, the regularity with which she moved homes.

The medical profession of the time should not be blamed too harshly for the fact it was only when she over-reached herself in West Auckland that the truth was finally suspected. Even as late as 1939 a survey in the neighbouring city of

Newcastle-upon-Tyne showed that a third of the certified causes of death were wrong, and faulty diagnoses are still far from unknown today.

The morning after the sentence, the *Newcastle Journal* described Mary Ann, somewhat predictably, as "a monster in human shape" and commented: "Murder grew with her. Perhaps the most astounding thought of all is that a woman could act thus without becoming horrible and repulsive. Mary Ann Cotton, on the contrary, seems to have possessed the faculty of getting a new husband whenever she wanted one. To her other children and her lodger, even when she was deliberately poisoning them, she is said to have maintained a rather kindly manner. We feel instinctively that the earth ought to be rid of her. Pity cannot be withheld, but it must be mingled with horror . . ."

Nevertheless, there were feelings of unrest about her death sentence on several grounds—the hanging of a woman, the haphazard way counsel for the defence had been appointed, the admission of evidence of deaths other than the one she was being tried for, the fact that no witnesses for the defence had been called. In prison, Mary Ann busied herself trying to obtain support for a petition for her reprieve. She also arranged for Margaret, her new baby daughter, to be cared for by a married couple who had been unable to have children of their own.

Variety tour

The Home Secretary refused all pleas that her sentence should be commuted to life imprisonment. Five days before her execution, Mary Ann's baby was forcibly taken from her. Then, on Monday, March 24, 1873, maintaining her innocence to the end, she finally went to the scaffold. She was a long time—three minutes—in dying.

She was by then already a legend. What was described as "a great moral drama", *The Life And Death Of Mary Ann Cotton*, was in rehearsal for a variety tour which started eight days later. Mothers of children who would not go to sleep or eat their cabbage threatened them with the spectre of "the monster in human shape".

In the streets the children themselves chanted a rhyme which began:
Mary Ann Cotton,
She's dead and she's rotten.
She lies in her bed
With her eyes wide open.
Sing, sing, oh, what can I sing?
Mary Ann Cotton is tied up with string.

The memories of her dark deeds faded with the years, however. It was not until 1973, a century after they hanged her, that she became the subject of a full-length book, *Mary Ann Cotton: Her Story And Trial*, by the north-country writer Arthur Appleton.

'SHE'S BEEN USED!'

When Helen Priestly disappeared, only one family in the area where she lived seemed unaffected. Amid the fears and desperate searchings which culminated in the discovery of Helen's body, the Donalds remained strangely unmoved . . .

DETECTIVE points out the position of the sack where it was found (below). The drab building (left) was where the Priestlys and the Donalds were living.

THE DEATH of eight-year-old Helen Priestly resulted in a trial and sentence for murder. But many people, including criminologists who were present at the trial, were of the opinion that the verdict should have been culpable homicide—a Scottish verdict which, in England, would be manslaughter.

The case began in a building inhabited by respectable working-class families just off King Street and close to the big City Hospital. This was 61 Urquhart Road, Aberdeen, which was divided into eight flats, two on each floor. From the front door, which was usually kept closed, a passage led to the rear of the premises and a yard from which there was no exit. A staircase led to the upper flats and beyond each staircase was a lavatory shared by the flat-dwellers directly concerned, the Donalds and the Priestlys.

On the ground floor one flat was occupied by the Donald family, which comprised Alexander Donald, a hairdresser, his 38-year-old wife Jeannie, and their daughter, also named Jeannie, aged 9. The Priestlys lived in the flat above the Donalds. The daughter of the family, Helen, was a mischievous but harmless child. Mrs. Priestly and Mrs. Donald did not speak to each other; this stemmed from a disagreement that was just five years old on Friday, April 20, 1934.

The weather was typical of April, a combination of cloud, sunshine, and some rain. It was reasonably bright when the children were released from school at noon. Helen Priestly arrived at her home at fifteen minutes past twelve; her mid-day meal, primarily consisting of meat and potatoes, was ready for her. After she had finished she rushed off to visit a friend, a Mrs. Robertson, of whom she was very fond. She was back home again at ten past one, when her mother sent Helen to the nearby Co-operative Store to buy a loaf of bread. In making such purchases the customer receives a voucher, the store portion being retained and endorsed by a salesman with the membership number of the customer. Helen bought her loaf and received her voucher, a thin slip of numbered paper bearing a green line; the store record was to show that the purchase was made about one thirty. She had to be back at school by two o'clock. As she ran home she was seen by several people, and then she completely vanished.

Perils

She was a bright, pleasant little girl, no better and no worse than the average; she was also obedient and responsible, so when she did not return with the loaf, Mrs. Priestly immediately went to see if her child was back with Mrs. Robertson. Both women, well aware of the perils which face small girls, took alarm, and began checking, speaking to neighbours who had seen Helen running home.

The women now sent to tell Mr. Donald at his place of work. The school, three minutes' walk away, was also visited, without result. Jeannie Donald was among those in the playing ground, and though the Donalds and the Priestlys did not usually speak, the two children were casual friends. Jeannie went through the school without success. Mr. Priestly, a painter and decorator, was informed, and he made his own search of the district. The police were told, and were at once on the alert, for a small girl had been abducted the previous November.

At six o'clock that evening Dick Sutton, a nine-year-old friend of Helen, reported seeing her being dragged, holding her loaf, along the street and into a tram-car by a middle-aged man of middle height in a dark coat with a tear in the back. The police swung into fast and all-out action. Searches were made throughout the city, particularly in hospitals.

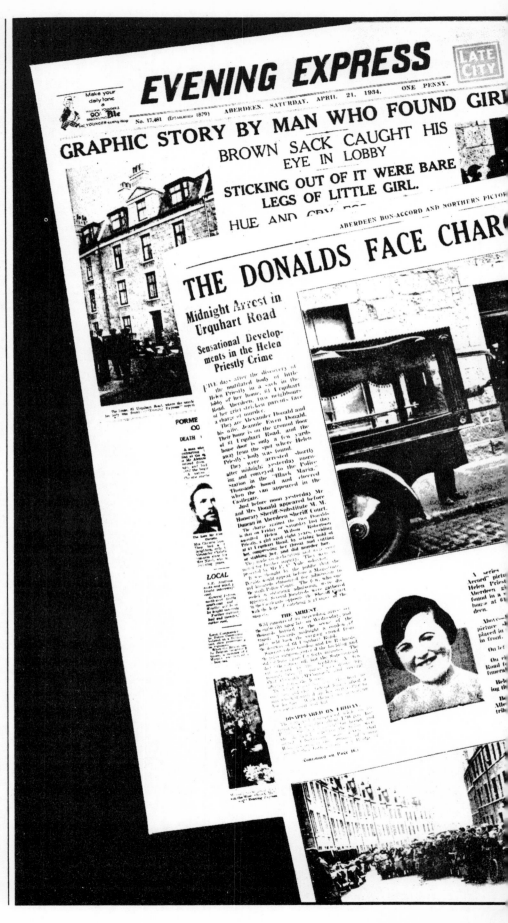

86

OF MURDER

Details were flashed on to cinema screens, and in Urquhart Street itself, the strong Scottish sense of community resulted in search-parties fanning out in every direction, and many individuals making their own forays into every possible corner.

By nightfall the weather had turned windy and chill, with a heavy rain falling at about eight o'clock, but the searchers kept untiringly at work, Mr. Priestly trailing round and round the streets in a friend's car until he returned home, tired out and exhausted, at midnight: at four in the morning he was up again and at the police station waiting for news. A neighbour in Urquhart Road was also up by five o'clock and went in to tell the Priestlys he was off again to resume searching. The street door of No. 61 was unlatched and he went into the building, pausing a moment as his eyes adjusted to the gloom.

Near hysteria

Near the back door by the lavatory there was a recess under the stairs, facing a store cupboard. In the recess, lying half way into the passage, was a sack; this struck the neighbour as seeming odd. He went up to see what it was, and, dimly, made out a child's hand and foot protruding from the sack. He gave the alarm and within minutes the building was a turmoil of excitement and near hysteria; Helen had been found, and one woman is said to have cried out: "She's been used!" But with all the uproar, the comings and goings, the two ground-floor flats remained quiet. One, where a Mrs. Topp was sleeping, was otherwise empty as her husband had gone to work; the other flat was that of the Donalds; their door was closed.

Time checks were easily made. The police, arriving almost at once, were able to show that they had made a final search of the public part of the premises the previous night at eleven. Priestly had come in at midnight; William Topp had used the ground-floor lavatory at halfpast one. The sack was not there at fourthirty when Priestly, a friend, and then Topp had passed by to resume the search. Police checks showed that the jute sack containing the body was dry, as was the small girl in it. But outside the back door was a pool of water and the yard ground surrounding the building was soggy, though there were no footmarks on the step. The streets were wet. The building had not been really deserted all night, but nobody had seen anything suspicious.

With morning the police began their most acute checks, together with a fresh questioning of Dick Sutton for more details of the mystery man. This time the boy lost his nerve and confessed that he had made up the whole story.

No. 61 Urquhart Road was full of policemen and neighbours, but the Donalds' door remained obstinately closed, except for being briefly opened when the milk was taken in. A little later, Donald looked out to ask a passing police officer: "Is there any word?" and was told of the discovery of the body.

Sutton's story had proved a frustrating red herring, since a visual check of Helen's body had shown strangulation marks on the neck and signs on the private parts which sent squads of policemen after the man in the torn coat, a hardpressed search only called off when Dick Sutton told the truth. The body was examined in detail at the post mortem. Vomited matter was found in the windpipe and small air tubes, bruises inflicted before death were found in the neighbourhood of the voice-box and the wind-pipe. The general condition of Helen Priestly was consistent with asphyxia from strangulation. When the stomach was opened it was seen that the paramount contents were meat and potatoes, so little broken up by digestive processes that it was finally decided that death must have taken place not later than two p.m. on the previous day.

The police were already questioning every man in the building where the Priestlys lived. Alibis turned out to be one hundred per cent as each male could prove he was at work at the pertinent times. At the post mortem table a Dr. Richards, and Professor Shennan, Professor of Pathology at Aberdeen University, had now finished with the upper parts of the body and began their examination in detail of the child's private parts. It was quickly established, both by the quality of the marks and the absence of semen, that Helen had not been raped; it was possible, however, to show that intrusion had been made by some sort of sharp stick, or perhaps a poker. This tended to confirm a theory that the false signs of rape were deliberately made by a woman in order to delude the searchers.

Solitary couple

Two new pieces of evidence now emerged through the painstaking police investigation. Helen had actually been observed on her return with the loaf at one forty-five inside 61 Urquhart Road, and, later, a workman said that he had been aware of a child screaming inside the building at about two o'clock. It was later supposed that Helen had been unconscious, or even dying, when the false rape attempt had been made but that this had aroused her and caused her to scream. It was known by the neighbours that the Donalds were a quiet, solitary couple who kept very much to themselves, but the fact they had taken no part in the search or had shown any obvious interest in it naturally caused gossip.

Thus, the following Wednesday the police, impressed by certain directing and most coincidental factors, went to see the Donalds with the intention of questioning them thoroughly. Donald, a decent and respectable man, had an alibi of having been at work at the time in question. His wife, a good-looking woman of equal respectability, was a church worker, a partaker in Salvation Army activities and a woman whose whole life was wrapped up in her daughter, for whom she worked hard.

The police were given permission to search the Donalds' flat, and found what appeared to be bloodstains in a cupboard. The Donalds were arrested at midnight and amid riotous scenes from people outside the building they were rushed in a police car to the station where they were taken into custody. Donald was later released when the police were satisfied with his alibi, but Jeannie Donald was committed for trial, to be held in the High Court of Justiciary, Edinburgh. It opened on July 16, 1934.

Fragment of paper

The paramount evidence was medical. It was shown that a benzedrine test for blood was made in the Donalds' flat, with some results. With the body of Helen Priestly in the jute sack were found some cinders, some household fluff and a number of hairs. The child's combinations bore bloodstains containing bacteria which had come from the rupturing of the intestinal canal (the spurious rape).

Professor Mackie, occupying the Chair of Bacteriology at Edinburgh University, was to say that there was an unusual variety of coliform bacillus of intestinal origin on the child's combinations; two imperfectly cleaned washing-cloths in the Donald flat bore closely similar bacteria. The Professor's view was that the three articles were contaminated from the same source. Bloodstains on various articles belonged to the same group as those on Helen's clothing.

It was shown that the child's thymus gland was enlarged. This meant that she would have been rendered unconscious more quickly than the normal child. Other supporting facts were produced, but one, not brought into evidence, was that a fragment of paper bearing a green line identifiable as belonging to the ticket Helen had received from the Co-operative Store was found in the debris of the Donalds' fireplace.

The trial ended without Mrs. Donald giving evidence. The jury returned within 18 minutes to give its verdict, 13 being for "Guilty" and two for "Not Proven". Sentence of death was passed but this was commuted to life imprisonment. Mrs. Donald was released on June 26, 1944.

The motive for the crime has never been shown, but it was certainly clear the

ARREST of the Donalds (below) took place after the most painstaking police investigation. The absence of an obvious motive made it into a "mystery murder".

child had been hidden in the Donalds' flat until the time arrived for her to be placed in the hall where she was found. It was also shown that Helen Priestly did not think much of Mrs. Donald, that she frequently "cheeked" her, and gave her the unflattering nickname of "Coconut". The late William Roughead, a noted authority on criminological matters, later wrote down his views on the case:

Sudden collapse

"Helen Priestly used to call Mrs. Donald 'Coconut', and plainly held her in low esteem," he said. "It may be that by a fatal chance on that Friday they met at the Donalds' door. The child may have done something to rouse the woman's wrath: kicked at the door, put out her tongue at her, or otherwise annoyed or mocked her. She lost her temper, seized the child by the throat, and shook her. Such a shock, owing to the child's physical defect [the enlarged thymus gland], would result in a sudden collapse, passing into coma.

"The woman, horrified, thought she had killed her. She carried her into the kitchen and frantically strove to revive her, but without avail. What was she to do? There was bad blood between them; doubtless she would be accused of deliberate murder. Then to her, panic-stricken and distraught, the very Devil suggested as the sole means of safety the vile expedient of simulated rape . . ."

THE BLAZING CAR MURDER

The burnt-out Morris Minor yielded a pitiful pile of charred bones. For bigamist A. A. Rouse it must have been a painful death, but so convenient. . . .

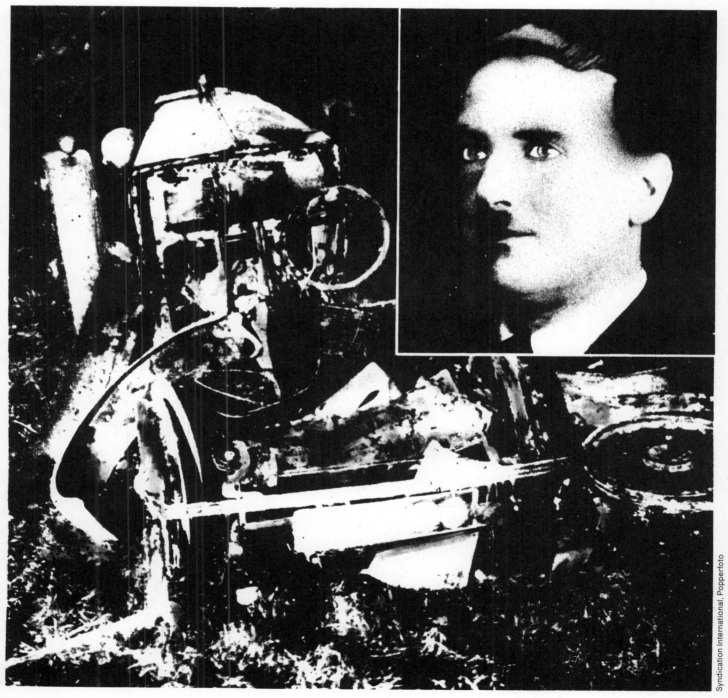

Syndication International. Popperfoto

THANKFUL at last to be almost home, the two young cousins, Alfred Brown and William Bailey, stepped out along the moonlit country lane. They had been to a Guy Fawkes' Night dance in Northampton, England, and now they were on the final half-mile lap of their three-mile walk from the town to their village of Hardingstone.

It was lonely in Hardingstone Lane, the air crisp and still, the moonlight so strong that the details of the surrounding countryside were silver-bright. At that hour — it was 1.45 a.m. on November 6, 1930 — Brown and Bailey felt sure they must be the only people about.

But, suddenly and astonishingly, they discovered they were not alone. Just ahead of them and out of the ditch on the south side of the lane emerged the figure of a stocky, hatless man wearing a light raincoat and carrying a small overnight case. What impressed Brown, as he later explained, was that such a "respectably dressed" man should be seen in such curious circumstances.

But that was not the only odd thing about the stranger so clearly observed in the moonlight. For, first, he hurried past the two young men without a word, towards the cross-roads where Hardingstone Lane met the main London-Northampton road. Then, having gone some little way beyond them, he half turned and shouted: "It looks as though someone is having a bonfire up there!"

Almost at that very same moment Brown and Bailey had themselves noticed a fire-like glow farther along the lane and closer to the village. Seconds later stalks of flame sprouted from the glow and the two cousins, forgetting the mysterious stranger momentarily, hurried towards the blaze

It was a frightening sight they came upon. A Morris Minor, a type of car then known as a "baby saloon", was parked close to the grass verge of the lane facing towards the cross-roads. It was totally bathed in flames that leapt as high as 15 feet. The heat was so intense that Brown and Bailey were forced to the opposite side of the lane, 20 feet away.

In the dazzling glare it was impossible for them to see whether anyone was in the

A BONFIRE, thought the two cousins (inset) when they saw the glow late on Guy Fawkes' night. But they found a frightening sight: a car bathed in flames.

car. They raced on to the village and returned with two local constables and buckets of water. It took them 12 minutes to quell the fire.

As the smoke cleared they saw that the car was almost completely destroyed. But in the midst of the ashes and the heat-twisted frame there remained a strange thing, a charred shape that at first puzzled the sweating fire-fighters. Then a closer look disclosed what it had been—a human being, now incinerated; whether man or woman none of the horrified on-lookers could guess.

Carefully the policemen went about the grisly task of gathering together what they could of the remains. Here they found a brittle, twisted stick that had been an arm, there a blackened leg burned off at the knee. A half-broken, rounded object retained just enough detail to show that it had been a human head.

By dawn the local policemen and senior officers from the Northamptonshire force had wrapped the pathetic remains in sacking and carried them to Hardingstone's Crown Inn. They had also begun positive moves to unravel the secrets of the blazing car. For, luckily, one decisive clue had survived the fire—the car's rear licence plate was intact and perfectly clear: MU 1468.

Life of the party

A check of registrations quickly disclosed the identity of the owner, a Mr. Alfred Arthur Rouse, of Buxted Road, Finchley, north London. But where, now, was this Mr. Rouse—so popular at local clubs and parties when he would sing the "Cobbler's Song" from *Chu Chin Chow*? His wife had no idea.

"I don't know whether it is my husband who is dead in the car or not," she told one reporter.

Perhaps that oddly fleeting figure, the hatless man seen by Brown and Bailey, could help? The police circulated a description ". . . aged between 30 and 35, height 5 ft. 10 ins., with a small round face and curly black hair." It might be that the small round face belonged to that same missing Mr. Rouse.

The next day, photographs of the burned-out car, under headlines like "Body found in a blazing car", and "Blazing car mystery", were given large-scale display in the national newspapers. A copy of one, the *Daily Sketch* for November 7, was bought in Gellygaer,

Glamorganshire, by Miss Phyllis Jenkins, a miner's daughter.

She showed it at once to a visitor to the household. This man had arrived at eight the previous evening with a tale of great misfortune. "I have been 18 hours on the road," he complained. "I lost my car round Northampton. I went in to have a cup of tea and when I came out my car was gone." He was told of a report, in that evening's local paper, of a burned-out car at Northampton. But, "Oh, no," he said, "that is not my car."

Next morning, here was Miss Jenkins with the *Daily Sketch* and some rather more specific information. "There is a photograph of your car," she told him. "How do you know it's mine?" he asked. "Your name, 'A. A. Rouse', is underneath."

For Alfred Arthur Rouse — smooth-tongued womanizer, bigamist, sex-hungry commercial traveller who later declared "my harem takes me to several places and I am not at home a great deal" — it was almost the end of the road.

Rouse had certainly travelled a long, confused and dangerous road since he was born to a genteel shopkeeping couple in London's Herne Hill on April 6, 1894.

It looked, in his early manhood, as though he might also follow a solid-citizen life. In November, 1914, he married Lily May Watkins, a quiet, domesticated woman. Before they could settle down he was with the army in France and, in May, 1915, suffered a head wound which had lasting effects.

Voracious sexual appetite

For a time his memory was defective and he was prone to frequent headaches. The slightest pressure on the scar of his wound caused severe irritation and for that reason he seldom wore a hat.

Psychiatrists later suggested that his injuries may have contributed to his voracious sexual appetite, and his almost total incapacity to tell the truth about any matter, however trivial. In the fantasies with which he regaled his women he had been educated at Eton College and Cambridge University, and had been a major in the army.

But his phoney charm worked with an endless succession of women — to their cost in many cases. His job as a salesman, covering a wide territory, served him well in his search for recruits to his "harem". By 1930 he almost certainly had at least 80 women on his visiting list — shop assistants, nurses, domestic servants, and married women who "entertained" while their husbands were out.

Several had his children. One girl was delivered of a son at the age of 15 — the child lived for only five weeks — and three years later bore him a second son. He went through a bigamous marriage with her and eventually, when the girl had

learned the truth about him, his real and childless wife took the boy into their home and brought him up as her own.

Four days before the destruction of his car another girl was in a London maternity hospital expecting her second child by Rouse. Down in Gellygaer a third girl, Phyllis Jenkins's sister, Ivy, was about to give birth. Rouse had promised her "marriage" and bragged to her family of the beautifully furnished—but needless to say non-existent—house he had bought at Kingston-on-Thames, near the capital.

But Rouse knew that in the great game of catch-a-woman it was he who was about to be caught. Payments on maintenance orders were piling up; his wife's tolerance of his extra-marital exploits was wearing thin. And, unlike many of the girls he cultivated, Ivy Jenkins was surrounded by fair-minded relatives determined to hold her "fiancé" to his promises.

Escape from the vortex into which his amorous adventures had dragged him was becoming urgent. He had somehow to "disappear" and, in doing so, collect enough money to keep himself going while he started a new life. That at least seems to have been the way his mind was working to judge from his subsequent confessions. But, as with so many other things, he was incapable of carrying out any project successfully.

Topix

His plan to solve all problems was, he said, suggested by a chance meeting with a down-and-out who "told me the usual hard luck story". He discovered the man had no relatives and no permanent home.

He seemed the ideal victim. He could die, burned in the Morris Minor and mistaken for Rouse, while the real A. A. Rouse faded from the sight of his women and their maintenance demands. Later he would collect the insurance money on his life and his car—although how that was to be done he had apparently not worked out. For the moment only the next step mattered. He arranged to pick the man up and drive him north on the evening of November 5.

Only a matter of hours

A clear indication of the simple-mindedness behind his brash man-of-the-world appearance was given by Rouse when he added in his confession that he had not thought "there would be much fuss in the papers" about his burning car. All the more shock for him, then, when Phyllis Jenkins confronted him with the front-page headlines; all the more certain that it could be only a matter of hours before the police would be inviting him to "assist" them in their inquiries.

Rouse, who had travelled from the scene of the fire to Gellygaer by way of London—on a lorry which he stopped at the Hardingstone cross-roads—and then by long-distance bus, decided that he had better put distance between himself and Wales. By the afternoon of November 7, he was on a return bus to Victoria Terminal, London.

But his departure was not unnoticed. Gossip about his visit had reached the Cardiff police, who now had urgent information to pass on to their London colleagues.

At 9.20 that evening. Detective-Sergeant Robert Skelly of the Metropolitan Police peered through the windows of a motor-bus which had stopped, on its way to Victoria, at Hammersmith Bridge Road coach station. He picked out one passenger and signalled to him to alight. The man was hatless, wore a light raincoat and carried a small overnight case bearing the initials A.A.R.

"Are you Mr. Rouse?" Skelly inquired politely.

"Yes, that's right."

Skelly indicated a constable with him and said: "We are police officers. You are to accompany us to the police station."

Rouse replied: "Very well. I am glad

Popperfoto

SMOOTH-TONGUED Rouse had at least 80 women on his visiting list, among them (from top left): Nellie Tucker, Helen Campbell (with their son) and Ivy Jenkins. The "real" Mrs. Rouse is pictured left.

it is over. I was going to Scotland Yard about it. I am responsible. I am very glad it is over. I have had no sleep."

So Rouse talked. The story he told he stuck to. He was making an overnight journey to, the Leicester headquarters of his firm when a man thumbed a lift. They drove north, saying little to each other, and, having made a mistaken right turn into Hardingstone Lane, Rouse decided to stop for a brief doze.

But first he needed to relieve himself and as he left the car he told his passenger: "There's some petrol in the can. You can empty it into the tank while I'm gone."

The man had a request, too, according to Rouse. "Have you got a smoke?" he asked. Conveniently, Rouse, a non-smoker, happened to have a cigar which he passed to the man.

Rouse then walked more than 200 yards from the car, taking his case with him — he had, he said, earlier seen the man's hand on the case in the car and didn't trust him. Almost as soon as he had found a secluded place out of sight of the car he "saw a light".

He described what happened then: "I ran towards the car which was in flames. I saw the man inside and tried to open the door but could not as the car was then a mass of flames . . . I was all of a shake. I did not know what to do and ran as hard as I could along the road where I saw the two men [Brown and Bailey] . . . I lost my head and did not know what to do and really don't know what I have done since."

"A certain man"

Accident followed by panic: in someone else's case it might have seemed a satisfactory explanation. But Rouse's behaviour after the fire, his failure to seek help from Brown and Bailey, his "looks like a bonfire" cry and his lies to people he met in Wales put the seal on the police suspicions. Rouse was taken under arrest back to Northampton, charged with the murder "of a certain man whose name is unknown".

From the opening of the proceedings at the magistrates' court Rouse did himself mortal harm. His statement to the police about his "harem" and evidence from a number of young women about his private life and illegitimate children were given nationwide publicity. His defence lawyers feared that no juryman able to read or even to overhear the public gossip could judge him impartially.

But Rouse was brought to trial at Northampton Assizes on Monday, January 26, 1931, with the late Lord Birkett — then plain Mr. Norman Birkett, King's Counsel — exercising the utmost fairness, as chief prosecutor for the Crown, by eliminating all the "immorality" evidence given at the magistrates' court.

Rouse made a sad spectacle in the dock. He was, by turns, wheedling, arrogant and over-talkative. He showed no remorse for the dreadful fate of his unknown passenger.

Why, when he got to the Jenkins' home in Wales, Mr. Birkett asked, had he told lies about what had happened to his car? "Because," said Rouse, "there are many members of the family, for one thing, and I should have to tell the story over and over again, and I did not like to tell it with ladies present."

Why, for 43½ hours between the fire and being called off the coach at Hammersmith, had he made no move to report the "accident" to the police?

To the fountainhead

"My reason is that I have very little confidence in local police stations . . . If you want my candid opinion I have not much faith in them. I was going to the fountainhead. One usually goes to the fountainhead if one wants things done properly."

No, in their five-hour journey together Rouse had asked no details of his passenger. He didn't know his name, home town, job; not even where the man eventually intended making for.

"He inferred that he did not do tramping on his feet," said Rouse who, as a teetotaller, added the pseudo-fastidious comment that he soon regretted giving the man a lift because "his breath smelt of drink".

Why had he told Sergeant Skelly he felt "responsible"? Ah, Rouse replied, that was a mere technicality for "in the police eyes the owner of the car is responsible for anything that happens to that car. Correct me if I am wrong"

Rouse's case was that the man had set the car on fire himself through trying to light the generously-given cigar while

UTMOST FAIRNESS was shown by Prosecutor Birkett (near left), who eliminated Rouse's "harem" statements. His wife was loyal to the end (right).

March. 7. 1931.

I have fought to the last ditch
to save my husband's life.
But alas. I have failed, and the law
will take its course.
Those who knew him well, knew the
good that was in Arthur, I did, and
so do others.
But I knew I was fighting a lost
cause. for before he went to the
Court of Criminal Appeal, he had told
me that the Jury's verdict was the
correct one, and he was guilty.

My own opinion is that he was
not in his right mind on Nov. 5th.

Lily May Rouse

Mirrorpic

pouring petrol. Rouse, as he told it to the jury, fled in panic, said nothing at all to Brown and Bailey, just ran to the cross-roads and thumbed a lift from a lorry driven by a Mr. Henry Turner.

Some of the conversation Rouse admitted to with Mr. Turner on the journey to London gave the jury a clear idea of the real man behind the panic-stricken motorist who had just seen a man roasted alive. Rouse told Mr. Turner: "I have been expecting a mate with a Bentley but I missed him . . . That's a good idea of yours, to have the floorboards up; because of the exhaust it makes a warm cab."

Technical evidence by a fire assessor and Rouse's own actions after the fire were the two strongest weapons in the Crown's armoury. Rouse was noticed to pale when the remnants of his car's carburettor were handed to him in the dock—an apparently clear sign, if not evidence in law, that he had deliberately tampered with it to ensure a swift, consuming funeral pyre.

It was impossible for the jury to be given any proof of the man's condition at the outbreak of the fire—had Rouse already killed him? (Much was made of a wooden mallet found near the burned-out wreck, but it almost certainly played no essential part in the crime.) But most criminologists now broadly accept Rouse's post-trial "confession" in which he said the man was befuddled by whisky—supplied by Rouse for the purpose.

At the end of the six-day hearing, on Saturday, January 31, 1931, the jury took only one hour and 15 minutes to arrive at their verdict of guilty. And they had spent part of that time examining a Morris Minor similar to Rouse's, as well as having lunch.

Just to be near him

Rouse's appeal was heard and dismissed on February 23 and he was hanged at Bedford Jail on March 10. His long-suffering wife had remained loyal to the end, even taking a job in a Northampton shop to be near him during his weeks under arrest.

Apart from its other aspects of notoriety, the blazing car murder remains a classic among crimes because of that shadowy figure who featured so promin-

ently, yet so fleetingly, in it: the victim.

His identity was never discovered. Only one witness, a Hertfordshire policeman, was able to give the jury even the vaguest glimpse of him. At 11.15 p.m. on November 5—a few hours before the murder—Police Constable David Lilley saw Rouse's car standing without lights near a small café a mile from Markyate.

He spoke to Rouse, who was sitting in the driving seat and who immediately apologized and switched the lights on. The man in the passenger seat, the constable told the jury, "appeared to me to be about 35 to 40 years of age. He was a man of small stature, had an oval, pale face and was dressed in a dark coat and trilby hat. I am not certain as to whether he had a moustache or not."

It was a meagre record, for history, of one man's life. But, for all its obscurity, that life was not too unimportant for the law to ignore its brutal and merciless end.

NIGHTMARE AT THE YWCA

The dark stranger appeared in the girls' hostel, then left.
Months later he was back on his fatal trail.

Sunday Mercury

'THE MIDLANDS' OWN SUNDAY NEWSPAPER

No. 2,131 ✱ ✱

PRICE 4D.

365 handkerchiefs GUARANTEED FOR 365 DAYS

THE GREAT CHRISTMAS MANHUNT FAILS

Mercury Staff Reporter

AS Birmingham's most intensive-ever Christmas manhunt enters its fourth day, the sadistic killer who murdered a young woman at an Edgbaston YWCA hostel is still at large.

And last night Det. Chief Supt. Jim Haughton, head of the City CID, asked: "Where are the 60 bus passengers who travelled with a bloodstained man on Wednesday evening?"

Despite Press, TV and radio appeals none of the passengers on the 7.40 p.m. No. 8 (Inner Circle) bus have come forward.

Yesterday, police announcements were made at Birmingham and West Bromwich Albion football grounds, and in Birmingham cinemas.

Notices appealing for any information were posted on buses and in public houses throughout the city.

The headless body of 29-year-old Miss Sidney Stephanie Baird was found in the YWCA annexe at Wheeleys Road, Edgbaston. She had been brutally murdered with a table knife.

After he had murdered Miss Baird, the killer attacked Miss Margaret Brown, who was also staying at the hostel.

Police believe the man caught a No. 8 bus at Wheeleys Road and travelled towards Five Ways, The Ivy Bush, Hockley

THE GIRL WHO ESCAPED

A holiday flash-back to a smiling Margaret Brown.

'My 10 seconds of horror'

...he spent a frightened Christmas, 21-year-...
...own yesterday told for the...

Woman of 66 and son die in house blaze

A 66-YEAR-OLD woman, and her 36-year-old son died in a Christmas morning fire at West Bromwich despite rescue attempts by five men.

The woman was Mrs. May Jones, of 14 Neal Street. Her son, who was spending the night with her and his step-father, Mr. George Jones (68), was Mr. Jack Hooper, father of a young daughter, of 9 Larchwood Road, Yew Tree Estate, West Bromwich.

Mr. Jones managed to escape from the blazing house, but firemen, wearing breathing apparatus, found the bodies of Mrs. Jones and Mr. Hooper in a smoke-filled bedroom.

It is believed that Mr. Hooper was trying to save his mother's life when he was overcome by smoke.

Mr. Thomas William Parsons, a 36-year-old welder, of 12 Neal Street, said: "We were opening the children's presents when we heard a milkman shouting that No. 14 was on fire. I saw Mr. Jones in the backyard. He was doubled up with coughing.

"Mr. Sidney Taylor and his son from No. 18, joined me and Mr. Bert Barnard, the care-taker of a nearby school. Mr. Barnard brought a ladder and I got to a bedroom window but was driven back by the heat and smoke.

"It was impossible to get in."

Flames rushed out

Mr. Taylor said: "My so... and I dashed along in our nig... clothes and with bare feet... burst the back door open... the flames rushed out at... making it impossible for us... get into the house.

"The milkman was also... ing but I don't know his n...

Mr. Jones was detained... hospital with severe sho...

Yesterday police and... officers were trying to es... the cause of the fire.

A Fire Brigade spo... said: "So far we have... how it started."

IT WAS 11.15 p.m. on a cold evening in March 1959. A beautiful young teacher who occupied a single room in the annexe of the Y.W.C.A. hostel in Birmingham, England was lying in bed. Outside all was quiet. She had heard the comforting sound of the porter as he made his rounds and felt that all was safe. Soon she would be asleep. Suddenly the door opened — the light was switched on and a dark figure stepped into the bedroom. "Hello," he said softly, "I'm looking for Kathleen Ryan."

The girl sat up in bed, her heart pounding with fear. She made a desperate effort to keep calm. "How did you get in?" she asked. "I climbed in through a window," came the reply. The man approached the bed with a purposeful look on his face. He stared fixedly at the girl's breasts outlined beneath her flimsy nightdress, and she realized that only a miracle could save her from assault.

"Please," she pleaded, "I'm engaged to be married. Perhaps you had better be going."

Something in her tone of voice seemed to calm the stranger. For a second he hesitated. Then the miracle happened: he turned and walked towards the door. The girl quickly jumped out of bed and with a bravado which astonished even herself, ordered the man to follow her. She led the way down the corridor, opened the front door, and let him out of the hostel. Seconds later she was on the telephone to the police; but there was no sign of the intruder when they arrived.

Clothes and presents

Nine months later, on December 23, 1959, another girl who occupied the next room in the Y.W.C.A. annexe came face to face with the same man. Her name was Stephanie Baird, a highly attractive but retiring girl who was totally uninterested in men. As before, the intruder climbed in through a small window at the rear of the building, and again, no one saw him. There were very few girls staying at the hostel that night since most of them had gone home to spend Christmas with their families. Stephanie, too, was packing a few clothes and presents with the intention of leaving on the following morning for her mother's house.

She moved confidently round her room in a red pullover and petticoat, little suspecting that she was already being watched. Outside in the corridor, the stranger found a chair, stood on it, and looked through the high glass panel set above Stephanie's door. Soon, however, he began to get bored. He jumped off

HOSTEL OF TERROR: In the annexe (left) Stephanie Baird died horribly. In the ironing-room (right) Margaret Brown's screams saved her from the same fate.

Syndication International, UPI, PA

the chair and was about to steal away when the door opened.

"What are you doing?" demanded Stephanie.

"I'm looking for somebody," the intruder replied.

Then, without warning, she was in his arms. He began kissing her frantically and edging her, at the same time, back into her room. Stephanie struggled desperately, and for a brief second managed to tear her face away long enough to scream. It was the last voluntary sound she ever made. To silence her the man closed his powerful fingers round her throat and squeezed. Under his weight she fell backwards, fracturing her skull on the floor. By this time she was already unconscious, but the man kept on squeezing until her body lay limp and lifeless in his arms. What followed led police and doctors to label Stephanie's killer as one of the most monstrous sexual psychopaths in the history of crime.

Panting and moaning with excitement, the man proceeded to make love, in a variety of ways, to the dead body. But this was only a beginning. Having satisfied his first urges, he remembered the chair outside and took the precaution of putting it back where he had found it. Re-entering Stephanie's room, he locked it from the inside and got undressed. Then, as if he were unleashing all the suppressed passions of a lifetime of ugly, frustrated desires, he attacked the girl's body with unprintable bestiality, running through the whole gamut of sexual activities which his warped imagination could invent.

Even this, however, lost its attraction to him. He was about to stop when he spotted a table knife lying on the shelf of an open cupboard. With it, he carved off Stephanie's right breast and flung it onto the bed. Next he tried to cut open her stomach, making deep scores on both the back and front of the body. Finally, when this failed, he attacked the head and succeeded—although he had no knowledge of anatomy—in cutting it off within the space of a few minutes. He then held it up by the hair and stared at it in the mirror.

At that moment a noise interrupted him. Startled for the first time, he dropped the head onto the bed, wiped his hands on Stephanie's underwear, dressed quickly and climbed out through the window. He left a note, scrawled in ballpoint, on the dresser. It said: "This was the thing I thought would never come." It was an extraordinary and horribly pathetic message; so much so, that police were unsure whether it was the remark of a madman or a disgusting joke.

She raised the alarm

Outside once more, the criminal composed himself for a further assault. He was still excited and breathing heavily and, after thoroughly inspecting the annexe for a second victim, made his way over to the main block. There was a light on in the hostel laundry. Twenty-one-year-old Margaret Brown was busy ironing some underwear. She, too, was preparing to go home for Christmas. Once, she put the iron down and walked through the adjoining washroom to close the outside door, which she had noticed had blown open. She returned and was about to continue ironing when she suddenly heard the door click open again. Once more she walked through the washroom to close it and returned. But as soon as she picked up the iron the same thing happened a third time.

The washroom lights went out almost at the same moment. Margaret, suspecting nothing, again turned to close the door. As she entered the washroom, she just glimpsed a shadowy figure before being struck a violent blow on the head. The man lunged forward and Margaret screamed and screamed again at the top of her voice. Unlike Stephanie, she was lucky. This time the intruder took fright and fled, and the terrified girl was able to raise the alarm.

When police arrived they had no inkling that Stephanie Baird had been murdered and mutilated in her room. They interviewed Margaret Brown, who gave them a reasonably accurate description of the attacker. "He was about 28 years old," she told detectives, "five feet eight inches high with a ruddy complexion and a well-defined chin." Some footprints were found outside an open window and plaster casts were taken. Then, as a matter of routine, the police decided to check on the other girls staying in the hostel. They found that Stephanie Baird's door was locked, and an officer was sent outside to look through a chink in the curtains. He could just see a pair of motionless, naked human legs.

"Batter down the door," came the order. Seconds later the police had burst in on the scene of blood and chaos left by the killer. One of the young officers was physically sick. All of them were numbed by the awfulness of the sight before them.

A televised warning

The news of the murder was quickly relayed to Birmingham Police Headquarters, and the entire local police force was placed on the alert. Detective Chief Superintendent James Haughton, head of Birmingham's Criminal Investigation Department, took over the case. Contact was made with every other police department in Great Britain, and also with various European countries through Interpol. In addition, Haughton called in the Press and also made sure that there would be radio and television news flashes on the murder; later he appeared on television programmes to warn the public of the possibility that the killer might strike again, and to ask for help in finding him. It was a nation-wide man hunt.

From the start, however, Haughton was beset by bad luck. A police dog picked up the murderer's scent, and was avidly on the trail when a traffic accident scattered the contents of an overloaded truck over the highway. The scent was lost. The Press was keen to support the police effort, but the date was against them. Late editions of the newspaper carried the

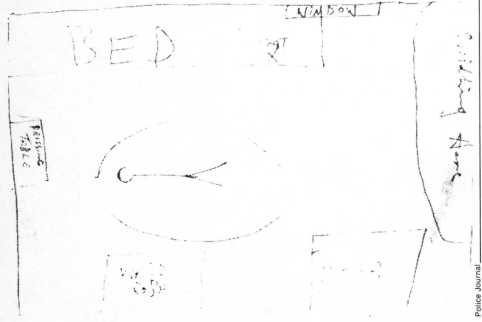

"I WANT TO TELL YOU . . . it's been on my mind." Pathetic psychopath and brutal killer Patrick Byrne even drew a "map" to help ensure his own conviction.

story on Christmas Eve, but no more editions were due to appear again until Sunday, December 27. Many local people had gone away for the national holiday whilst others had come into the area from elsewhere, thus increasing the difficulty of checking on possible suspects.

Then, just as Haughton was preparing for what looked like a long and arduous inquiry, he seemed to get a break. At a police check point some distance from the scene of the crime an officer had stopped a bus and questioned the conductor. He learned that earlier on the same evening a man whose description coincided with that of the suspect had boarded the bus near the Y.W.C.A. He was heavily soaked in blood—so much so, that it had dripped from his arms onto the seat. Days were spent trying to trace this man and all the other passengers on the bus who might possibly have seen him. Tests on the blood confirmed that it was of the same group as Stephanie's. Detectives drove the conductor round and round the bus route in an effort to help him remember where the man had left the bus. He had to be traced, if only to be eliminated from the inquiry.

Despite the most urgent appeals, however, he never came forward and police were forced to continue their search without ever discovering his identity. Eventually, a reconstruction of the crime satisfied detectives that the blood-stained passenger was not the murderer. He was *too* covered in blood; for it was soon realized that since there was no trace of blood en

THE KNIFE of a madman? And what of the note? Was that some kind of sick and disgusting joke? There were clues by the score, but from the start the police were dogged by bad luck. Even an apparently lucky break set them on the wrong track.

route from the hostel to the bus stop the murderer probably had very little on his clothes. Because of this, Haughton guessed that he had undressed before mutilating the body.

The two who confessed

When this avenue of investigation failed, Haughton realized that he had no choice but to begin a house to house search, radiating outwards from the hostel. A questionnaire was carefully prepared so that every detective would ask exactly the same questions, and this was given out to small teams who visited all the houses in their area to check out the movements of every adult male. The initial investigation resulted in 20,000 completed questionnaires. Gradually, as no new information appeared, the area was extended until it covered a three-quarters of a mile radius round the Y.W.C.A. The number of people interviewed in the death area alone reached the total of 100,000.

Because the intruder had been seen in the hostel on at least one other occasion, Chief Superintendent Haughton was convinced that he was a local man. Nevertheless, thousands of criminals who lived outside the area were interviewed, and everyone in Birmingham and surrounding districts who had a record of conviction for peeping, or indecency, or accosting, or assaulting women, was methodically checked. They were all eliminated. So were two men who actually confessed to the crime.

Then came a further blow. The fingerprint men had been working day and night in an attempt to produce a legible set of prints. They finally admitted defeat. The night had been so cold and wet that insufficient sweat exuded from the killer's fingers to make prints. Even the paper on which he had written the strange message yielded nothing.

There was only one clue left: the footprints left by the killer under the annexe window. The police had been anxious to keep photographs of these from the Press for fear that the criminal would destroy his shoes if he thought that they might

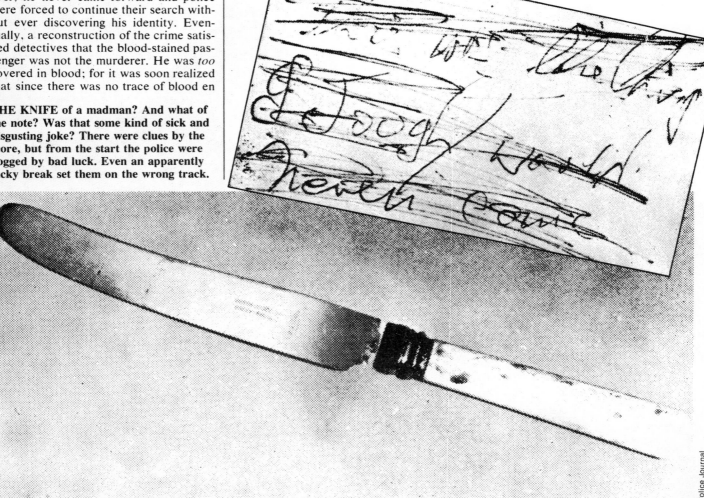

Police Journal

Keystone

trap him. With every other line of investigation drawing a blank, however, Haughton decided that the risk must be taken. The pictures were released along with an appeal to anyone who had seen a man wearing this type of shoe to come forward.

Unknown to the police, the shoes, with their distinctive pattern of transverse bars on both soles and heels, were being driven round in a Birmingham City Corporation garbage truck – the discarded property of an Irish labourer named Patrick Joseph Byrne. Byrne was already known to the police. He had, until Christmas Eve, been living in lodgings quite close to the Y.W.C.A. During the exhaustive house to house inquiries, his name had appeared on the police lists. The fact that he had left his lodgings the day after the murder had not made him a suspect. He had told his landlady well before December 23 that he intended to leave and was going to stay with his mother in Warrington, Lancashire. His previous employers had also been notified.

On the night of the murder his landlady confirmed that she had seen him leave the house at 5.30 p.m., and again at 8 p.m. and 10.30 p.m. – at which time Byrne asked if he could stay an extra night as

he had drunk too much to go to his mother's house. The landlady agreed, and he left early the next morning. A friend of Byrne's testified to police that they had been drinking together during the evening. He seemed to have a sound alibi.

On leaving, Byrne placed the shoes and the suit he had worn on the murder night into a paper carrier bag and gave them to the landlady to throw out. The landlady left the bag beside her garbage can and, as a result, the garbage collector spotted them and decided to rescue them. "They were too good to throw out," he said later.

We mustn't let him go

Byrne, now safely in Warrington, had forgotten all about the discarded shoes. But when the police released the pictures of his footprints – and he saw them splashed over the front page of his newspaper – he remembered them with a shock. Suppose his landlady had forgotten to throw them away? Suppose she had recognized them and was on her way to the police? He began to worry; soon he was on the verge of panic.

Meanwhile, Chief Superintendent Haughton was suffering agonies of frustration. He spent days travelling through-

WITNESSES: The bus conductor (left); the fortunate Margaret Brown (with fiancé, centre); and the landlady. On the London train for a visit to Scotland Yard.

out the City of Birmingham and the surrounding districts showing slides of the murder to groups of policemen. "The majority of the police had not been to the scene," he said later, "and hadn't seen the gruesome nature of it. These slides helped to give them impetus and have them going away saying, 'We must find this person!' and conveying this enthusiasm to everyone in the area: 'We mustn't let him get away. We've got to find him.'"

In this way, an attempt was made to retain police interest through the long, hard weeks of fruitless searching. Finally, Haughton decided that the only answer lay in repeating the house to house search. He felt sure that somewhere, some minute detail had been missed which held the key to the killer's identity. The only way to obtain this was by interviewing the 100,000 people again.

Almost immediately, a flaw in the original search was noticed. It was pointed out that none of the men who had left the area during the Christmas period and

103

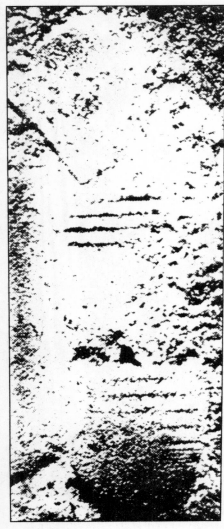

Police Journal

failed to return had been interviewed *personally* by the police. Perhaps the killer was one of these. Accordingly a list of their names was made up and among them was that of Patrick Joseph Byrne. He was quickly traced to Warrington and a message was sent to the local police requesting them to interview him.

On February 10, 1960, Byrne, clearly terrified, called at Warrington Police Station. He was seen by Detective Sergeant George Welborn, who observed Byrne's agitation. Nevertheless, the Irishman made a good attempt to appear unconcerned. He freely answered the sergeant's questions about his movements on the murder night, and everything he said coincided with what the police already knew. Welborn, however, was a highly professional officer. To satisfy his professional conscience, he asked one extra question which didn't appear on the questionnaire: "Would you have any objection to having your fingerprints taken?"

There was a moment of silence. Byrne made an effort to reply, but the words refused to come. In those few seconds his resistance collapsed and panic took over.

He became sure that the police knew more than they said. They probably already had the shoes. It was a trap. Sensing that the silence had been a little too long, the astute policeman asked a further question: "Have you anything you care to mention about your stay in Birmingham?"

Without warning Byrne blurted out, "I want to tell you about the Y.W.C.A. I have something to do with it." The sergeant then pointed out to Byrne the seriousness of what he had said.

"I know," replied the killer, "I cannot sleep. It's been on my mind. I was coming down to see the police. These last seven weeks have been no good to me."

Within hours Chief Superintendent Haughton had driven to Warrington to collect the suspect. He had had two confessions already, but he soon realized that this one was different. The facts tallied. Byrne related details which only the real murderer could know. Later, the tell-tale shoes were picked up and definitely identified as belonging to him. At his trial, Mr. John Hobson, representing the Crown, read out in full the remarkable statement Byrne made to police after his arrest. It

FOOTPRINTS TO FATE: The evidence that the police held back from the public . . . yet these traces were enough to spur the killer's blurted revelations.

told, in graphic and obscene detail, the story of his nightmarish attack on Stephanie Baird and the bestial feelings which prompted·it.

"I wanted to get my own back on them for causing my nervous tension through sex," he said at one point. "I felt I only wanted to kill beautiful women. I watched her for a time, and stood close to the window . . . the urge to kill her was tremendously strong."

Byrne was subsequently found guilty of murder and sentenced to life imprisonment. On appeal, the Lord Chief Justice, Lord Parker, substituted for the verdict one of manslaughter on the grounds that Byrne was on the borderline of insanity. The sentence, however, remained the same. As Chief Superintendent Haughton later stated, it was only by "unremitting effort" and police tenacity that the brutal psychopath was put where he belonged—behind bars.

THE FATAL FANTASIES OF RONALD TRUE

His name belied his nature: a blusterer, a braggart, a devious teller of tall tales. A harmless party bore, perhaps . . . but for the seeds of violence rooting in the depths of his perverted imagination.

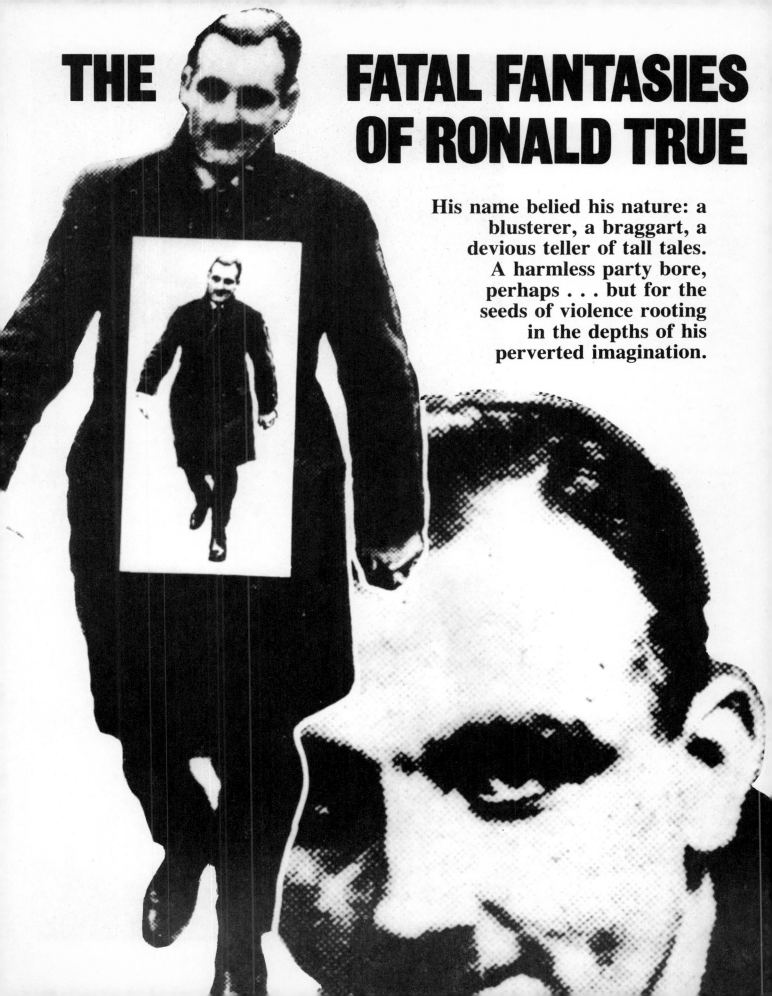

PUNCTUAL as always, Miss Emily Steel arrived at 9.15 a.m. at the basement flat in Fulham for her regular five hours' stint as cleaning woman to the tenant, Miss Olive Young.

She let herself in with her latch-key and was not surprised to find the bedroom door still shut, for her employer often slept late. She was equally not surprised to see a man's coat, scarf and gloves on the table in the small sitting room.

For Miss Steel was under no illusions about her employer's profession—it was, as the saying goes, the oldest in the world. Olive Young, whose real name was Gertrude Yates, was a prostitute of what some later called "the rather better class".

Many of her clients were "regulars" who could afford the cost of entertaining her to meals and staying all night with her.

So, accepting what seemed to be a routine situation at No. 13a Finborough Road, London, S.W. 10, Miss Steel went into the kitchen and began to prepare some sausages for her own breakfast.

She noticed that a teapot contained the dregs of still-warm tea, and two cups and saucers were gone from the dresser. Clearly Miss Young or her friend had been up and about in the flat not so very long before.

Impressive and sleek

Leaving the sausages to cook, Miss Steel returned to the sitting room to tidy up. She had barely begun when she saw a man appear from the direction of the bedroom. She recognized him at once as Major True, whom she had seen at the flat with Miss Young two weeks previously.

The impressive, six-foot visitor with the sleek, dark hair and neat moustache addressed her in quiet confidential tones.

"Don't wake Miss Young," he said. "We were late last night and she is in a deep sleep. I'll send the car round for her at twelve o'clock."

Miss Steel helped the Major on with his coat and received in return a tip of half-a-crown—a handsome gratuity for 1922. From the top of the basement steps she watched Major True hail a taxi and drive off down the Fulham Road.

Back in the flat, Miss Steel tapped at the bedroom door and, receiving no reply, went in. The bed was empty, but when she drew back the bedclothes she was alarmed to find two pillows laid lengthways down the middle of the bed and covered with blood. Under the eiderdown was the kitchen rolling-pin.

The dressing-table drawers were open, and it was obvious that someone had been

A PROSTITUTE of "the rather better class", Gertrude Yates, alias Olive Young, lay brutally battered about the head with a cord knotted around her neck.

THE DAILY MIRROR, Tuesday, March 7, 1922.

As Good as Sunshine:

Pip, Squeak and Wilfred will che up the dullest day. See Page

The Daily Mirro

NET SALE NEARLY TWICE THAT OF ANY OTHER DAILY PICTURE NEWSP.

Registered at the G.P.O. as a Newspaper

TUESDAY, MARCH 7, 1922

No. 5,724.

GIRL'S MURDER IN LONDON FLAT

VANISHED

An official of Scotland Yard sketching the house in Finborough-road at which the tragedy occurred.

The Rev. F. S. Kinder, the from Lewsham. He left his h ruary 14, and no news his a to have resigned

NEW LAW APPOINTMENTS

Mr. Leslie Scott, Solicitor-General.

EX-UNDERGRADUA

rummaging through the contents. With growing apprehension she went to a cupboard near the bed where she knew Olive Young kept her jewel box. Some of the more valuable pieces of jewellery were missing.

There was only one room left in which Miss Steel could look for her employer—the bathroom. Fearfully she pulled open the door and there on the floor, almost completely naked and brutally battered about the head, lay Olive Young.

Not only had the 25-year-old prostitute been bludgeoned but, as the subsequent police examination showed, a piece of rough towelling had been thrust into her mouth with such force that her tongue was doubled back. And a dressing-gown cord had been knotted tightly around her neck.

The police, led by Chief Inspector William Brown of Scotland Yard, knew at once the name of the man they must

A CERTAIN SURFACE POLISH enabled True to be charming in the most unlikely circumstances . . . even at the inquest (below) after Olive Young's death.

seek to "help" them with their inquiries. Miss Steel gave the information. But, more than that, the ferocious murderer had even left his own calling card on the sitting-room sideboard "Mr. Ronald True," it said in print, and below that, in handwriting, "23 Audley Street, W.1." The name was correct, the address false.

In such circumstances most murderers would have used every ounce of energy and every second of time to disappear from public view. But not True. He behaved almost as though he were deliberately setting out to lay a trail for himself, like the "hare" in a paper-chase.

He went, by the taxi Miss Steel had seen him hail, to an outfitter in Coventry Street, just off Piccadilly Circus, and bought a bowler hat, collar and tie and a ready-made brown suit—for a total cost of £16 16s. 10½d.

Mr. James Milne, assistant in the tailoring department, noticed that True's trousers were stained in front by a large patch of blood.

To his surprise True volunteered a unique explanation. "This came from an

aeroplane accident," he said. "I'm a pilot flying the Marseilles express and I had a smash on landing this morning."

True changed into his new suit in the shop's fitting room and asked Mr. Milne to wrap his bloodstained clothes in a parcel. As True emptied the pockets of the old suit Mr. Milne saw him open a small jewel case containing a wrist-watch and a string of pearls. These, and the money he was spending, had belonged to Olive Young.

From the outfitter's he went to a barber's, where he had a haircut and shave and asked if he could leave his parcel, "while I pop across the road". He did not return for the parcel, and it was eventually retrieved by the police.

True's next call was at a pawnshop in Wardour Street, Soho, where he produced two of Olive Young's rings and asked for a loan on them of £70. The assistant, Mr. Herbert Elliet, told him that was "an absurd price" and offered him £25, which True promptly accepted.

By then it was time for True to go to the entrance to the Prince of Wales theatre, in Coventry Street, where he

was due to be met by the hired car he had been using for the past five days for a series of idle trips around London with his friends. His usual driver, Luigi Mazzola, was sitting at the wheel.

The previous night Mr. Mazzola had driven True to 13a Finborough Road and been told: "I am staying here the night. Meet me tomorrow at 11."

Now, at this next day's meeting, True's first words were: "Sorry I dismissed you last night, because I stopped only 20 minutes in the flat and left a man and woman fighting there."

But still True showed no anxiety to disappear. He picked up a friend and they were driven off on another of True's aimless wanderings—calling at Hounslow first for a drink, then driving out to Croydon and Richmond and finally to the Hammersmith Palace of Varieties.

The Palace was True's last stopping place in freedom. Detectives had traced him through the hired car company, and just before 10 p.m. four senior police officers walked quietly into the box where True was sitting with his friend.

Detective Inspector Albert Burton grasped True with both hands and ordered him out into the corridor behind the box. There another officer frisked him and found a loaded revolver in his hip pocket.

Charged with the murder of Olive Young, True denied any knowledge of the crime, but told a rambling story of

ONCE ARRESTED (by Detective Inspector Burton, left), True faced a line of ominous witnesses from driver Luigi Mazzola (above) to Miss Emily Steel the maid (centre left). . . .

seeing, on the night of the murder, a "tall man running along Fulham Road coming from Finborough Road".

It was the first of a series of fantasies the police were to hear from True. And when his trial opened at the Old Bailey on May 1, 1922, it was evident that he was either a schizophrenic or was trying to appear like one. His general behaviour in the weeks before the murder had been "strange", to say the least.

One of the stories he told his friends was that a man was visiting West End pubs and clubs impersonating him and using the name Ronald True. This man, so the fantasy went, was passing out dud cheques which eventually the real Ronald True's mother was having to honour.

For that reason the "real" True carried a loaded revolver which he frequently brandished, even in the company of strangers. He also produced bullets which had been cut so as to turn them into the dum-dum variety, which cause tearing wounds.

Curiously, most of the men he met seemed to believe his impossibly tall stories. The women he knew did not. Rightly they suspected that True was in fact living most of his life in a self-created never-never land.

True was born in 1891, so that by the time of Olive Young's death he was 30. He was illegitimate, but his mother, who was only 16 at the time of his birth, looked after him well and later married a prosperous businessman who was able to give young Ronnie True a good start in life.

The good start proved to be of little value, for True was shiftless and unreliable. He was sent out to New Zealand to try his hand at farming, but that failed, and for several years he drifted around the world.

He went to the Argentine and then to Canada, where he had a brief and inglorious career in the North-West Mounted Police. Then he was off to Mexico, and

111

finally to Shanghai where, in 1914, he learned of the outbreak of war and decided to return home and become a hero.

True was by now a morphia addict, but despite the effects of that and his general fecklessness, he had a certain surface "polish".

He could be charming and observe the social graces when he wasn't being foul-tempered and moody. And it was that superficial charm that helped to get him into the Royal Flying Corps as a student-pilot with commission prospects.

To the amazement of some of his fellow trainees, True passed his pilot's examination. He immediately ordered an insignia of wings for his uniform jacket, three times the size of the regular type and worked in silks of rainbow colours.

Guy Dent, another pilot who trained with him at Gosport, Hampshire, said: "He had a feverish air about him. He was always rushing about and laughing with a loud voice, and he seemed deficient in common sense. When I saw the case in the paper I thought if this is the same True, he was unstable six years ago."

Crashing aircraft

Inevitably, and despite his "wings", the only thing True could do with aircraft was to crash them. After one accident, in which he was seriously injured, he was invalided out of the air force.

By the end of the war True had invented the "other True". In a nursing home, where fruitless attempts were made to wean him from his daily dose of 30 grains of morphia, he went into a rage when any bill was presented to him and declared: "It's not meant for me—it's for the other one."

Once out of the nursing home he adopted the title of "major" and announced that he was a wartime fighter ace who had shot down at least five German aircraft.

Exhibiting his loaded revolver, he shouted that he was "out to get the other Ronald True". If any of his friends had anyone they wanted removed he would do the job, he offered, at "a bob a nob"—a shilling a head.

He told a woman friend: "I'll murder someone one of these days. You watch the papers and see if I don't. There'll be a big case about it."

This woman decided there and then that True was insane. Yet his circle of friends increased, and many found him amusing. With his fantastic stories and sudden outbursts of maniacal anger he became something of a party clown—for the men around him, at least.

On the night of February 18, 1922, True paid his first visit to Olive Young at her Fulham flat. They had met a few days previously in London's West End. Olive Young had once been a shopgirl. She drifted into prostitution, and because

RONALD TRUE REPRIEVED.

CONVICT CERTIFIED TO BE INSANE.

Ronald True, who was found guilty and sentenced to death at the Central Criminal Court on May 5 for the murder of Olive Young, has been certified to be insane, and the death sentence has been respited.

The following official notice was issued last night:

The Home Secretary, ac...

THE GREATEST TRAGEDY of all was that so many people who knew of his illness did nothing to help him—and so save the life of Olive Young.

of her intelligence and attractiveness had built up a successful "business". She had money in the bank and, unlike a common street-walker, could be choosey about her clients.

She quickly decided that Major True was not her type. During his first night's visit to Fulham he had frightened her by his routine with the revolver. After he had left she found that a five-pound note from her handbag had gone with him.

From then on she tried to avoid him. She made sure that each night no light was visible from her flat. She let him hammer at the door in vain. She would not speak to him on the telephone.

Close to midnight on Sunday, March 5, a near-penniless True, who was keeping his hired car until the final moment of payment arrived, ordered the faithful Mazzola to drive him to Finborough Road.

For once Olive Young had relaxed her vigilance. Through the glass of the front door True saw a light in the hallway. He knocked, and Olive opened the door.

In view of her efforts to dodge True the girl must have been dismayed when she saw the tall figure of the "major" looming in the doorway. But in her profession she could not afford to create a "scene" in the quiet, respectable street.

She had no option but to let him in and so bring about her own violent death.

The medical evidence given later showed that she had died at between 7 a.m. and 8 a.m. on Monday, March 6. It was clear that, on the pretext of making tea, True had gone to the kitchen in search of a murder weapon and had found the rolling-pin.

While the girl sipped her tea he moved behind her and struck her five savage blows on the head. He then used the towel and the dressing-gown cord to ensure that she was quite dead.

The fact that True so stupidly remained in the flat until the "daily" arrived was made much of at the trial by his defence counsel, the brilliant Sir Henry Curtis Bennett. That, and the wild spending spree that followed, were clear pointers to True's insanity, Sir Henry pleaded.

Sentenced to death

All the same, a cautious jury found True guilty as charged, and he was sentenced to death. From Pentonville Prison he wrote to a friend: "If you come to the same place I'm going to I'll have a drink of nice cold water ready for you."

But True did not go to that place. Instead, on the intervention of the Home Secretary, he was sent to Broadmoor. He lived out the rest of his life there and died in 1951, at the age of 61—one of the happiest, most popular and longest-staying patients the criminal mental asylum had ever had.

The greatest tragedy of True's case is that so many people who realized how split and mentally ill he was did nothing to help him—and so save the life of Olive Young, who loathed and feared him.

THE SPANISH FLY MURDERS

Innocent Arthur Ford thought a magic love potion would send the girl of his dreams flying into his arms. But the "potion" was a deadly poison. . . .

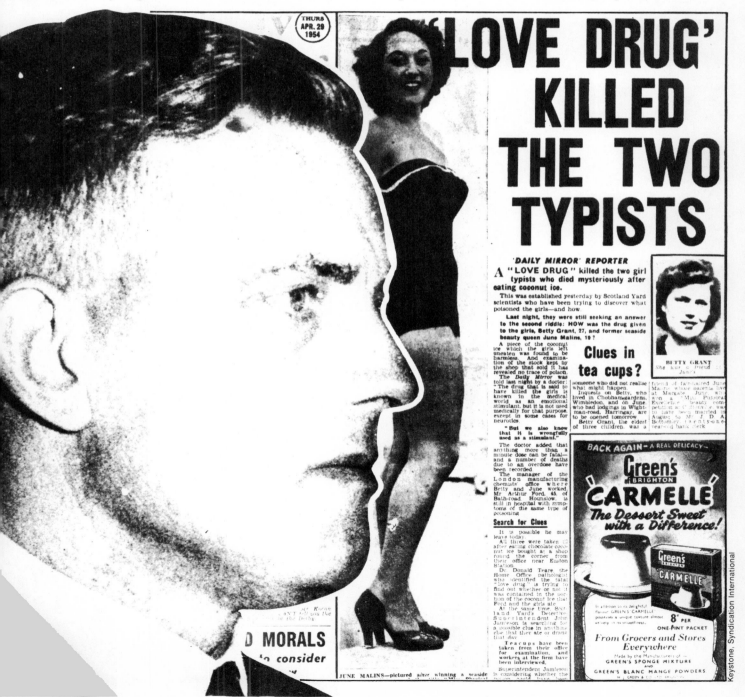

THURS APR. 29 1954

"LOVE DRUG' KILLED THE TWO TYPISTS

'DAILY MIRROR' REPORTER

A "LOVE DRUG" killed the two girl typists who died mysteriously after eating coconut ice.

This was established yesterday by Scotland Yard scientists who have been trying to discover what poisoned the girls—and how.

Last night, they were still seeking an answer to the second riddle: HOW was the drug given to the girls, Betty Grant, 27, and former seaside beauty queen June Malins, 19 ?

A piece of the coconut ice which the girls left uneaten was found to be harmless. And examination of the stock kept by the shop that sold it has revealed no trace of poison.

The *Daily Mirror* was told last night by a doctor: "The drug that is said to have killed the girls is known in the medical world as an emotional stimulant, but it is not used medically for that purpose, except in some cases for neurotics.

"But we also know that it is wrongfully used as a stimulant."

The doctor added that anything more than a minute dose can be fatal—and a number of deaths due to an overdose have been recorded.

The manager of the London manufacturing chemists' office where Betty and June worked, Mr. Arthur Ford, 45, of Bath-road, Hounslow, is still in hospital with symptoms of the same type of poisoning.

Search for Clues

It is possible he may leave today.

All three were taken ill after eating chocolate coconut ice bought at a shop round the corner from their office near Euston Station.

Dr. Donald Teare, the Home Office pathologist who identified the fatal "love drug" is trying to find out whether or not it was contained in the portion of the coconut ice that Ford and the girls ate.

At the same time, Scotland Yard's Detective Superintendent John Jamieson is searching for a possible clue in anything else that they ate or drank that day.

Teacups have been taken from their office for examination, and workers at the firm have been interviewed.

Superintendent Jamieson is considering whether the poison could have been

Clues in tea cups?

someone who did not realise what might happen.

Inquests on Betty, who lived in Chobham-gardens, Wimbledon, and on June, who had lodgings in Wightman-road, Harringay, are to be opened tomorrow.

Betty Grant, the eldest of three children, was a

BETTY GRANT
She was a friend of June's

friend of fair-haired June Malins whose parents live at Margate. June, who won a "Miss Paignton Excelsior" beauty competition a year or so ago, was to have been married in August to Mr. J. D. A. Bottomley, twenty-one-year-old bank clerk.

D MORALS
to consider

JUNE MALINS—pictured after winning a seaside

Keystone, Syndication International

113

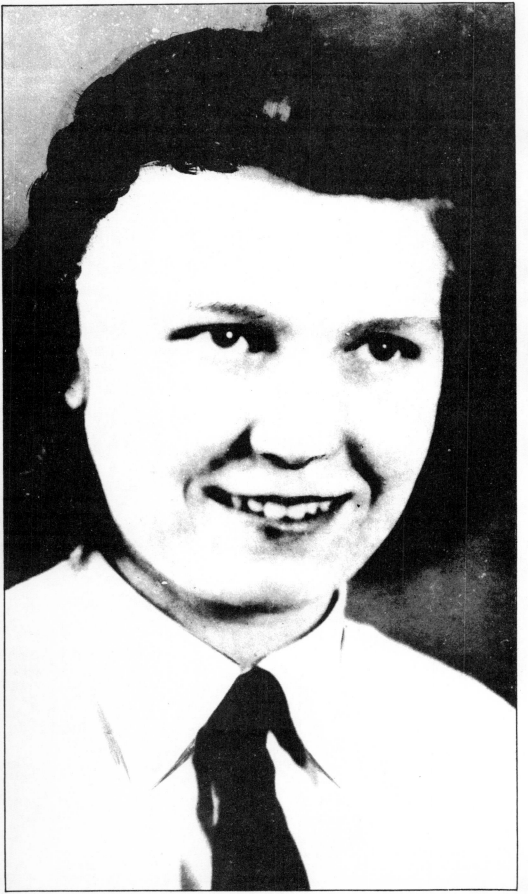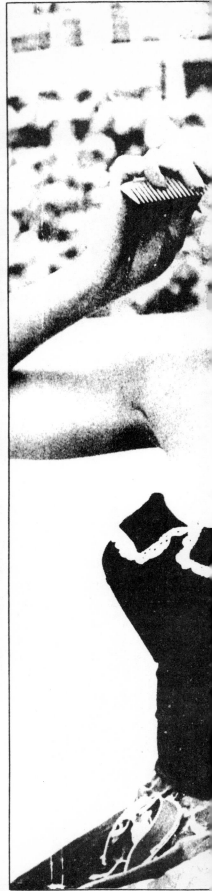

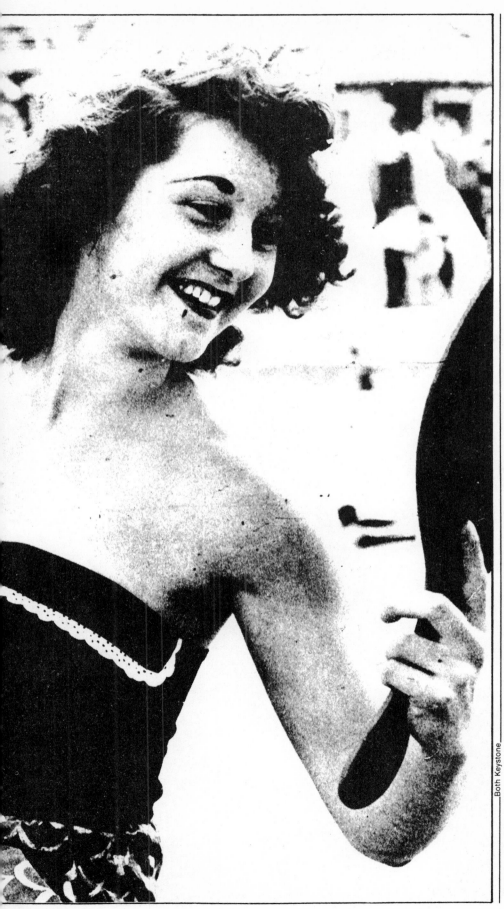

HIS eyes glazed and near to collapse, 44-year-old Arthur Kendrick Ford heaved himself up the stairs from the underground cells at the Old Bailey and into the prisoner's dock. He reached out with shaking hands to grip the polished wooden sides of the dock. Then, in a strained voice, he pleaded guilty to the manslaughter of Betty Margaret Grant, aged 27, and June Florence Malins, aged 19.

Watching him closely, her eyes rarely shifting their gaze from his face, was his wife, Marjorie, sitting in the well of the court. In front and above him on the bench sat Lord Goddard, the Lord Chief Justice of England.

Ford seemed only half aware of the proceedings and was obviously in a state of shock. He had, after some initial hesitation, admitted to one of the strangest office killings on record. But, at the same time, it was clear that he had not intended to kill, and the nightmare realization of what had actually happened now seemed visibly branded upon him, and destined to remain with him for the rest of his life.

The detailed story of what had happened on the fateful day of April 26, 1954, had been told at the preliminary hearing in the magistrate's court that led to the Old Bailey trial. There it was that the scene was set in the general office of a wholesale chemist's firm in London's Euston Road—where Ford, as office manager, had charge of a staff of 22 women and four men.

Stomach pains

Mr. John Claxton, for the prosecution, explained the events of the afternoon of that day. At 2.30, he said, Ford "went to his chair in the main office and had with him a paper bag marked with the name of a local sweetshop. From that bag he took several pieces of coconut ice—half white, half pink, with a chocolate covering. He did not offer the bag to any of the girls there, but with his fingers handed a piece to Miss Betty Grant, then to another girl, and then to a Miss Glover and a Miss Dodds.

"He was not seen, in fact, to hand Miss June Malins a piece, but she was seen to be eating a piece. All these girls consumed what had been given to them, but about 3.30 p.m. Miss Grant took Miss Malins up to the sickroom. Miss Malins was sick and complaining of stomach pains. Miss Grant herself did not complain at that time of feeling ill, but 20 minutes later she went back to the

"HERE YOU ARE, GIRLS" . . . and an hour or two later office typists Betty Grant (far left) and June Malins, a seaside beauty queen, were dying in agony, their internal organs seared by the cantharidin hidden in Ford's chocolate-covered coconut ice.

sickroom and had all the symptoms that Miss Malins had.

"About 4 p.m. Ford himself started to complain of head pains. He was seen by several people in his office, and he appeared to be wavering on the edge of unconsciousness, but made no complaint of stomach pains."

The mysterious sickness, the prosecutor said, worsened in the three afflicted people, Ford and Miss Grant and Miss Malins, and they were all taken to London's University College Hospital. There, the next day, April 27, the two girls died, and there the police turned their attention to the survivor, Ford—still sickly

pale in his hospital bed, but clearly on the way to recovery.

By April 28, the court was told, autopsies had disclosed that both girls had died from poisoning by cantharidin, a highly dangerous drug which—if taken in anything except an absolutely minimal dose of something like one two-hundredth of a grain—would cause swift death. Cantharidin is better known to laymen as Spanish-fly, and is said to have the property of stimulating sexual excitement. It was this supposed property which was at the heart of Ford's actions and his subsequent trial.

Mr. Claxton went on to recount Ford's

response when the police told him of the cause of the girls' deaths, and asked if he could help them with their inquiries. Ford was at once thrown into an acute state of agitation. "Oh, dear God," he moaned, "what an awful thing I have done! Why didn't somebody tell me? I have been a fool. Let me tell you the whole story."

That whole story was bizarre. On a homeward-bound ship, after war service in the Far East, he had heard gossip among his fellow-soldiers about Spanish-fly and its supposed sexual value. He had listened with interest, but had pushed the matter to the back of his mind,

returned home to his job with the wholesale chemists, married and had his domestic life consolidated by the arrival of two children to whom he was devoted.

Then, Ford told the police, in late March or early April, 1954, a minor event occurred that was to have devastating consequences. To Ford at his office came a customer's query about cantharidin. When he made the necessary inquiries, he discovered to his surprise that cantharidin was the medical term for Spanish-fly.

His thoughts flew back to the gossip he had overheard on his returning troopship. His curiosity was further aroused

Syndication International

"MY MOTHER always told me to tell the truth," said Ford, pictured weeping as he is escorted from the hospital by police. But the truth may have been yet another victim of this unfortunate man's wild imagination. . . .

when, taking part in stock-taking at his firm, he came across a bottle bearing the name of the drug. Making sure that no one else was around, he emptied 40 grains of the poison into an envelope.

At first, although he admitted taking the drug himself, he denied giving the cantharidin to any of the girls in the office. But later, unable to continue with the deception, he burst out:

"I have been thinking a lot about this. My mother always told me to tell the truth. . . . When I said I did not give Miss Grant and Miss Malins cantharidin I was not telling the truth. I now wish to say I took a little of the cantharidin and put it on the desk. I then picked some of it up on the blade of a pair of scissors and put it into two of the pieces of coconut ice. I pushed it into the coconut ice with the scissors.

"I gave one of the pieces to Miss Grant. We were very fond of each other. She kept putting me off and I made up my mind to give her cantharidin in the coconut ice to stimulate her desire for me. It seemed to me the best way to give it to her. I cannot say how Miss Malins got the other piece except that it must have been by accident. The only girl I was interested in was Miss Grant. I am deeply sorry I gave Betty Grant the drug. I now realize that I caused the death of these two girls by doing this crazy thing at the expense of losing my dear wife and children."

Reckless gossip

It might have seemed at that stage of the hearing that Ford had merely been a simpleton who had acted upon reckless gossip—and had not troubled to find out whether the drug had other, and possibly more dangerous, properties than that of sexual stimulation. But the prosecution had some crucial facts to add—which came from its key witness, Mr. Richard Lushington, the senior chemist at Ford's firm.

His appearance in the witness-box was brief but decisive. At around 10 o'clock on the morning of April 26, he testified, Ford went to him and asked if he had any cantharidin. He was interested, he said, because one of his neighbours was breeding rabbits and had heard that the drug might play a useful part in the mating process. Yes, said Mr. Lushington, he had the drug in stock and showed Ford the bottle (the same bottle which Ford had already seen during the firm's stock-taking).

"But," Mr. Lushington told the court, "I added, 'This is a number one poison.' Ford then said to me, 'Oh, well, if that's the case I don't want it.' He went away and later a check of the stock showed that nearly 40 grains of the drug were missing."

Soon afterwards to the witness-box came Mr. Lewis Nickolls, director of Scotland Yard's laboratory, to confirm that cantharidin had been found in the bodies of the dead girls, and to add the significant point that once it was absorbed they were beyond hope.

"It is not possible," Mr. Nickolls stated flatly, "to use any reasonable method of eliminating that poison."

Luckless moment

The total interest of the court was centred upon Miss Dodds, another member of Ford's office staff, when she took the oath and stood ready to answer questions. For she had been one of the lucky ones in that luckless moment. She had been given a piece of coconut ice by Ford. She ate it and enjoyed it, but suffered no sickness from it. She well remembered Ford's words as he passed his generous gift around the office. "Here you are, girls," he said. For two of those girls it was the last gift they were ever to receive.

It was on the basis of that evidence, at the preliminary proceedings, that Ford found himself in the dock at the Old Bailey, gazing around him as though only some improbable force had brought him there. Once he had pleaded guilty there was little for him to say—although Mr. R. E. Seaton, for the Crown, pointed out that, so far as Ford knew, young June Malins had been a victim purely by accident.

Onlookers in the court, observing Arthur Ford, were bewildered that any supposedly intelligent man should have thought that, by administering a dangerous drug, he could make a girl feel some strong personal desire for him.

Ford hung his head as Mr. Seaton told the Lord Chief Justice that both girls had died in agony, their internal organs literally burned away by the deadly cantharidin. It seemed that Ford might well have been a victim of his own wild imagination about Betty Grant's interest in him. For, Mr. Seaton declared, Ford had told the police:

"I had intercourse with Betty in the office about three months ago. Don't write that down, for her sake." Yet, the prosecutor added, the post-mortem examination of Betty Grant appeared to show that she had died a virgin.

No one, it seemed, could be sure what Ford had intended. His defence counsel, Mr. Richard Elwes, referred to the "intercourse" statement, but told the Lord

117

Chief Justice that "my instructions had been to make no reference to the relationship between Miss Grant and Ford. But I would like to point out that what Ford did is not to be regarded as having been done to commit an odious offence by subterfuge".

In fact, the truth, as Mr. Elwes patiently went on to explain, was that even Ford did not really know what advantage he had expected to gain from giving Betty Grant the Spanish-fly.

"Those instructing me," Mr. Elwes declared, "have failed to get any coherent instructions out of him. The result of this case on this man is that he is physically and mentally something like a wreck. One thing that emerges clearly is what he did was certainly not a considered thing . . ."

Here the Lord Chief Justice intervened. He had been actively scribbling notes, in the way that British judges have of not looking as though they are following every word, and yet missing nothing. "Of course he did not intend to murder—everybody understands that," he said. "But I do not understand how you can say it was not considered."

Mr. Elwes bowed and replied: "His ignorance of the ways of wickedness has contributed to this dreadful tragedy. If he had more wicked knowledge than he has, he would never have done what he did. The memory of what he has done will never leave him for the rest of his life. His wife has completely forgiven him, showing very great moral courage, and is standing by him."

Moistening eyes

The Lord Chief Justice commented: "He gave this stuff to her [Miss Grant] in the hope that she would be sexually inclined to him. Whether she was sexually inclined is another matter. Evidently at the time she was not." Ford raised his saddened, moistening eyes to the judge as if he, too, wished to stress the terrible futility of what he had done. He was evidently close to collapse.

There was little left for anyone, except the judge, to say. There was, in the Old Bailey courtroom, something of an air of disbelief about the whole situation. A man had, for some immature reason, committed an utterly stupid act. As a result of it, two young, attractive girls were dead, and men in wigs and gowns, with documents tied with pink ribbon, were gathered solemnly to consider the idiocy.

As he stared around him it was a

CLOSE TO COLLAPSE, at his trial Ford could only plead ignorance and naïveté. "The memory of what he has done will never leave him for the rest of his life," said counsel for the defence. Was this punishment enough?

thought like that which seemed to be edging across Ford's haunted mind.

Lord Goddard shuffled his papers and looked towards the ashen-faced prisoner. It was not a moment that such a distinguished judge could enjoy. But what he had to say he must say without any show of emotion. Tonelessly, he addressed the unhappy man in the dock—whose knuckles now whitened to a fine parchment tint as he grasped at the wooden rail.

"Arthur Kendrick Ford," the Lord Chief Justice began, and the prisoner appeared totally surprised by that form of address. To his wife and his friends Ford was "Arthur", occasionally Arty. Who, he seemed to wonder, could this "Arthur Kendrick" be? But it is a requirement of justice that, whoever may stand arraigned, he must be formally identified. Therefore, the judge proceeded:

"Arthur Kendrick Ford, you were determined to administer to Miss Grant an aphrodisiac, or what you believed to be an aphrodisiac. You asked a qualified chemist to give you some of this substance, giving him an untrue reason why you wanted it. He gave you a serious warning that it was a dangerous poison."

Number one poison

Lord Goddard paused, as though wishing to remind counsel on both sides of the evidence of Mr. Lushington, the chemist who had pointed out that cantharidin was "a number one poison". Then the judge continued: "Nevertheless, after that warning you went out to a shop and bought a sweetmeat and treacherously administered this poison in the sweetmeat to the young woman."

The lawyers—and some of the spectators—exchanged glances. It seemed odd

DAILY MAIL, SATURDAY, MAY 1, 1954

GIRL'S DEATH: FORD CHARGED

He said: 'What an awful thing I have done,' Yard allege

CID HOLD HUNDREDS IN SEARCH

Stratford street sealed off

Mother sails 3,000 miles to claim baby

'I DARE NOT HOPE TOO MUCH'

Last chance

Cars stopped

Pigeons fly to port and like it

HOMERS NOD—IN PASS ON TIP

By Daily Mail Reporter

Still there

ARTHUR FORD: Helped from dock.

'MANSLAUGHTER? I DID NOT KILL HER'

By Daily Mail Reporter

ARTHUR KENDRICK FORD, 44-year-old office manager, when charged with the manslaughter of Miss Betty Margaret Grant, a 27-year-old secretary, kept calling out: "Oh, Betty, I did not kill you," it was alleged at Clerkenwell yesterday.

COSTLY
Norwegian
British

RUBBER FREED

Restrictions off exports to Iron Curtain nations

Mystery bang cracks a house

Wife waits

NO OV
Dockers
ban no

'RARE POISON' KILLED GIRLS

Woman

Daily Mail

in that so-modern year of 1954 to hear such an apparently archaic word as "sweetmeat". No layman in Britain would ever have thought of using it. "Sweet", yes, the British would have acknowledged, and "candy" Americans would have recognized immediately; "confectionery", the more pompous might have employed. But "sweetmeat" had a Dickensian ring about it. Yet, after consideration, it did seem to carry a solemn note, and there was no doubt that such an experienced judge as Lord Goddard was aware of that.

Literary usage

His Lordship showed no signs of registering the onlookers' reactions to his literary usage. He went on: "You put the poison in coconut ice and did not take the precaution to see that no one else got it. The death of these two girls is at your door, and I have no doubt you bitterly regret it. I have not the slightest doubt that the last thing you intended was to kill these girls."

A DICKENSIAN RING about Lord Goddard's summing-up suggested that his verdict would be severe. Ford's sentence was five years for "the most terrible case of manslaughter . . ."

But it was, continued the judge, "the most terrible case of manslaughter it has ever been my lot to try and you must go to prison for five years". Ford's head fell forward, and he seemed to be struggling to decide what next to do. Yet, although he said nothing, it was apparent that it was not the sentence that shocked him, but the words of the judge reminding him of the memory of events that he would carry with him, into prison and beyond.

The judge rose, the lawyers bowed low, their bewigged heads nodding in ceremonious unison, and a gentle official arm was laid upon Ford's, directing him down to the cells below the court. A few miles away, in the London suburbs of Wimbledon and Harringay, two families continued in their own way to mourn daughters who had set out to work, cheerful as

usual, back in April, and had not returned alive.

But it was not quite the end of the "trial" of Arthur Kendrick Ford. He still had certain "pleas" to make, and he made them in the pages of a Sunday newspaper. He had always, he said, been deeply in love with his wife, "yet I still fell in love with Betty Grant". He would have married her had he been single, he declared. Then he proceeded to add to the mystery about his fatal actions, of which his defence counsel remarked at the Old Bailey.

Betty's love for him, he wrote, "was not a passionate one. Her love for me was a gentle sort of love. She disliked sex. But it was not Betty Grant's dislike of sex which caused her death. It is not true that I gave her cantharidin as an aphrodisiac, hoping it would sexually stimulate her. I had no intention of giving her the drug at all—it was all a ghastly mistake." Then he added, obscurely, "And to prove that I can tell the world no inducement was necessary. Her objection to the actual act of sex was a physical objection only and not an emotional one."

One in a million

His wife, Marjorie, told her own story in the same newspaper and described Arthur Ford as "what we wives call a husband in a million". Betty Grant, she said, had been to their home and even acted as a baby-sitter, "but she was not the type a wife gets jealous about". Since her husband's arrest she had learned that "once he and Betty were lovers. This took place at the office. I do not blame Arthur for this lapse. I blame Betty's personal unhappiness."

She ended her article: "Arthur Ford and I are still desperately in love with each other, and some day, somehow, we hope to regain the happiness we have known and restart our lives together."

The full truth, as it was shown at the trial, was perhaps more prosaic than newspaper confidences. Arthur Ford had thought, as countless men before him had thought, and countless more will think over the ages, that somewhere is to be found the miracle inducement that will bring the most hesitant woman flying into a man's arms.

Perhaps for most men in the world's offices, casting longing glances at young women colleagues, the extent of their approach is a lavish dinner they can ill afford. For the girl on whom Arthur Ford had set his sights—and her innocent colleague—the tragedy was that the pursuer continued with his fatal plan even after he had been warned of the acute danger of the inducement he had chosen.

It was that ignored warning that weighed most with the judge at Arthur's trial.

THE HONEYMOON MURDER

They found her tiny body sprawled by a remote mountain pool. But who had strangled her, and why? The inscrutable Mr. Miao wasn't talking. . . .

CUMBERLAND had not had a murder for 40 years. But when violent death came at last to the remote and beautiful county, it took the form of a bizarre crime, bizarre because of the nationality of victim and killer, because of the inept way it was carried out, and bizarre—above all—because it was committed in England.

HONEYMOON MURDER: STRANGLED CHINESE BRIDE shrieked the headlines. The bride who died was Wai-Sheung Siu, daughter of a rich Chinese merchant. She was tiny (4 ft. 11 in.), 29, a shrewd and intelligent businesswoman who travelled the world marketing Chinese art treasures. On May 12, 1928, after a whirlwind courtship, she had been married in New York to Chung Yi Miao, 28—who claimed to be the son of a rich Shanghai family, and to have taken law degrees both in China and at Loyola University in Chicago.

A month later the couple sailed for Scotland. Then, on Monday, June 18, they travelled to the picturesque Lake District to continue their honeymoon. They took a room in the Borrowdale Gates Hotel at the foot of Derwentwater. Next morning, like so many honeymooners before them, they set out on a walk to enjoy the fresh Cumberland air and some of England's most striking scenery. At two o'clock, after lunch, they went out again. But when Miao was seen

returning two hours later, he was alone.

At 7.30 that evening, a farmer named Tom Wilson found the bride's body, half hidden under a brown umbrella, lying beside a natural pool called Kidham Dub, which was sometimes used for bathing. She had been strangled with three pieces of string and blind cord. She lay on her back with her knees slightly drawn up and opened. Her skirt and underskirt were around her hips, and her knickers slightly torn. The rings she had been wearing were missing from her bare left hand, beside which lay a white kid glove, partly inside out as if it had been peeled from her.

Sexually assaulted

The impression was that she had been sexually assaulted, murdered and robbed. But, by midnight, her husband had been taken, under suspicion, to the police station at Keswick, the town at the opposite end of the lake, for the start of the questioning that would lead to his arrest.

Then—at Carlisle Assizes on November 22, 1928, five months after the killing—began the trial to decide whether Miao was a strangler. There had been big queues, and the public galleries were packed as the sallow, sleek-haired Chinese, looking alert and unperturbed, was escorted into the dock. In a firm voice, he pleaded: "Not guilty." The

hearing, which would prove a classic case of conviction by circumstantial evidence, was to last three days.

After returning to the hotel around four o'clock, Miao had gone to his room. At 7 p.m., he dined alone. A woman guest at a nearby table told the court how she had asked: "What has happened to your wife?" He replied, she said: "She has gone to Keswick to buy warm underclothes." After dinner she felt Miao was worried about his wife's failure to return and reassured him: "You need not be nervous. Your wife is a woman of the world who has travelled a good deal."

Miao added that he had not accompanied his wife because he had a slight cold and she had suggested he would be better off in bed. At 8.15, Miss Crossley, owner of the hotel, also asked what had happened to Mrs. Miao. Miao repeated his earlier explanation: "She has gone to Keswick to buy warmer underclothing."

A little later, Miss Crossley mentioned that there was a bus due from Keswick at 9 p.m. and offered to meet it. Miao made the odd reply: "It's no use. She won't come by the bus. She doesn't like the bus. She will come by private car."

Nevertheless, Miss Crossley had gone to the terminus, which was near the Post Office, to see if there was any sign of Mrs. Miao off the nine o'clock bus. During her absence, Miao wandered into the kitchen looking for the proprietress. "She has gone to see if your wife is coming back," a maid named Holliday told him. According to her evidence, Miao asked: "Where would she go to?"

Noose around the neck

Then occurred a curious exchange which, with other circumstantial evidence, went a long way towards tying a noose around Miao's neck. The maid went on: "I said: 'To the Post Office.' He said: 'Would she go to the place where they bathe?' I said: 'No, to the Post Office.'"

The significance of the maid's evidence was not lost on Mr. John Jackson, K.C., appearing for Miao. She agreed with the lawyer that Miao did not speak English well. But she would not accept counsel's suggestion that what Miao had actually said was: "Has she gone to where people take the bus?" Mr. Jackson tried pronouncing "bus" with a slight lisp and "bath" with a short "a" to make the words sound alike. The maid refused to agree she might have misheard.

At 11 p.m. that night, Inspector Graham of Keswick police called at the hotel.

THE BRIDE who died was Wai-Sheung Siu, a shrewd dealer in Chinese antiques. Her husband, Chung Yi Miao, said he was the son of a rich Shanghai family. They were last seen together leaving the Borrowdale Gates Hotel (left).

"Miao was in bed," he said. "I explained I was a police inspector and told him to get up and dress. 'What do you want me for?' he asked. I cautioned him, told him that his wife had been found dead and that he would be detained on suspicion of having caused her death by strangling. 'What do you say?' he asked. 'My wife dead? Suspicion? What do you mean by that?' He appeared very emotional," the inspector went on, "but I had the impression he was acting a part."

While Inspector Graham stayed behind to search the hotel room, Miao was driven to Keswick police station where, in the charge room, he had another curious conversation—which Mr. Jackson tried to explain away by saying Miao had been misunderstood because of his poor English pronunciation.

Had she knickers on?

P.C. Scott then stated that, shortly after arriving, Miao suddenly said: "May I ask you a question, sir?" He replied: "You may." "Did you see my wife?" asked Miao. "I did," said Scott. Then, according to the constable, Miao inquired: "Had she knickers on?" Scott had refused to answer. Mr. Jackson tried to establish that what Miao had actually said was: "Had she a necklace on?" Scott, however, insisted that there had been no misunderstanding.

An hour later, while being searched, Miao had suddenly begun to speak in his halting English. "She had one necklace on," he said. "She had one white one on yesterday afternoon. She had pocket book with her. She had diamond ring on. Had she these with her now?" Inspector Graham, who had arrived after searching the hotel room, did not answer.

The following morning, at 6.45, Superintendent Barron, the Deputy Chief Constable, had arrived to interview Miao. Once again the prisoner had something unusual to say. "It is terrible—my wife assaulted, robbed and murdered," he told the Superintendent. Up to that time nothing had been said to him about the position in which his wife's body had been found and the rings missing from her left hand. Again, that afternoon, Miao asked about his suit and overcoat, which had been taken from him earlier. Superintendent Barron explained that they had been sent away to be examined for bloodstains.

"The bloodstains on my overcoat were got in New York," said Miao—another odd reply in the light of subsequent medical evidence that, in fact, no bloodstains had been found on his clothing.

That was by no means the end of the circumstantial evidence. String and blind cord—although the cord was of a different colour from that found around the dead bride's neck—were discovered in a cupboard in the Miaos' bedroom and an easily-accessible drawer in the hotel kitchen. A week after the murder, Inspector Graham gave two used films, found in Mrs. Miao's unlocked suitcase, to a local photographer to develop. Wrapped up in silver paper with one of the films were two rings. They had quickly been identified as the wedding ring and diamond solitaire Mrs. Miao had been wearing the night before her death.

Then came the medical testimony. Dr. Crawford, who had examined the body at 9.30 p.m. on the night it was found, put the time of death at 3.30 to 4.30 in the afternoon. Professor John McFall of Liverpool, an expert in forensic medicine, said the bride's knickers were slightly stained in front, but there was nothing to suggest "discharge from a man". The tear, exactly at the seam, suggested "a certain amount of force having been used". "I have seen many of these cases," he said, "and it seems to me a very good imitation of an assault."

Mrs. Miao had bled from the nose, mouth and left ear. Professor McFall was able to show from the nature of bloodstains on her left glove that it had been removed—almost certainly after death—by pulling the body of it over the fingers, which is not the way a woman normally removes a glove. On the skirt there were ten horizontal stains of blood. They suggested "a crumpling of the cloth, the ten smudges being the result of one large smear, as if the material had been gathered up by a bloody hand.

"When it is opened out, you see the smudges. They were therefore made by someone tampering with the body after the injuries had been inflicted."

Mr. Justice Humphreys, the judge: Does this all mean that, in your opinion, it is more probable that the clothes of the woman, her skirt and underskirt, were pulled up after bleeding had begun?

Professor McFall: Yes.

Showing off her jewels

It took the prosecution a day-and-a-half to present this formidable mass of circumstantial evidence. Mr. Jackson began his assault on it after lunch on the second day by an address to the jury. His main points were:

1) Miao had been arrested solely on the evidence of witnesses that he had been seen with his wife at 2.30 and alone at 4 on the afternoon she died.
2) Mrs. Miao was fond of showing off her jewellery, even to comparative strangers. This, together with the publicity given to her New York wedding, had made her the target of international jewel thieves. Miao had noticed two Orientals following them in Glasgow, Edinburgh and in Grange, the Derwentwater village where their hotel was situated.
3) Mrs. Miao had sent her husband home at 3 p.m. — 30-90 minutes before the time of her death—because he had a cold. She had gone shopping in Keswick, saying she would get a lift from a passing car because she did not like buses. The jewel thieves, who had been waiting to catch her alone, took the opportunity to kill her and rob her. Although a pearl necklace had been found among the £3500-worth of jewels in her room, another necklace was missing.
4) Miao had gone home as his wife suggested. Finding the fire out in their room, he had gone out again with his camera. He returned again at four o'clock when there was a rain shower.
5) Because of Miao's poor accent, witnesses had confused "bathe" with "bus" and "necklace" with "knickers". To Superintendent Barron he had said "rudely murdered", not "robbed and murdered".

That was the melodramatic story Miao told confidently. How had the two rings got into the Kodak film spool wrapper where the photographer accidentally discovered them a week after the murder? "My wife put them there after lunch," he said. "I was not surprised. I had seen her hide them for safety on top of the wardrobe and in other odd places before." He added that he had never heard the word "knickers". Nor did he know that there was a pool in the vicinity used for bathing.

Impossible to have sex

Mr. John Singleton, the prosecutor, began his cross-examination by trying to establish two possible motives for the murder. First he questioned Miao about his financial affairs, seeking to show that, despite his claims, he was not a man of substance but had married for money. Secondly, there was the matter of an operation performed on the bride on May 25, before they sailed for Scotland, because she had found it impossible to have sexual intercourse. Miao agreed the operation had taken place, but he denied that either his wife or her doctor had told him it would be impossible for her to have children.

The defence then called several witnesses who had seen other "Orientals" in the area on or about the day of the murder. That was the end of the evidence. Mr. Jackson's speech for the defence on the third day of the trial lasted 45 minutes. "What motive was there behind the murder?" he asked. "Both these young people were well-furnished with this world's goods and both were happy. If

THE FIRST MURDER in 40 years in Cumberland was so bizarre and inept that it created a furor out of all proportion to its importance. Most amazing was that it was committed in England at all.

The HONEYMOON TRAGEDY

Chinese Bridegroom on Trial for his Life ... Carlisle Assizes.

PROSECUTION

CHINAMAN'S APPEAL DISMISSED.

CHINAMAN FOUND GUILTY

Close of the Wife Murder Trial ... Carlisle Assizes.

... VERDICT"—THE JUDGE

... of Death Received with ...tations of Innocence.

... Chung Yu Miao, at Carlisle Assizes on a charge of murdering
... in a verdict of Guilty. The Judge passed sentence of death,
... verdict to be a true one. Prisoner, who had excitedly affirmed
... the Judge's summing up, received the death ... calmly
... was not guilty.

THE VALUE OF THE JEWELLERY.

Norman Grant, jeweller, Carlisle, who had examined the contents of the jewel case,

THE CO...

stated that he est...

CHINAMAN TO DIE.

"A TRULY DIABOLICAL AND CALCULATED MURDER."

APPEAL DISMISSED.

LORD CHIEF JUSTICE FINDS AMPLE
EVIDENCE FOR CONVICTION.

RAIL...

MANSL...

TRI...

Ernest
Frances
driver of
mail tra...
field on...
trates
day, ...
Doro...
Mrs

the prisoner had wanted to murder his wife," he went on, "why did he come to England to do so? Why did he not take the opportunity in the liner on the voyage from America and simply push her into the sea?

"The jury's verdict," he pointed out "must be based on evidence and not on theory. It has been shown that the dead woman was rather vain about her jewellery. There are crooks at almost every port who never miss such opportunities as were offered here. What were those Oriental men doing in Keswick?

"The police arrested Miao when the only evidence against him was that he had been seen with his wife in the afternoon. Since then they have simply tried to build up theories. There is no proof that the girl was even murdered where she was found. She might well have been murdered in a car in which she had asked for a lift to Keswick. The prosecution is relying upon a chain of circumstantial evidence,

each link of which can be explained, and on the prisoner's ignorance of English pronunciation."

The summing-up

With the defence case concluded, some of the main points referred to by Mr. Justice Humphreys in his summing-up were:

Miao's command of English in the witness-box.
You may have noticed that, when he was answering questions put by his learned counsel, he seemed as clear and quick, almost, as an Englishman. But when he was cross-examined you may have noticed that his hesitation was very much greater and more marked. When you come to consider his evidence, you will have to make up your minds whether in the answers he gave to counsel for the prosecution [in cross-examination] he was acting the part of a person who did not understand, or whether he honestly did

want time to be quite sure that he followed what the questions were.

The departure of Mrs. Miao at 3 p.m. (according to her husband) to buy warm underclothes in Keswick.
Do you believe the story that this woman suddenly decided, about three o'clock, to go to Keswick, and if so how did she get there? She certainly did not go by omnibus . . . Do you think it possible that that woman could have gone off to Keswick without being seen by any human being? The police have not been able to find anybody who saw her, and the defence have not been able to trace anybody who saw her.

The removal of Mrs. Miao's left glove and the finding of her rings wrapped up with the spool of film.
If it was done by the person who killed her, why did he do it? Can you entertain any doubt that he had done it for the purpose of taking off the rings? Does the evidence satisfy you that the murderer had taken off the rings? If it does, the significance of that evidence is quite important. If they *were* taken off by the murderer, how did the prisoner get hold of them?

Could the murder have been committed by robbers?
She was found to have been killed by the application very tightly round her throat of a piece of string which had been twisted so as to make it double. Who did it? Can you imagine a robber killing a woman in that way? This was a little woman, only five feet high. Do you think a person who wanted to take her jewellery would have got so near to her without her knowing it as to be able to put round her neck that piece of string and strangle her? Of course, if the person who did it was a person in whom she had every confidence, you may think she would have no objection at all to his putting his hands round her throat or doing anything else he liked . . .

Miao's apparent knowledge, before anyone told him, of his wife's exact fate.
The prisoner made this observation [to Superintendent Barron]: "It is terrible. My wife assaulted, robbed and murdered." The prosecution draws your attention to the word "robbed". How did this man know that his wife had been robbed? All that had been told him was that her body had been found strangled in a wood. The prisoner says what he really said was: "This is terrible. My wife has been *rudely* murdered." There it is . . .

Of Miao's evidence that, before going out, his wife had herself hidden the two

THE HEARING, which was to prove a classic case of conviction by circumstantial evidence, took three days, almost half of which was needed by the prosecution to present all its evidence.

THE KING WITH A BUTTONHOLE.

—AND A WALKING-STICK.

The King, taking advantage of the warm sunshine yesterday, walked with the Queen for about 100 yards to the sea wall in front of Cragwell House.

He left his bath chair in the grounds and sat for half an hour in a wicker chair on the sea wall reading newspapers. He had a large pink flower in his buttonhole and carried a walking stick.

Six women who arrived at the Princess Mary Home of Rest, Bognor, yesterday, learned that the Queen had left Easter presents for them during her visit the previous day. The nature of the gifts, however, is being kept secret from them until Easter Monday.

CLEANER FOOTBALL.

MORE PUNISHMENT FOR FOUL PLAY.

An important move to "clean-up" football will be made when the Council of the Football Association meets in London to-morrow.

Recommendations will be considered which aim at giving more effective punishment for foul play. All the rules regarding free-kicks and penalties will be reviewed.

"The Man in the Corner" deals with this problem on Page Twenty-three.

COUPLE WOUNDED.

MAN IN HOSPITAL WITH THROAT INJURY.

Philip Phillips, of Humberstone-road, Commercial-road, Aldgate, is lying in Ilford Emergency Hospital, with a wound in the throat.

Bessie Phillips, of Roman-road, Ilford, is suffering from slight cuts. She was not taken to hospital.

It is not known if the couple are related.

A CHINESE BRIDE'S DEATH SECRET.

KILLED TO SAVE HER HUSBAND'S SOUL.

"SHE COULD NOT GIVE ME A SON."

BEHIND the mysterious murder of a Chinese bride by her husband in the Lake District on June 19, 1928, lies a strange secret of the inscrutable Orient.

Chung Yi Miao, the young husband, was executed at Strangeways Gaol, Manchester, on December 6 last year. Throughout his trial he denied that

THE MURDERED GIRL.

he murdered his rich bride, Cheung Miao.

Before he died, however, he revealed the secret. And this is the strange story he told:—

"I killed my wife, but it was not murder according to my faith and the

stormy sea.

This was the epic story, told day lightheartedly, unemotion Mr. H. M. Morris, then an year-old lieutenant in the Ro Force, who, with Air Mechan Wright, also aged eighteen, hero of this amazing war d 1917.

I found Mr. Morris, who is tain the Essex County cricket t season, about to start out on a golf. He was playing for school, Repton, in the Halford cup—and he told me frankly was much more interested in the story about which I wanted talk to me.

DAWN SEARCH.

Finally, after a lot of persua said :—

"It was early in the morning 23, 1917, that I was roused f sofa in the mess at Westgate where I was on night duty in emergency.

"I was sleeping in my unifo I was told that a 'hornet' wh gone in chase of a raiding Zepp not returned, and they wante look for it.

"Air Mechanic Wright was same duty, and when we had him we set off, without ou clothes, in a Short seaplane.

"I should like to make it cl we went without our flying because the picture in the War Museum, South Kensingt ing with our rescue, shows us overcoats.

"We had lots of time late regret that we did not equipped!

"We searched the sea f hours, without observing anyth at last I decided to turn back running short of petrol, and more than forty miles from :

THIRST TORTURE

"Almost as soon as I turned of the machine homewards, th stopped, and I was obliged down into a sea infested wit

"We had then travelled a miles towards the coast. We the engine, and found that it neto trouble, and as we did a spare, there was nothing f to wait for rescue.

"It was then about midday sea was calm, but during the a squall blew up, and a gr caught our craft a terrific b sank her, tail first.

"We swam about for a litt and Wright was suddenly bu the boat, which had broken a the machine.

"As it was our only hope to it, and it became our nearly a week.

THE ILLUSTRATED POLICE NEWS—JUNE 28, 1928.

LABOUR'S STORMY PETREL.

THE
ILLUSTRATED
POLICE NEWS

LAW COURTS
AND WEEKLY RECORD
THE OLDEST AND BEST POLICE JOURNAL IN THE WORLD.
WITH WHICH IS INCORPORATED
GREAT GLOVE FIGHTS.
ESTABLISHED 1864

No. 3357. [REGISTERED AT THE G.P.O. AS A NEWSPAPER.] **THURSDAY, JUNE 28, 1928.** TWOPENCE

SCENE OF THE TRAGEDY

THE BORROWDALE VALLEY.

THE CHINESE BRIDE AND HER HUSBAND WERE SEEN WALKING.

FOUND STRANGLED.

ARREST OF THE HUSBAND.

PRETTY NEWLY MARRIED CHINESE GIRL STRANGLED IN LAKELAND

SCENE OF THE MURDER

CHUNG MIAO

THE MURDERED BRIDE.

EXECUTION OF CHUNG MIAO

rings in the Kodak film spool.
He says: "I asked her why she put the rings there." She said: "I do not want to open the jewel case. We are in a hurry." If you think you can accept that story, I should think you would be able to accept everything else the prisoner tells you. If you think you cannot accept that story, you are in a position that you have a man whose evidence you are asked to accept with regard to whom in one important matter you say: "That man is lying" . . .
Of the other "Orientals" in the neighbourhood.
There is no witness called to say that those persons were seen just at the critical time at Grange Bridge with a motor car, hanging about . . .
It took the jury only an hour on the afternoon of the third day of the trial to find Miao guilty. He responded, when

"ACCURSED is the man who has no son to revere his memory" . . . according to a statement published posthumously, this may have been the reason Miao decided to murder his young bride.

asked if he had anything to say, with a truculent attack in which he complained that his point of view had never been put properly to the jury. He also made the observation: "The last word I say is this. You say: 'How clever he is.' Now you have tried my life and the verdict is I am guilty. If I did that, I must be very nervous. Now you see I am not nervous . . ."

Mr. Justice Humphreys sentenced him to death. Miao appealed immediately. His appeal was heard—by the Lord Chief Justice, Mr. Justice Avory, and Mr. Justice Acton—on November 19 and 20. It was an unusual appeal. Miao decided

to dismiss Mr. Jackson and conduct it himself. He was allowed—probably as a concession to the fact that he was a foreigner—the abnormal privilege of calling new witnesses, who testified to seeing two "Orientals" near the scene of the crime at about the time it was committed.

His basic case, apart from a reiteration of the story that he had told at his trial, was that prosecuting counsel and the judge were so prejudiced that he had not been given a fair hearing.

The Lord Chief Justice, reviewing the evidence, laid great stress on the hiding of the rings with the film spool. "It may well be," he said, "that in this case the jury thought that his cupidity had got the better of his cunning." Of the question of possible misunderstanding of the words "knickers" for "necklace" and "bath" for "bus", he remarked: "Miao complained he was misunderstood. His difficulty is not that. His difficulty is that he *was* understood."

Manacled and in tears

There was no evidence that the "Orientals" in Grange had ever been seen with Mrs. Miao. The summing-up at the trial had been "extremely careful and impartial". No point of law had been raised. Therefore the appeal was dismissed. Manacled and in tears, Miao was driven off from the Law Courts in London on the first stage of his journey back to Strangeways Prison, Manchester—where he was executed on December 6.

All that remains is to try to fathom not only why he killed his bride, but also why he chose to kill her in England when there would have been so many advantages in a simple shipboard accident, or even in waiting until their return to China.

A variety of reasons have been put forward—that he was insane; that he wanted to get his hands on his wife's money and property; sexual desire, thwarted by the fact that, even after her operation, she was still unable to have intercourse; dismay, born of the Chinese tradition of ancestor worship, that his wife could not bear him children; that he was a crypto-member of a Chinese *tong* (secret society) dedicated to duping, or even murdering, rich women to raise money.

There are objections to all these theories. More than three months after Miao went to the scaffold, the London *Sunday Express* did publish an article which claimed to give, in his own words, the reason for the murder. It said:

"We were told we could never have a son to grace our union and to perpetuate my name. The strongest of all religious feelings in China, especially in the south where I come from, is reverence for our ancestors. Thus a man who has no son to revere his memory is accursed."

ON THE TRAIL OF A RAPIST

A GIRL of four was snatched from a hospital bed, sexually assaulted and murdered at the spot arrowed. The only real clues were the fingerprints on a bottle . . . but they were enough to trap killer Peter Griffiths (inset).

THE child's cry brought Nurse Humphreys out of the kitchen, where she was preparing breakfasts for her charges in Ward CH3, which was at the back of Blackburn's sprawling Queen's Park Hospital in the northwest of Britain.

The sound came from Michael Tattersall, one of the six small children sleeping on that night of May 14, 1948. The light in the ward was dim, but the children, in their high-railed cots, were quiet except Michael, who was whimpering quietly.

The nurse comforted him, freshening his cot, soothing him for perhaps 15 minutes. She saw him asleep, and paused for a moment at the next cot. It belonged to June Ann Devaney, a bright, clever child of barely four—even though she looked much older than her age. She had suffered from pneumonia but was now cured and due for discharge the next day; she also was safely asleep.

It was just after midnight when Nurse Humphreys, back in the kitchen, thought she heard a girl's voice. She looked in the ward again, glanced out of the porch door, at the back of the cots; all seemed well. When another toddler began to cry the nurse took it out of bed and into the kitchen for a warm drink.

Quietness reigned until 12.45. Nurse Humphreys went into the ward once more. Her acute senses, always wary, felt something was wrong. She found June Devaney's cot empty; under it was a Winchester bottle, a bottle about 15 inches high used for various liquids. What horrified the nurse was the sight, by the cot, of what looked like the imprints of two bare adult feet, clear against the highly polished wooden floor.

She did not waste a moment on possibilities, and aroused the staff of the sleeping hospital. An immediate search began for June—intensified when it was found the porch door near her cot was open, as was a window at the other end of the ward which gave access to a small room next to the lavatories.

At five minutes to two that morning Blackburn Police Headquarters had been alerted. Policemen collected the father, Albert Devaney, from his home to advise them. An inch by inch check of the hospital began.

The grounds were surrounded by brick walls and railings, which protected some 70 acres of grounds. Nearly 300 feet from Ward CH3, huddled against the wall, the police found June. The strongest man felt sick at the sight on the ground.

Extraordinary swiftness

June was lying face down in the grass, her nightdress pulled up so that her buttocks were exposed. Her body was covered with dirt. Under the revealing police Wootton lamps the newest probationer could read the answer—June Devaney had been horribly raped, and battered to death.

The police moved with extraordinary swiftness. By 4 a.m. that same morning the Chief Constable of Blackburn, with a police surgeon and a high police official of the Lancashire Constabulary, were on the spot.

By 5.10 a.m. Detective Chief Inspector Colin Campbell, of the Force Fingerprint Bureau at Hutton, was on the scene but no chances were being taken. Within hours Scotland Yard was called in.

Blackburn had some 110,000 inhabitants and one man had to be found, a man, indeed, who might not even live in the town. The words are easily written, but visualization is difficult. Looking, for example, for a man's own brother in a chain store full of people is a good parallel.

Imagine that same search in a conglomerate of 110 chain stores, each holding a thousand people, but this time a search for a man nobody even knew by

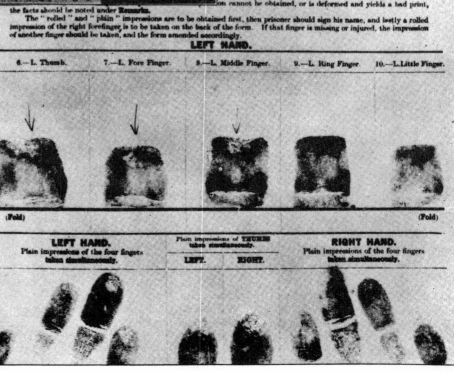

A TOWN'S FINGERPRINTS . . . there were 35,000 homes in Blackburn, and every male was asked to help the police. Then the team of checkers matched the fingerprints (right) of Peter Griffiths with those found at the murder scene. He had taken the child while Nurse Humphreys (below) was in the hospital kitchen.

Syndication International

130

name or by sight. This is how the case already looked to the investigating officers.

Footprints

The outbreak of public fury was alarming, for here was a little girl stolen from the apparently safe and secure confines of a great hospital, and brutally murdered. National anger was as great. The country was sick of war and blood, and this was a crime that belonged to the too-close horrors of World War II.

The clues discovered were factually ample. The Winchester bottle had obviously been picked up from a trolley in the ward, intended as a weapon or for protection. It bore a number of clear fingerprints. There were imprints of stockinged

feet from the little anteroom to the ward, almost to the door through which Nurse Humphreys had gone to the kitchen, then they went back down the ward again.

The early sun spotlighted the prints with remarkable clarity, and the first officers on the scene were grateful to the hospital rule which demands highly waxed, highly polished ward floors.

Each footprint was ringed with white chalk, and photographed. To the naked eye the prints seemed made by bare feet; but this was not so. A strong light was directed on each print, at an angle of between 45° to 60°. On the other side, at the same angle, a camera was placed. The resultant print revealed that the marks had been made by the socks of a grown man.

Every surface in the ward was photographed after each fingerprint had been "dusted". The prints on the Winchester bottle got special attention. Some of the prints were old and by fingerprinting the hospital personnel, the police were able to eliminate many of the prints. It would seem the few remaining, which were certainly "fresh", were those of the intruder.

Forensic investigation

Over half a day's hard work showed that none of the hospital staff had gone into Ward CH3 in stockinged feet; that the Winchester bottle had been kept on its usual trolley and not under June's bed; and that no member of the staff had touched it.

THE HOSPITAL layout was well known to Griffiths (right), who had been a patient there as a child. He got drunk, then found an entrance to the hospital, and took the girl. His statement said nothing about the assault and murder. Griffiths, who had served in the Welsh Guards, had a low intelligence quotient, and was a schizophrenic. He was sentenced to death . . .

It was score one—the prints remaining on the bottle *must* be those of the intruder. It was a vital weapon with which to start the great search.

The Preston Home Office Forensic Laboratory technician had, while the police were investigating, begun his own probe—gathering a motley collection of probably invaluable items.

From the open window in the little anteroom to the ward, fibres were collected, and so were fibres from the well waxed ward floor. These fibres were so fine they were not much more than short "hairs", which had been shed by a woollen sock, or stuck to the floor as the intruder crept about. But under the microscope each fibre would be almost rope-like, fully capable of comparison with a stocking, when it was found.

Other, less material, clues recovered by the Laboratory were valuable, and tragic. From the hospital boundary wall, where June Devaney's body was found, were removed blood and hairs. Foreign fibres (that is, not from her clothes) were found on her body. A single pubic hair was recovered from her own bare genitals.

The Laboratory was to receive a lock of June's hair, her nightdress, blood taken from her heart, and swabs from vagina and rectum, to serve for purposes of comparison when the time came.

Macabre post-mortem

Meanwhile the post-mortem table was telling its macabre story. The child's nightdress was wet, and her body dirty —which indicated that she had been rolled about. There was extensive bruising over the whole of the face and under the hair. There was some blood exuding from the nose.

There was blood on the thighs, the abdomen, and coming from the vagina. There were two clear bruises, one on each of the inner and upper parts of both thighs which, to the examiner, suggested severe thumb pressure of large, certainly male, hands.

A generalized bruise across the front of the throat suggested it had also been gripped; also there were bite marks present. There were other bruises, all caused before death.

On the left foot the examining doctor saw several small punctured wounds, which were less wounds than sharp little bruises. They baffled him for some moments, then he saw the revolting answer. The child had been gripped round the leg, the murderer's fingernails making the small marks, and she had been dashed against the hospital wall, ending with a multiple fracture of the skull.

Every injury the child had suffered was shown to have occurred before death. The doctor decided that the injuries were the result of a ferocity only explicable by a maniacal frenzy on the living body of a small girl just one month under four years old.

Then the police search began. First of all the prints on the Winchester bottle had to be qualified, and false trails eliminated. Inquiries began among patients, ex-patients, visitors to, and employees of, Queen's Park Hospital going right back for two years—a mammoth task in itself.

A total of some 642 people were traced, and fingerprinted, who had, at some time or another in two years, had access to the hospital. Staff members were carefully screened—it was clear that the intruder to the ward was someone familiar with the hospital and its grounds.

Whole population

By June 15 no less than 2017 people had been dealt with, and every single one had been eliminated as a murder suspect.

To simplify the search the chief keyprints on the bottle were seen as a thumb and three fingerprints, all made at the same time by the same hand. A startling decision was then taken. It was decided to fingerprint the whole population of Blackburn comprising every male over 16 years of age.

The Mayor of Blackburn made an appeal, set the process going by giving his own prints. He banked on one certain factor: the fury of all decent people against the murder, and he was right. Save for the odd objector here and there, Blackburn rallied to a man.

Special collecting points were set up. The police made a frank and clear statement to the effect that every print, except for the one vital reward to the search, would be destroyed in due course.

There were some 35,000 houses in Blackburn. Electoral rolls were used as the primary guide. Police officers carrying specially condensed fingerprint cards and ink pads set out to call on each house, seeking males who had been present on the night of May 14-15.

This inquiry was to become worldwide, for many men on leave from the armed forces had returned to their units; sailors, and travellers to other lands, had departed.

Every set of prints had to be "bought" by police officers using tact, courtesy, and charm—they had no power to force a man to supply his prints. Seldom has sympathy and understanding between police and public been so manifest; prints poured in.

Copies of the Winchester bottle prints had also gone all over the country, each police force seeking companions to the infamous prints. Every fingerprint bureau in the world was circularized in case the prints were known or recognized.

Headquarters at Hutton checked steadily on. By the end of June all Blackburn males had been printed, without result. To make sure nobody had been missed out, the records maintained for the issue of wartime ration books were all called in to ensure the work was complete.

As the checkers were drinking quick cups of tea on the afternoon of August 12, one of the experts suddenly stood up, crying out: "I've got him!"

The prints had been made by a Peter Griffiths, aged 22, of Birley Street, Blackburn. The following night he was arrested, and made a statement admitting his guilt.

The scientists stepped in, clinching fact after fact. The fibres removed from the anteroom window to Ward CH3 were shown as identical with those of Griffiths' suit; fibres taken from June's body also tied with the suit, as did some fibres found on her nightdress. The minute fibres taken from the footprints in the ward itself were red and blue, matching a sock taken from Griffiths' home.

Blood on the fly of Griffiths' trousers was group A, as was June's blood. Bloodstains were also found on the linings of both trouser pockets, on the bottom of each sleeve of the jacket, each of the two lapels and other places.

Peter Griffiths knew the hospital and its grounds very well indeed; he had been a patient there for a period when he was about nine years old.

He was a tall, willowy young man who had served briefly overseas in the Welsh Guards. He had a low intelligence quotient, and was a schizophrenic.

Mild-faced

It seemed difficult, at the trial, to associate the mild-faced, slightly vacant-looking young man in the dock with the murder. But in his statement he admitted that, on the fatal night, he had taken a number of drinks—beer, rum, and such— and then he had set out to get "sobered up".

Later, he found himself outside the railings of Queen's Park Hospital. But he did not mention the rape and the murder, and only gave facts about his entry to the hospital—adding that he ". . . picked the girl out of her cot . . . carried her in my right arm and she put her arms round me neck . . ."

June Devaney died on the night of May 14. Precisely three months later Peter Griffiths was arrested; two months and two days later he had been tried and condemned to death—a condemnation made certain by police and scientists working together as a team in the service of justice.

Deutsche Presse

THE VAMPIRE OF DUSSELDORF

His mild manners and soft-spoken courteousness placed him above suspicion, and to most people he appeared to be totally harmless. Yet his bourgeois exterior concealed one of the most brutal sadists of modern times . . .

AS NIGHT fell across the city that had lived through a year of terror, the streets rapidly emptied. People hurried through the narrow lanes to their homes. Children were plucked from playgrounds and sent to bed. Doors were bolted and curtains drawn. The people were in dread of a creature—a vampire—which had no face, no name, no shape. Already, it had committed 46 violent crimes, displaying every kind of perversion. Five bodies had been taken to the mortuary. But still it remained little more than a spectre.

As the lights went out on the night of August 23, 1929, the people of Düsseldorf, in the German Rhineland, felt almost inured to horror. Nothing more, they thought, could shock them now. As they slept fitfully, they little foresaw that the next few hours would demonstrate the full bestiality of the man they had labelled The Düsseldorf Vampire.

There was one bright and cheerful patch of light that evening. In the suburb of Flehe, hundreds of people were enjoying the annual fair. Old-fashioned merry-go-rounds revolved to the heavy rhythm of German march tunes, stalls dispensed beer and *würst*, there was a comforting feeling of safety and warmth in the closely-packed crowd.

A shadow

At around 10.30, two foster sisters, 5-year-old Gertrude Hamacher and 14-year-old Louise Lenzen, left the fair and started walking through the adjoining allotments to their home. As they did so a shadow broke away from among the beansticks and followed them along a footpath. Louise stopped and turned as a gentle voice said:

"Oh dear, I've forgotten to buy some cigarettes. Look, would you be very kind and go to one of the booths and get some for me? I'll look after the little girl."

INSTRUMENTS used by Kurten during his murder rampage. The knife (left) is the one used in the attack on Gertrude Schulte and (below) is the broken fragment found in Miss Schulte's back.

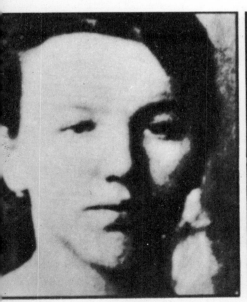

Louise took the man's money and ran back towards the fairground. Quietly, the man picked up Gertrude in his arms and carried her behind the beanpoles. There was no sound as he strangled her and then slowly cut her throat with a Bavarian clasp knife. Louise returned a few moments later and handed over the cigarettes. The man seized her in a stranglehold and started dragging her off the footpath. Louise managed to break away and screamed "Mama! Mama!" The man grabbed her again, strangled her and cut her throat. Then he vanished.

Twelve hours later, Gertrude Schulte, a 26-year-old servant girl, was stopped by a man who offered to take her to the fair at the neighbouring town of Neuss. Foolishly, she agreed. The man introduced himself as Fritz Baumgart and suggested they take a stroll through the woods. Suddenly, he stopped and roughly attempted sexual intercourse. Terrified, Gertrude Schulte pushed him away and screamed, "I'd rather die!"

The man cried "Well, die then!" and began stabbing her frenziedly with a knife. She felt searing pains in her neck and shoulder and a terrific thrust in her back. "Now you can die!" said the man and hurled her away with such force that the knife broke and the blade was left sticking in her back. But Gertrude Schulte didn't die. A passer-by heard her screams and called the police and an ambulance. By then, the attacker had disappeared.

In barely more than half a day, the Düsseldorf maniac had killed two children and attempted to rape and kill another woman. The citizens were stunned as they read their morning papers. Day by day, the attacks continued. Their increasing frequency and ferocity convinced medical experts that the Vampire had lost all control of his sadistic impulses.

In one half-hour, he attacked and wounded a girl of 18, a man of 30, and a woman of 37. The Bavarian dagger gave way to a sharper, thinner blade and then to some kind of blunt instrument. It was the bludgeon that hammered to death two more servant girls, Ida Reuter and Elisabeth Dorrier; the thin blade that killed five-year-old Gertrude Albermann, her body shredded with 36 wounds.

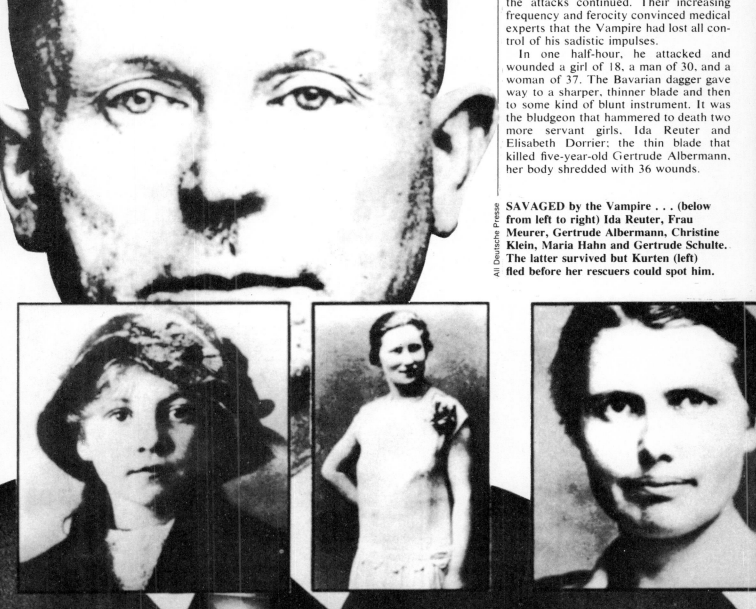

All Deutsche Presse

SAVAGED by the Vampire . . . (below from left to right) Ida Reuter, Frau Meurer, Gertrude Albermann, Christine Klein, Maria Hahn and Gertrude Schulte. The latter survived but Kurten (left) fled before her rescuers could spot him.

Mettmannerstrasse

Twenty miles away, in the cathedral city of Cologne, a 21-year-old "domestic" named Maria Budlick read the anguished headlines and said to a friend: "Isn't it shocking? Thank goodness we're not in Düsseldorf."

A few weeks later, Maria Budlick lost her job. On May 14, she set out to look for work and boarded a train for Düsseldorf . . . and an unwitting rendezvous with the Vampire.

On the platform at Düsseldorf station, she was accosted by a man who offered to show her the way to a girls' hostel. They followed the brightly-lit streets for a while, but when he started leading her towards the dark trees of the Volksgarten Park she suddenly remembered the stories of the Monster, and refused to go any farther. The man insisted and it was while they were arguing that a second man appeared, as if from nowhere, and inquired softly: "Is everything all right?" The man from the railway station slunk away and Maria Budlick was left alone with her rescuer.

Walk in the woods

Tired and hungry, she agreed to accompany him to his one-room flat in Mettmannerstrasse, where she had a glass of milk and a ham sandwich. The man offered to take her to the hostel, but after a tram ride to the northeastern edge of the city, she realized they were walking deeper and deeper into the Grafenburg Woods. Her companion stopped suddenly and said:

"Do you know now where you are? I can tell you! You are alone with me in the middle of the woods. Now you scream as much as you like and nobody will hear you!"

The man lunged forward, seized her by the throat and tried to have sexual intercourse up against a tree. Maria Budlick struggled violently and was about to lose consciousness when she felt the man's grip relax. "Do you remember

GENTLE vampire's apartment . . . It was to this humdrum room that Kurten led Maria Budlick for a sandwich and a glass of milk before attacking her.

Deutsche Presse

where I live?" he asked. "In case you're ever in need and want my help?" "No," gasped Maria, and in one word saved her own life and signed the death warrant of the Düsseldorf Vampire. The man let her go and showed her out of the woods.

Misdirected letter

But Maria Budlick *had* remembered the address. She vividly recalled the nameplate "Mettmannerstrasse" under the flickering gaslight. And in a letter to a friend the next day, she told of her terrifying experience in the Grafenburg Woods with the quiet, soft-spoken man. The letter never reached her friend. It was misdirected and opened by a Frau Brugman, who took one look at the contents and called the police.

Twenty-four hours later, accompanied by plainclothes detectives, Maria Budlick was walking up and down Mettmannerstrasse trying to pinpoint the quiet man's house. She stopped at No. 71. It looked familiar and she asked the landlady if "a fair-haired, rather sedate man" lived there. The woman took her up to the fourth floor and unlocked a room.

It was the same one in which she had drunk her milk and eaten her sandwich two nights earlier.

She turned round to face even more conclusive proof. The quiet man was coming up the stairs towards her. He looked startled, but carried on to his room and shut the door behind him. A few moments later, he left the house with his hat pulled down over his eyes, passed the two plainclothes men standing in the street and disappeared round a corner.

Maria Budlick ran out and told the officers: "That's the man who assaulted me in the woods. His name is Peter Kurten." So far, nothing linked Kurten with the Vampire. His only crime was suspected rape. But he knew there was no longer any hope of concealing his identity. Early the following morning—after meeting his wife as usual at the restaurant where she worked late—he confessed: "I am the Monster of Düsseldorf."

On May 24, 1930, Frau Kurten told the story to the police, adding that she had arranged to meet her husband outside St. Rochus Church at three o'clock

that afternoon. By that time the whole area was surrounded by armed police. The moment Peter Kurten appeared, four officers rushed forward with loaded revolvers. The man smiled and offered no resistance. "There is no need to be afraid," he said.

Grisly exhibits

After exhaustive questioning, during which he admitted 68 crimes—not including convictions for theft and assault, for which he had already spent a total of 20 years in prison—the trial of the Düsseldorf Vampire opened on April 13, 1931. He was charged with a total of nine murders and seven attempted murders.

Thousands of people crowded round the converted drillhall of the Düsseldorf police headquarters waiting to catch their first glimpse of the depraved creature who had terrorized the city. A special shoulder-

SIXTEEN names appeared on the police list of vampire victims of whom nine were murdered. At the trial, Kurten related the details with obvious relish.

Straftaten und Urteil im Mordprozeß gegen Peter Kürten 13.4. / 22.4. 1931.

Lfd Nr	Name des Opfers	Anklagebehörde Straftat	Beantragte Strafe	Anträge des Verteidigers	Urteil des Schwurgerichts	Gesamturteil
	Kind Christine Klein	Mord Die unzüchtigen Handlungen sind verjährt	Todesstrafe	Totschlag daher bereits verjährt	Todesstrafe	
	Frau Ida Reuter	Mordversuch in Tateinheit mit versuchter Vornahme unzüchtiger Handlungen	10 Jahre Zuchthaus	gefährliche Körperverletzung	10 Jahre Zuchthaus	
	Kind Rosa Ohliger	Mord in Tateinheit mit gewaltsamer Vornahme unzüchtiger Handlungen	Todesstrafe	Totschlag	Todesstrafe	
	Maschinist Rudolf Scheer	Mord	Todesstrafe	Totschlag keine Überlegung	Todesstrafe	
	Hausangestellte Maria Hahn	Mord in Tateinheit mit gewaltsamer Vornahme unzüchtiger Handlungen	Todesstrafe	Totschlag keine Überlegung	Todesstrafe	
	Fräulein Anni Goldhausen	Mordversuch	10 Jahre Zuchthaus	gefährliche Körperverletzung	10 Jahre Zuchthaus	
	Frau Mantel	Mordversuch	5 Jahre Zuchthaus	gefährliche Körperverletzung	5 Jahre Zuchthaus	
	Arbeiter Hornblum	Mordversuch	5 Jahre Zuchthaus	gefährliche Körperverletzung	5 Jahre Zuchthaus	
	Kind Hamacher	Mord in Tateinheit mit gewaltsamer Vornahme unzüchtiger Handlungen	Todesstrafe	keine Überlegung Totschlag	Todesstrafe	
	Kind Luise Lenzen	Mord in Tateinheit mit gewaltsamer Vornahme unzüchtiger Handlungen	Todesstrafe	keine Überlegung Totschlag	Todesstrafe	
	Gertrud Schulte	Mordversuch in Tateinheit mit versuchter Notzucht	15 Jahre Zuchthaus			
	Hausangestellte Ida Reuter	Mord in Tateinheit mit vollendeter Notzucht	Todesstrafe			
	Hausangestellte Elisabeth Dörrier	Mord in Tateinheit mit gewaltsamer Vornahme unzüchtiger Handlungen	Todesstrafe			
	Frau Meurer	Mordversuch in Tateinheit mit versuchter Vornahme unzüchtiger Handlungen	10 Jahre Zuchthaus			
	Frau Wanders	Mordversuch in Tateinheit mit vollendeter Vornahme unzüchtiger Handlungen	5 Jahre Zuchthaus			
	Kind Dietlieben Hartmann	Mord in Tateinheit mit gewaltsamer Vornahme unzüchtiger Handlungen	Todesstrafe			
		Gesamte beantragte Strafe siehe Urteil			Gesamtstrafe 9 x zum Tode 60 Jahre Zuchthaus	

Urteil:
9 × zum Tode, 15 Jahre Zuchthaus, Stellung unter Polizeiaufsicht und Aberkennung der bürgerlichen Ehrenrechte auf Lebzeit.

high "cage" had been built inside the courtroom to prevent his escape and behind it were arranged the grisly exhibits of the "Kurten Museum"—the prepared skulls of his victims, showing the various injuries, knives, scissors and a hammer, articles of clothing, and a spade he had used to bury a woman.

The first shock was the physical appearance of the Monster. Despite his appalling crimes, 48-year-old Peter Kurten was far from the maniac of the conventional horror film. He was no Count Dracula with snarling teeth and wild eyes, no lumbering, stitched-together Frankenstein's Monster. There was no sign of the brutal sadist or the weak-lipped degenerate. With his sleek, meticulously parted hair, cloud of Eau de Cologne, immaculate suit, and well-polished shoes, he looked like a prim shopkeeper or minor civil servant.

It was when he started talking that a chill settled over the court. In a quiet, matter-of-fact voice, as if listing the stock of a haberdasher's shop, he described his life of perversion and bloodlust in such clinical detail that even the most hardened courtroom officials paled.

Drunken brute

His crimes were more monstrous than anyone had imagined. The man wasn't a mere psychopath, but a walking textbook of perverted crime: sex maniac, sadist, rapist, vampire, strangler, stabber, hammer-killer, arsonist, a man who committed bestiality with animals, and derived sexual satisfaction from witnessing street accidents and planning disasters involving the deaths of hundreds of people.

And yet he was quite sane. The most brilliant doctors in Germany testified that Kurten had been perfectly responsible for his actions at all times. Further proof of his awareness was provided by the premeditated manner of his crimes, his ability to leave off in the middle of an attack if disturbed, and his astonishing memory for every detail.

How did this inoffensive-looking man become a Vampire? In his flat, unemotional voice, Kurten described a life in which a luckless combination of factors—heredity, environment, the faults of the German penal system—had conspired to bring out and foster the latent sadistic streak with which he had been born.

Kurten described how his childhood was spent in a poverty-stricken, one-room apartment; one of a family of 13 whose father was a drunken brute. There was a long history of alcoholism and mental trouble on the father's side of the family, and his father frequently arrived home drunk, assaulted the children and forced intercourse on his mother. "If they hadn't been married, it would have been rape," he said. His father was later jailed for three years for committing incest with Kurten's sister, aged 13.

Bestiality

Kurten's sadistic impulses were awakened by the violent scenes in his own home. At the age of nine, a worse influence took over. Kurten became apprenticed to a dogcatcher who lived in the same house, a degenerate who showed him how to torture animals and encouraged him to masturbate them. Around the same time, he drowned a boy while playing on a raft in the Rhine. When the boy's friend dived in to rescue him, Kurten pushed him under the raft and held him down until he suffocated, too.

His sexual urges developed rapidly, and within five years he was committing bestiality with sheep and goats in nearby stables. It was soon after that he "became aware of the pleasure of the sight of blood" and he began to torture animals, achieving orgasm stabbing pigs and sheep.

The terrible pattern of his life was forming. It only needed one more depraved influence to transfer his sadistic urges from animals to human beings. He found it in a prostitute, twice his age, a masochist who enjoyed being ill-treated and abused. His sadistic education was complete and they lived together for some time.

Far from straightening him out, a two-year prison sentence for theft left him bitter and angry at inhuman penal conditions—particularly for adolescents—and introduced him to yet another sadistic refinement, a fantasy world where he

ENCAGED in court, Peter Kurten looked anything but a savage killer. He was smartly dressed, polite and tranquil.

could achieve orgasm by imagining brutal sexual acts. He became so obsessed with these fantasies that he deliberately broke minor prison rules so that he could be sentenced to solitary confinement. It was the ideal atmosphere for sadistic daydreaming.

Shortly after being released from prison, he made his first murderous attack on a girl during sexual intercourse, leaving her for dead in the Grafenburg Woods. No body was ever found and the girl probably crawled away, keeping her terrible secret to herself. More prison sentences followed, for assault and theft. After each jail term, Kurten's feelings of injustice were strengthened. His sexual and sadistic fantasies now involved revenge on society.

THE EVIDENCE . . . Kurten, it turned out, was also a dab hand at arson and police had managed, in several cases, to recover the matches he had used (below). But the killer himself supplied most of evidence, like the map (right) which he drew to show where he buried a victim.

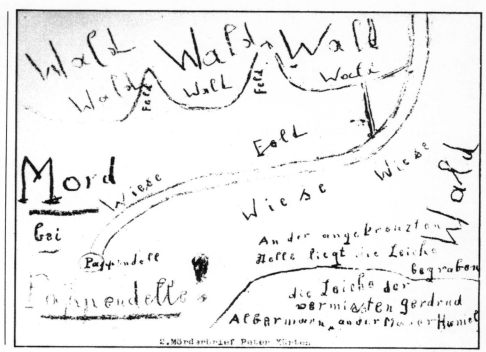

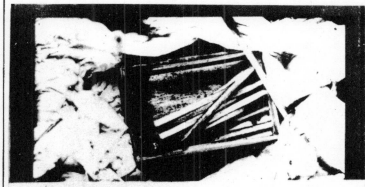

"I thought of myself causing accidents affecting thousands of people and invented a number of crazy fantasies such as smashing bridges and boring through bridge piers," he explained. "Then I spun a number of fantasies with regard to bacilli which I might be able to introduce into the drinking water and so cause a great calamity.

"I imagined myself using schools or orphanages for the purpose, where I could carry out murders by giving away chocolate samples containing arsenic which I could have obtained through housebreaking. I derived the sort of pleasure from these visions that other people would get from thinking about a naked woman."

The court was hypnotized by the revelations. To them, Kurten's narrative sounded like the voice of Satan. It was almost impossible to associate it with the mild figure in the wooden cage. While hysteria and demands for lynching—and worse—reigned outside the court, the trial itself was a model of decorum and humanity, mainly due to the courteous and civilized manner of the Presiding Judge, Dr. Rose. Quietly, he prompted Kurten to describe his bouts of arson and fire-raising . . .

"Yes. When my desire for injuring people awoke, the love of setting fire to things awoke as well. The sight of the flames delighted me, but above all it was the excitement of the attempts to extinguish the fire and the agitation of those who saw their property being destroyed."

The court was deathly quiet, sensing that the almost unspeakable had at last arrived. Gently, Dr. Rose asked, *"Now tell us about Christine Klein . . ."* Kurten pursed his lips for a second as if mentally organizing the details and then—in the unemotional tones of a man recalling a minor business transaction—described the horrible circumstances of his first sex-killing.

"It was on May 25, 1913. I had been stealing, specializing in public bars or inns where the owners lived on the floor above. In a room above an inn at Köln-Mülheim, I discovered a child of 13 asleep. Her head was facing the window. I seized it with my left hand and strangled her for about a minute and a half. The child woke up and struggled but lost consciousness.

"I had a small but sharp pocketknife with me and I held the child's head and cut her throat. I heard the blood spurt and drip on the mat beside the bed. It spurted in an arch, right over my hand. The whole thing lasted about three minutes. Then I locked the door again and went back home to Düsseldorf.

"Next day I went back to Mülheim. There is a cafe opposite the Kleins' place and I sat there and drank a glass of beer and read all about the murder in the papers. People were talking about it all round me. All this amount of indignation and horror did me good."

In the courtroom, the horrors were piling up like bodies in a charnel house. Describing his sexual aberrations, Kurten admitted that the sight of his victims' blood was enough to bring on an orgasm. On several occasions, he drank the blood—once gulping so much that he vomited. He admitted drinking blood from the throat of one victim and from the wound on the temple of another. In another attack, he licked the blood from a victim's hands. He also had an ejaculation after decapitating a swan in a park and placing his mouth over the severed neck.

Everyone in the courtroom realized they were not just attending a sensational trial, but experiencing a unique legal precedent. The prosecution hardly bothered to present any evidence. Kurten's detailed, almost fussy, confession was the most damning evidence of all. Never before had a prisoner convicted himself so utterly; and never before had a courtroom audience been given the opportunity to gaze so deeply into the mind of a maniac.

Bitter sting

Every tiny detail built up a picture of a soul twisted beyond all recognition. Kurten described with enthusiasm how he enjoyed reading *Jack the Ripper* as a child, how he had visited a waxwork Chamber of Horrors and boasted "I'll be in there one day!" The whole court shuddered when, in answer to one question, Kurten pointed to his heart and said: "Gentlemen, you must look in here!"

When the long, ghastly recital was over, Kurten's counsel, Dr. Wehner, had the hopeless task of trying to prove insanity in the face of unbreakable evidence by several distinguished psychiatrists. During Professor Sioli's testimony, Dr. Wehner pleaded:

"Kurten is the king of sexual delinquents because he unites nearly all perversions in one person. Can that not change your opinion about insanity? Is it possible for the Kurten case to persuade psychiatry to adopt another opinion?"

Professor Sioli: "No."

Dr. Wehner: "That is the dreadful thing! The man Kurten is a riddle to me. I cannot solve it. The criminal Haarman only killed men, Landru only women, Grossmann only women, but Kurten killed men, women, children, and animals, killed anything he found!"

Professor Sioli: "And was at the same time a clever man and quite a nice one."

Here was the final twist to the conundrum. The face peeping over the wooden cage was recognizably only too human. Witnesses had spoken of his courteousness and mild manners. Neighbours had refused flatly to believe he was the Vampire. Employers testified to his honesty and reliability. He could charm women to their deaths, indeed was regarded as a local Casanova. His wife had been completely unaware of his double life and had only betrayed him on his insistence, so she could share in the reward for his arrest. Right at the beginning of the Düsseldorf Terror, a former girlfriend who suggested he might be the Vampire was fined by the police for making a malicious accusation.

Some of the bourgeois puritanism which made Kurten so plausible burst out in his final statement before sentence was passed. Speaking hurriedly and gripping the rail, he said:

"My actions as I see them today are so terrible and so horrible that I do not even make an attempt to excuse them. But one bitter sting remains in my mind. When I think of Dr. Wolf and the woman doctor—the two Socialist doctors accused recently of abortions performed on working-class mothers who sought their advice—when I think of the 500 murders they have committed, then I cannot help feeling bitter.

"The real reason for my conviction is that there comes a time in the life of every criminal when he can go no further. And this spiritual collapse is what I experienced. But I do feel that I must make one statement: some of my victims made things very easy for me. Manhunting on the part of women today has taken on such forms that . . ."

At such self-righteousness, Dr. Rose's patience snapped. "Stop these remarks!" he ordered, banging his desk. The jury then took only 1½ hours to reach their verdict: Guilty on all counts. Dr. Rose sentenced him to death nine times.

On the evening of July 1, 1932, Peter Kurten was given the traditional *Henkers-Mahlzeit*, or condemned man's last meal. He asked for Wienerschnitzel, fried potatoes, and a bottle of white wine—which he enjoyed so much that he had it all over again. At six o'clock the following morning, the Vampire of Düsseldorf, a priest on either side, walked briskly to the guillotine erected in the yard of Klingelputz Prison. "Have you any last wish to express?" asked the Attorney-General. Without emotion, almost cheerfully, Kurten replied "No."

For in the few minutes before that walk, and the blow that separated his head from his body, he had already expressed his last, earthly desire. "Tell me," he asked the prison psychiatrist, "after my head has been chopped off, will I still be able to hear, at least for a moment, the sound of my own blood gushing from the stump of my neck?" He savoured the thought for a moment, then added: "That would be the pleasure to end all pleasures."

MURDER MOST FOUL

SHOT
27·9·1927

Was it simply an excess of viciousness, or was there something more that drove the killer of Police-Constable Gutteridge to shoot out the dying man's eyes? A dark streak of superstition, perhaps, deep inside a brutal soul . . .

IT WAS just before six o'clock on the morning of September 27, 1927. The English country lanes of Essex, between Ongar and Romford, were still damp from the patchy, overnight fog.

Along one of those lanes a Mr. William Ward, a motor engineer, was driving from the village of Stapleford Abbotts towards Stapleford Torney.

As he turned a bend in the lane near the hamlet of Howe Green he saw, on his right-hand side, "a huddled-up form" of a man. The man seemed to be lying in a half-resting position, as though resting against the earthen bank skirting the lane. His legs stretched into the road.

Mr. Ward stopped and went across to the man. As a local resident he immediately recognized who it was: Police-Constable George William Gutteridge, of Stapleford Abbotts. He spoke to the policeman but there was no reply. He took hold of his left hand and found that it was cold. P.C. Gutteridge was dead.

He had been shot four times and two of the shots had been fired, at close range, into each of his eyes. Clutched in his right hand was a pencil; nearby lay his notebook and helmet. There was blood all around the body and a trail which stretched to a larger, bloody pool in the middle of the lane.

Torch in his pocket

When Gutteridge's colleagues from the Essex Constabulary arrived at the scene they noticed three other significant facts. The dead policeman's whistle was hanging from its chain outside his uniform jacket, but his torch was still in his pocket and his truncheon in its pouch.

Moreover, a doctor who made an on-the-spot examination estimated that Gutteridge had been killed at around four in the morning. It was obvious, of course, that it would have been dark at the time of his death.

Apparently he had taken out his whistle to signal to someone and clearly he had been about to write something in his notebook. Equally clearly, he had not needed the light of his torch to see by.

So what had he been doing in the moments before he was shot? The circumstances suggested an almost certain possibility to the investigating officers. Gutteridge must have been about to write by the light of a car's headlamps. He must have been killed when, in the glare, he could not see what his murderer or murderers were about to do.

The bullets collected from in and

SHOT FOUR TIMES at close range, the corpse of P.C. Gutteridge was already cold as the overnight fog dispersed along the remote country lane. He seemed to have died in the glare of headlamps, blind to the movements of the murderers.

around the body were of great importance. They were of an obsolete Service type, withdrawn from army issue as far back as 1914. One had been propelled by black powder not in normal use since 1894.

If the police could find a revolver capable of firing the shots and a cartridge case they would be close to the killer.

The first two direct clues in the murder hunt appeared swiftly. Soon after the discovery of Gutteridge's body a Dr. Edward Lovell, of Billericay, some 14 miles from the murder site, reported that during the night his blue Morris Cowley car, TW6120, had been stolen from the garage at his home.

At 6.45 on the evening of September 27 the car was found abandoned in Brixton, S.W. The nearside mudguard was damaged and around it were scrapings of a substance that looked like the bark of a tree. Dr. Lovell's cases of medical instruments, which he had left in the car, were missing.

There were splashes of blood on the car's running board and, under the front passenger seat, an empty cartridge case was found. It was a rare and obsolete type and matched one of the bullets fired at the policeman. Mr. Robert Churchill, the famous London gunmaker, was able to tell the police that this and other bullets used in the crime had been fired from a Webley revolver.

A quiet little business

But after those early clues the police investigations, led by Chief Inspector James Berrett, of Scotland Yard, seemed to have reached a dead-end. Then, nearly three months after the murder, missing pieces from the detectives' jigsaw suddenly began to fall into place.

At 7.50 p.m. on January 20, 1928, a grey Angus-Sanderson car, driven by a man named Frederick Guy Browne, rolled into the Globe garage in Northcote Road, Battersea, S.W. Its arrival was watched by detectives who had been keeping the garage under observation for several days. They suspected that Browne, the owner, was running a quiet little business in stolen vehicles.

The police waited until Browne, dressed as a chauffeur in blue uniform and peaked cap, had got out of the car. Then they moved in and arrested him on a charge of stealing a Vauxhall car from Tooting, S.W., the previous November.

About 10 officers took part in the arrest — at first sight a formidable number to tackle one suspected car thief. But Browne was well known to the police as a tough, professional "villain" who had devoted his life to crime, and whose record included the unlicensed possession of firearms.

Browne, who was 47, had served sentences of more than seven years since the

THE BULLETS were an important clue: all were long obsolete, one even propelled by black powder not in use for more than 30 years. The trail led straight to a Webley revolver—and to Frederick Browne (right) and William Kennedy.

age of 30. During one four-year "stretch" at Parkhurst he earned a reputation as a vicious convict who attacked prison officers and smashed-up his cell.

Now, while he was held at Tooting police station, one group of detectives searched the Battersea bed-sitter where he lived with his wife and young daughter. Another group searched his garage, and a third group searched Browne himself.

Each search provided a valuable haul of evidence. At Browne's home the police found a small nickel-plated gun loaded with six cartridges. From the pocket by the driver's seat in the car they took

a fully-loaded Webley and, from the garage, 16 cartridges and various doctor's instruments including a pair of forceps.

The search of Browne himself yielded a pair of artery forceps, a dozen ·45 cartridges which fitted the Webley, and a stocking mask with apertures cut for eyes, ears and mouth.

Up to the point at which all these "finds" were laid out at Tooting police station (on the billiard table in the recreation room), the detectives still thought they were dealing only with a dangerous car thief. But the facts about the murder of a colleague are fairly

144

understandably printed clearly in every policeman's mind. The moment that the officers examined the Webley and the doctor's instruments they began to suspect a link between Browne and P.C. Gutteridge's murder.

Browne himself, an over-talkative, snarling-tempered hoodlum, helped to underline those suspicions by his reckless outburst when the various articles were shown to him.

"Ah, you've found that, have you?" he sneered, looking at the Webley. "I'm done for now . . . What I can see of it, I shall have to have a machine gun for you bastards next time!"

The next day another loaded Webley was found at the garage. Chief Inspector Berrett then went to Tooting, told Browne he was investigating the murder and asked him to account for his movements on the night of September 26, and to explain his possession of arms and ammunition.

Browne insisted that he was at home on the night of the killing. "I have no connection with the murder of P.C. Gutteridge," he said, "and it doesn't interest me."

As for the revolvers: the one found in the driver's seat pocket he "gave £3 for down at Tilbury Docks from a sailorman whose name I don't know, neither can I describe him"; the second Webley and its ammunition were also his, he admitted, "but I decline to give any explanation of where I got them".

Meanwhile, still pursuing their inquiries into the Vauxhall car theft, the police began to centre their attention on 36-year-old William Henry Kennedy, an associate of Browne and a criminal with an equally black record.

More serious matters

On January 25 Kennedy was arrested in Liverpool on suspicion of being concerned in the theft. The following day he was brought to London and taken to Scotland Yard, where Chief Inspector Berrett had far more serious matters to discuss with him.

"I have been making inquiries for some time past respecting the murder of P.C. Gutteridge in Essex. Can you give me any information about the occurrence?" the bearded investigator asked.

In his faintly Irish accent—he had been born in Scotland of Irish parents—Kennedy replied: "I may be able to tell you something, but let me consider awhile. . . . Can I see my wife?"

Mrs. Kennedy, who had travelled down on the same train from Liverpool as her arrested husband, and was already at the Yard, was called into the room. She stared anxiously at the red-faced, balding man she had married only eight days before—and whose miserable "career"

ranged from army desertion to stealing a bicycle while armed with a loaded revolver.

The dialogue that followed between husband and wife was one of the oddest ever heard and recorded by police in a murder investigation.

"Well, my dear," said Kennedy, "you know when I was arrested at Liverpool yesterday I told you I thought there was something more serious at the back of it. Well, there is. These officers are making inquiries about that policeman murdered in Essex."

No, Kennedy said in answer to his wife's urgent first question, he hadn't murdered him. But he was there and he knew who had. If he were found guilty he might hang or, if not, he might go to prison for a long time as an accessory. Would she wait for him?

"Yes, love," Mrs. Kennedy assured him. "I will wait for you any time. . . . Tell them the truth of what happened."

A classic account

The story Kennedy then proceeded to dictate to Berrett is a classic among first-hand accounts of what the law used to call "murder most foul".

On the evening of September 26, he and Browne (Kennedy said) went by train to Billericay where Browne had previously earmarked a Raleigh car ripe for stealing.

A persistently barking dog scared them off and, since it was then after 11 p.m., Browne said: "We can't get back by train now, so we'll try somewhere else."

They then "cased" Dr. Lovell's house and garage, and waited in a nearby field until all the house lights were switched off soon after midnight. Then they crept up to the garage, which was at the top of a sloping driveway, and Browne forced the doors with a tyre lever.

For secrecy's sake they let the doctor's car run down the driveway under its own weight, and pushed it about a hundred yards along the road before starting the engine. Browne took the wheel and "drove off around country lanes at a great pace".

After several misdirections they found themselves on a road to Ongar and were speeding along when "we saw someone who stood on the bank and flashed his lamp as a signal to stop".

They drove on but heard the blast of a police whistle and Kennedy (so his story went) told Browne to stop, "which he did quite willingly".

The policeman, P.C. Gutteridge, came up to the car on Browne's side and asked them a series of questions. Where were they going? "Lea Bridge Road garage," said Browne. "We've been out doing repairs." Did Browne have a driving licence? He did not. Was this his

car? "No," Kennedy chipped in quickly, "it's mine."

A beam from the policeman's torch flashed in their faces as Gutteridge asked: "Do you know the number of this car?" Too cocky, as always, Browne replied: "You'll see it on the front of the car."

"Yes," said Gutteridge, "I know the number, but do you?" Kennedy answered: "It's TW6120."

Gutteridge put his torch back in his pocket, took out his notebook and pencil and was about to write in the light of the headlamps when, said Kennedy, "I heard a report, quickly followed by another one.

"I saw the policeman stagger and fall over by the bank at the hedge. I said to Browne 'What have you done?' and then saw he had a large Webley revolver in his hand.

"He said, 'Get out, quick.' I immediately got out and went round to the policeman who was lying on his back. Browne came over and said, 'I'll finish the bugger.' I said, 'For God's sake, don't shoot any more, the man's dying,' as he was groaning.

"The policeman's eyes were open and Browne, addressing him, said, 'What are you looking at me like that for?' and, stooping down, shot him at close range through both eyes."

After the murder they drove off even more wildly, blundering around country roads in the mist that had begun to settle. At one point Browne drove off the road and grazed the car against a tree.

Unimpressed

On the way, said Kennedy, Browne told him to re-load the Webley. He did so nervously, dropping an empty cartridge case on the car floor. At 5.30 a.m. they abandoned the car in Brixton and journeyed to Browne's garage by tram.

On Monday, April 23, 1928, Browne and Kennedy went on trial at the Old Bailey before Mr. Justice Avory, jointly charged with the murder.

Browne, arrogant and argumentative to the end, simply denied the charge as "absurd", and dismissed Kennedy's story as "a concoction". Kennedy's plea that he was "terrified" of Browne made no impression on the jury—especially after it came out in evidence that he had tried to shoot a detective when he was being arrested in Liverpool.

At the end of four days both men were found guilty and sentenced to death. From the death cell Kennedy wrote a final, highly emotional letter to his wife expressing the hope, because of his need for her, that she would soon be joining him in the hereafter.

On May 31 Browne was hanged at Pentonville and Kennedy at Wandsworth.

It is certain that Kennedy's story of

the murder was fairly accurate except for his professed horror at the events. Certainly Browne fired the fatal shots but Kennedy was his willing accomplice.

But one mystery will always remain: why, when P.C. Gutteridge was already dead, or on the very point of death, did Browne add unnecessarily to the night's brutality by shooting into the policeman's eyes?

Maybe it was merely a further manifestation of his viciousness. Or perhaps it was, as some people have suggested, that Browne, the tough, small-time "hood", had a dark streak of superstition in his soul.

Perhaps he believed the old wives' tale that the last thing a dying man sees is "fixed" like a photograph in his eyes.

ACE GUNSMITH Robert Churchill (right) identified a rare cartridge case and the bullets as having been fired from Browne's Webley. The killer (shown with wife) was arrogant and argumentative to the end, dismissing as a "concoction" the testimony of his "terrified" accomplice William Kennedy.

THE MAIDS OF HORROR

Everything appeared to be cut and dried. The brutally slaughtered bodies had been found, along with the murder weapons, and the two killers had immediately confessed to the crime. Yet something, surely, was wrong. These were not hardened criminals; they were not even psychopaths. They were two ordinary housemaids. What had driven them to hack their employers to death?

THE newspapers had called them "the monsters of Le Mans", "the diabolical sisters", and "the lambs who had become wolves". But as Christine Papin, 28, and her sister, Lea, 21, took their seats in the courtroom of the provincial French town of Le Mans on the morning of September 20, 1933, it was difficult to believe that these were the girls who had inspired those black headlines.

They were impassive. No emotion showed on their peasant-like, but not coarse, faces; they kept their heavy-lidded eyes on the floor. It was almost as if they were in a trance or under heavy sedation. On their way to the dock they moved like robots.

And yet they were charged with a double murder which has been described as "one of the most awesome recorded occurrences of motiveless ferocity"—a crime which "shocked France, baffled psychiatrists, and has yet to be satisfactorily explained".

The men and women in the public seats were hushed as they heard—from the principals this time, not from the columns of their daily newspaper—the macabre details of the crime committed in a middle-class home in Le Mans on a dark winter's evening nearly eight months earlier.

The date was February 2, 1933. Monsieur René Lancelin, an attorney who had been away on business all day, was due to

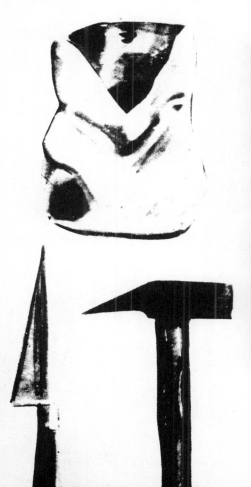

BLOOD RED staircase (above) leading to the servants' room where Christine and sister Lea lay huddled together in a single bed. The landing is where the bodies of Madame and Mademoiselle Lancelin were left, horribly mutilated. The weapons used by the "monsters of Le Mans" were a knife, a hammer, and a severely battered pewter pot (left) and all three were found beside the lifeless bodies.

THE SCENE awaiting Monsieur Lancelin on arrival at his house (below). The front door was locked and the only light came from the maids' room. Inside, his wife and daughter lay hacked to pieces.

meet his wife and 27-year-old daughter Geneviève, for dinner at the home of a friend. "They were not there," he told the court. "After waiting for a while, I tried to telephone my home. There was no answer. I excused myself and went to the house.

"The front door was locked from the inside and the house was in darkness except for a faint glow from the upstairs room occupied by the two maids, Christine and Lea Papin. I was unable to get in so I called the police."

Deep wounds

The story was then taken up by the police inspector who arrived in response to M. Lancelin's call and forced his way into the house. The ground floor was deserted, but on the first-floor landing . . .

"The corpses of Madame and Mademoiselle Lancelin were lying stretched out on the floor and were frightfully mutilated. Mademoiselle Lancelin's corpse was lying face downward, head bare, coat pulled up and with her knickers down, revealing deep wounds in the buttocks and multiple cuts in the calves. Madame Lancelin's body was lying on its back. The eyes had disappeared, she seemed no longer to have a mouth and all the teeth had been knocked out.

"The walls and doors were covered with splashes of blood to a height of more than seven feet. On the floor we found fragments of bone and teeth, one eye, hair pins, a handbag, a key ring, an untied parcel, numerous bits of white, decorated porcelain and a coat button."

That was not all. There were more discoveries—a kitchen knife covered with blood, a damaged pewter pot and lid, a blood-stained hammer. But where were the maids? The police found them, naked and huddled together in a single bed, in their room. Christine, the elder, immediately confessed to the crime.

In the horror-struck courtroom, she kept her eyes downcast as her words —spoken in a sullen, dull monotone— were recalled.

"When Madame came back to the house, I informed her that the iron was broken again and that I had not been able to iron. She wanted to jump on me. My sister and I and our two mistresses were on the first-floor landing. When I saw that Madame Lancelin was going to jump on me, I leaped at her face and scratched out her eyes with my fingers.

"No, I made a mistake when I said that I leaped on Madame Lancelin. It was on Mademoiselle Lancelin that I leaped and it was her eyes that I scratched out. Meanwhile, my sister Lea had jumped on Madame Lancelin and scratched her eyes out in the same way.

"After we had done this, they lay and crouched down on the spot. I then rushed down to the kitchen to fetch a hammer and a knife. With these two instruments, my sister and I fell upon our two mistresses. We struck at the head with the knife, hacked at the bodies and legs, and also struck with a pewter pot, which was standing on a little table on the landing.

"We exchanged one instrument for another several times. By that I mean that I would pass the hammer over to my sister so that she could hit with it while she handed me the knife, and we did the same with the pewter pot. The victims began to cry out but I don't remember that they said anything.

"When we had done the job, I went to bolt the front door, and I also shut the vestibule door. I shut these doors because I wanted the police to find out our crime before our master. My sister and I then went and washed our hands in the kitchen because they were covered with blood.

"We then went to our room, took off all our clothes, which were stained with blood, put on a dressing-gown, shut the door of our room with a key and lay down on the same bed. That's where you found us when you broke the door down.

"I have no regrets or, rather, I can't tell you whether I have any or not. I'd rather have had the skin of my mistresses than that they should have had mine or my sister's. I did not plan my crime and I didn't feel any hatred towards them, but I don't put up with the sort of gesture that Madame Lancelin was making at me that evening."

No regrets

Lea Papin confirmed her sister's statement. "Like my sister," she said, "I affirm that we had not planned to kill our mistresses. The idea came suddenly when we heard Madame Lancelin scolding us. I don't have any more regrets for the criminal act we have committed than my sister does. Like her, I would rather have had my mistresses' skins than their having ours."

The murders had been triggered off by the iron mentioned in Christine's statement. Lea had damaged it at some time during January. On February 1, the day before the killings, Madame Lancelin had deducted five francs from her month's wages to pay for the repair. Then, while the maids were ironing in the otherwise empty house on February 2, the iron fused, putting out all the lights. "What will Madame do to us when she gets back?" Lea had asked anxiously.

It seemed certain that, on her return, Madame Lancelin had been irritated and might have raised her hand to one or both of the sisters. But how could such a trivial incident have led to such savagery —two healthy women having their eyes gouged out and then, blinded and in agony, battered almost beyond recognition with the hammer and pewter pot, and finally their bodies further mutilated with a knife?

Even the judge found it difficult to credit both the story and the lack of emotion of the two sisters as it was related. Lea, looking very much the younger of the two, her dark coat buttoned to the neck, her hands thrust deep into her pockets, gazed vacantly in front of her.

Christine still gazed rigidly at the ground. She might have been asleep but for a strange smile, almost of contentment, that strayed across her lips.

Barely audible

The judge, speaking quietly and calmly, as if to two children, went over the salient facts with them again, almost as if seeking reassurance that he had heard correctly the first time. He said to Christine:

"You knocked Madame Lancelin down with a blow from a pewter pot. As she cried out, your sister came running. What did you say to her?"

"I told Lea to tear her eyes out."

A murmur of horror ran through the listeners in the public seats. The judge then asked Lea: "When your sister saw that Madame Lancelin wanted to get up again, did she say to you: 'Tear her eyes out'?"

"Yes," replied Lea in a barely audible voice.

"You came rushing up. You knocked her out by banging her head against the floor and then you tore her eyes out. How?"

"With my fingers," Lea replied in a flat, matter-of-fact voice.

There was a renewed hubbub in the public seats. "Death to them!" someone shouted. "Death to them!" The judge threatened to clear the court if there was any further disturbance.

Drunkard father

As peace was restored, he resumed the interrogation. What, he wanted to know, had happened after Lea had torn out Madame Lancelin's eyes and helped to batter her to death?

"I slashed her body with the knife," she responded.

"Have you any excuses for your action, any explanation, any regrets?" asked the judge.

Lea made no reply. Nor did Christine when the same question was put to her.

Could there be anything like a deep-rooted resentment of their lives as maids to account for the ferocity of their sudden assault? That suggestion, too, led the court nowhere.

Christine had gone straight into domestic service on leaving her convent school. Lea had followed her after being brought up in an orphanage (their father was a drunkard). They had worked

FLANKED by gendarmes (right), Lea Papin stares grimly at the judge while sister Christine, head bowed, stares stonily at the ground. Pictured (above) is a general view of the court in session during the trial and (left) the outside of the Palais de Justice at Le Mans. The courtroom was always packed with eager spectators fascinated by this bizarre story of monstrous murder. They were not disappointed by what they heard and saw: there were sensational and horrific confessions from both girls as well as a succession of gory exhibits. The verdict of guilty seemed inevitable.

together and changed jobs frequently before joining the Lancelins. Changing employers had been motivated by nothing more sinister than better wages, and all their references spoke of them as "willing, hard-working, and honest".

Both agreed that they had been well treated by the Lancelins. They were sufficiently well paid to have saved 24,000 francs; they ate the same food as the Lancelins; they even had electric heating in their room—considered something of a luxury for servants.

"What *did* you have against the Lancelin family?" the judge asked, sounding almost desperate in his anxiety to find some clue that would explain the sisters' violent action. "There has been mention of the social hatred of the employee for the employer. But this was not the case. You have said that you suffered from no feeling of inferiority, that 'a servant's profession is as good as any other'. Did you love your employers?"

Lea answered: "We served them and that was all. We never talked to them."

Totally indifferent

With that avenue of exploration apparently closed, the court turned to the personal relationship between the two sisters. Were they lesbians? It wasn't merely the fact that the police had found them naked in bed together after the killings. They had always lived what seemed an odd life for two young girls.

They spent nearly all their spare time together in their room, never going to the cinema or to dances. They had no friends of either sex. In fact, they seemed totally indifferent to everything except their work and each other.

Why had Madame Lancelin and her daughter gone home unexpectedly when they were due to meet M. Lancelin at a friend's? The parcel which the police found on the first floor had contained meat. Why had Madame Lancelin—or her daughter—taken the parcel upstairs instead of, as would have been normal, taking it straight to the kitchen?

Could it be that the mistress and her daughter suspected an illicit relationship,

and had caught the maids in a compromising situation—and that this had sparked off the horror?

Evidence to support this theory came from Christine's behaviour during the seven months she and Lea had been in prison awaiting trial. She, like Lea, had ceased to menstruate. When they were separated and placed in separate cells, she at first wept, then screamed threats, and howled like a dog.

Once, like a distraught lover, she cried all night for her "darling Lea". Another time, she rolled on the ground, screaming obscenities. "It seemed she was tormented by sexual desires," said a warder.

She begged for Lea to be reunited with her. When they were kept apart, she went on hunger strike and became so violent that she had to be placed in a straitjacket. Finally, they were allowed to meet for a brief reunion. Witnesses gave two slightly differing accounts of the meeting, both bizarre and both suggesting there was more—at least from Christine's point of view—in their relationship than mere sisterly love.

One version claimed that, as soon as Lea entered the cell, Christine leaped upon her and hugged her so hard they had to be forcibly separated before the younger girl choked. Then, as they sat on a bed, Christine tried to tear Lea's blouse off and to kiss her on the mouth, pleading with her: "Say yes to me, Lea, say yes to me."

Hysteria

In the second version, Christine, in a fit of hysteria, pulled her skirts up above her thighs, and, apparently in a paroxysm of sexual desire, begged her sister: "Come to me, Lea, come to me." Both accounts agreed that, for her part, Lea had remained calm and passive.

The medical evidence for the prosecution discounted this behaviour. The director of the lunatic asylum at Le Mans, in a joint report with another doctor, declared: "Christine and Lea are in no way depraved. They are not suffering from any mental illness and are in no way labouring under the burden of a defective

heredity. From an intellectual, affective, and emotive point of view, they are completely normal."

Three other doctors appointed to examine the sisters came to the conclusion "there is no question of an attachment of a sexual nature".

The exact nature of the relationship between the two girls proved a point on which the judge was anxious to satisfy himself and the jury. Once again he spoke almost like a parent trying to coax the truth out of a couple of reluctant youngsters.

Sexual relationship?

There were, he pointed out—somewhat hesitantly as if choosing his words carefully—several strange aspects to the life they lived in the Lancelin household. They never indulged in the kind of social activities that most young people enjoyed. They had no boy friends, and on breaking down the door of their room, the police found them in the same bed.

"I am bound to ask you," he said, "whether there was anything sexual in your relationship?"

Christine answered that they had merely been sisters. "There was nothing else between us," she shrugged.

And that was basically that. They had committed two brutal murders which, for their ferocity, were virtually without parallel in modern times . . . they had confessed . . . they were, despite their grim crime, sane and normal girls according to all the medical opinion produced by the prosecution.

In prison, awaiting trial, Christine had often said stoically: "I shall be punished—my head cut off, even. *Tant pis!*" Now it looked as if her prediction would be fulfilled.

The slender basis of the defence plea of not guilty was that the two sisters were not, in fact, sane and normal girls. In support of that contention, however, the only witness of distinction they could produce to try to refute the overwhelming medical evidence amassed by the prosecution was a Dr. Logre, a well-known psychiatrist of the era.

All Keystone

LA TRAGÉDIE DE LA RUE BRUYÈRE, AU MANS

LES DEUX SŒURS CRIMINELLES
PRÉCISENT DEVANT LE JUGE D'INSTRUCTION
LES CIRCONSTANCES DE LEUR FORFAIT

On a procédé
dans la Galerie
de France, en
t Lebrun, pré-
ue, aux opéra-
dernier tirage
nationale « la
profit des qua-
ns de mutilés :
s », « l'Union
e », « les Plus
les Ailes bri-

ui était accom-
colonel Bonas-
militaire, a été
gouverneur de
ce, et par les
s ainsi que par
président des

lités présentes,
ment : M. Micl-
sions, le maré-
nard, préfet de
réfet de police,

nercia tout d'a-
la République
honorer de sa
nonio du der-

Hier soir dans les couloirs du Palais de
LÉA à gauche) et **CHRISTINE**
(Photos

Un no
qui dét
en c

Bordeaux
comparait
Gironde le
Bressand,
millions d
fut arrêté
l'inculpatio
faux et us

L'instruc
cier minist
dans sa c
que de no
taient en c
pour se liv
bourse.

Rosset-B
Mᵉ Jean O
de, et M.
soutient l'
l'accusé p
rapelle se
notariale.

Il acheta
de temps
Après la g
et fut cite

The prosecutor's case was simple. Christine and Lea Papin were fully responsible for their actions. They had committed a crime which he described, in a ringing phrase, as "the most horrible, and the most abominable, recorded in the annals of justice." And nobody need look beyond sheer bad temper for a motive.

The defence restricted itself to the plea that psychiatry was a complicated and incompletely-understood science. The question of whether the sisters were of sound mind was still a matter of debate.

The argument carried little weight with the jury. At 1.25 a.m., after 100 minutes, they brought in their verdict. Both sisters were guilty. From the public benches came an audible sigh of relief and a ripple of applause.

Christine showed her first sign of emotion when the judge sentenced her to death. She slumped to her knees for a moment before her lawyer helped her back to her feet. Lea, for whom the jury had found extenuating circumstances in the way she was dominated by her sister, received a sentence of ten years' hard labour. Neither sister appealed.

Later, however, Christine's punishment was commuted to a life sentence of hard labour. But she served only four years, during which she refused to work and showed signs of insanity. She was finally transferred to a psychiatric hospital where she died in 1937. During that time she never once asked for Lea who, when her own term of punishment was over, was released to live in obscurity.

3f50
AU POUVOIR
DES
FORCES OCCULTES
PAR
ACHEFF

LA
VÉRITÉ
sur

LE CRIME INEXPLIQUE
DES SŒURS PAPIN

EDITIONS STYLEX

La Sarte

FIELD DAY for the press . . . Details
of the trial provided reporters with
plenty of headline copy (left). Le Mans
prison (this page) is where the two sisters
were jailed while awaiting trial — and
where they returned afterwards.

AN EXPERT
SLAUGHTERMAN

AT FIRST the attendant at Charing Cross cloakroom paid little attention to the well-built, dark-skinned man who brought a large black trunk for deposit. After all, some 2,000 pieces of luggage were left at the station each day, and in time one traveller came to look much like another. But this particular man seemed anxious to make himself known.

"You must take very great care of my property," he said as he received a ticket for the round-topped, wicker-work trunk. "I shall be travelling later today, and the contents must not be disturbed."

Having issued his instructions the man —who could have been an army officer from his upright stance and short, narrow moustache—strode off into the station yard. He hailed a taxi, and as he was driven away he did an extraordinary thing.

He lowered the window of the cab, put out his hand, and dropped the cloakroom ticket onto the cobbled ground. He was seen to do this by the station shoe-black, whose pitch was nearby the left-luggage office.

The shoe-black helpfully picked up the ticket, and gave it to Mr. Glass, the head of the cloakroom staff. To them, the man appeared to be just another careless traveller, who would later have to identify his trunk by its contents.

Severed head

The porters and attendants then went on with their work, and nothing more was thought about the man, the trunk, or the thrown-away ticket. Nothing, that is, until five days later when—on May 11, 1922 —a peculiar and offensive smell was noticed to be coming from the still unclaimed article.

Mr. Glass examined the outside of the trunk, consulted his immediate superior, and was told to take the box from the rack and place it in an adjoining room. There, in the presence of several mystified officials, a number of keys were tried on the massive brass lock.

None of the keys fitted the lock, and it was then decided to force the lid open with a hammer and chisel. This was duly done and the railwaymen were confronted with several brown-paper parcels tied up with string, a pair of high-heeled shoes, and a leather handbag.

A porter was ordered to open one of the parcels at random and see what it contained. He chose the parcel nearest to him—round-shaped and about the size of a football. He cut the string, unfolded the paper, and found himself holding a woman's severed head!

The horrified Mr. Glass made a phone

A CUT ABOVE the average killer, Robinson (top) carried out everything with military precision. He carved his victim (right) with immaculate skill.

call to Bow Street station, and shortly before 1 a.m. a Detective-Inspector and a police doctor came and took the trunk and its gruesome contents to Westminster mortuary. There it was discovered that the five parcels contained the amputated body of an apparently young woman.

The torso itself lay under some blood-stained clothing — a pair of corsets, a vest, knickers and silk stockings — and the limbs had been sawn off at the shoulders and hip-joints. The remains were examined by the famous Home Office pathologist, Sir Bernard Spilsbury — who, due to his defective sense of smell, could work in conditions which other doctors often found unbearable.

Putrefaction was then in an advanced state, but even so Sir Bernard concluded that the cause of death was: "Asphyxia from pressure over the mouth and nostrils whilst unconscious from head injury and other injuries."

The woman — who had been dead for about a week before the discovery of the body — had been around 35, short, rather stout, and with dark fashionably-bobbed hair. "The clean dismemberment of the parts," added the pathologist, "suggests the work of an expert slaughterman."

TELL-TALE contents of the trunk . . . But even with so many clues upon which to work, the police were in difficulties.

This clue — misleading as it proved to be — was something for the police to work on. The case was put in the hands of Chief Inspector Wensley of Scotland Yard, and after interviewing the cloak-room attendant, he put out the following description of the wanted man:

"Height 5 ft. 7 ins. or 5 ft. 8 ins.; military build; dark, sunburnt complexion; a closely cropped black moustache. Speaks with a slight Midland accent. Believed to be wearing a navy blue suit. Handsome face; features sharply defined; piercing black eyes."

Apart from this, there were other, even more definite leads to follow up. The dead woman's knickers bore a small white

linen tab with the name "P. HOLT" marked on it in block capitals. On another garment there were two laundry marks — H 581 and H 447. And there was also a duster of the kind used in public houses to wipe the glasses clean.

With all this in the police's favour — and with a photograph of the trunk issued to the Press — it seemed as if the case would soon be solved. This false optimism was increased when two of the clues provided speedy and satisfactory results.

First of all a dealer named Ward, who ran a second-hand luggage shop in Brixton Road, came forward and identified the trunk as the one he had sold on May 4. Mr. Ward told the police that it had been bought by a "distinguished, military-looking gentleman", who had been most particular about the size and the price of his intended purchase.

"I'd like a fair-sized trunk for one journey only," the man had said.

THE CLOAKROOM at London's Charing Cross Station where the "military gentleman" deposited the trunk. It was inevitable that the body would be found.

"I've got this one here," replied the dealer. "It belonged to a family in St. Leonards."

The would-be traveller inspected the trunk and nodded his satisfaction.

"That's fine," he said. "I shall be shipping it abroad and shall put a few clothes and oddments in it. I don't want to pay more than a pound for it."

Very attractive

A bargain was struck at 12s. 6d. To the dealer's astonishment, the customer then hoisted the trunk onto his back and proceeded to carry it away.

"I haven't far to go," the man explained. "Just up the road a bit to where my office is."

This airy reference to an office — which turned out to be opposite the police station in Rochester Row, Victoria — was typical of the coolness of a murderer who cut up his victim in a room overlooking the station and the local police court!

After this promising start, the police were further encouraged when the laundry marks were traced to a Mrs. Minnie Bonati, who had been employed as a cook by a Mr. and Mrs. Holt of Tregunter Road, Chelsea.

Mrs. Bonati was described by her former employers as a friendly, vivacious woman who was "very attractive to men". A short while later the cook's husband, Bernard Bonati, an Italian waiter, was run to earth.

He accompanied the Chief Inspector's men to the mortuary, where he identified the remains of his wife by her teeth formation, and by a crooked index finger on her right hand.

As in most cases of this kind, the husband is the first person to be suspected by the investigating officers. Bonati, however, was able to prove that he and his wife had been living apart for some time.

"She was always fond of dancing and having a good time," he stated. "She went with other men and finally ran off with a lodger we had. After he left her, she sometimes came back to me for money, which I gave to her rather than see her on the streets."

Mrs. Bonati's last address was discovered to be in Limerston Street, Chelsea, where she had last been seen alive at four o'clock on the afternoon of May 4.

She had then been visited by a Receiving Officer who was making enquiries into the many debts she had incurred.

Accomplice

And it was there—and with that information—that the police ran up against a seemingly blank wall. The mysterious "military gentleman" was no nearer to being caught, and for the next few days Chief Inspector Wensley, and his colleague, Chief Inspector Cornish, followed up one false trail after another.

Finally, on May 14, a conference was held at Scotland Yard when the theory was put forward that the murder, or its

aftermath, had been the work of two men. No one person, it was argued, could have taken the heavy trunk to Charing Cross station. The murderer must have had help—either from an accomplice, or from someone who did not know what was in the "death box". Then, as every avenue turned out to be a dead-end, three more people gave evidence which was to put a rope around the elusive killer's neck.

A taxi-driver named Waller read about the case, and said that on the morning of

A DEFECTIVE sense of smell helped Sir Bernard Spilsbury (below) to cope with the task of examining Minnie's body.

May 6 he had been picked up by a man in Rochester Row. He helped his fare put a "very heavy trunk" into the cab, and then drove him to Charing Cross.

Missing agent

Detectives immediately hurried to the office block opposite the police station in Victoria, and stared curiously at the front of No. 86 Rochester Row. On entering the building, they learnt that a Mr. John Robinson—who ran a one-man estate agent's business—had not been seen for several days.

At the same time, other detectives succeeded in tracing the duster which had been found in the trunk. It proved to have been taken from an inn, the Greyhound Hotel, in Hammersmith. There one of the barmaids had a lot to say about Mr. Robinson, who had suddenly stopped visiting the inn to see his wife.

Astounded by their luck, the officers interviewed Mrs. Robinson who was separated from her husband and forced to work in the hotel. She told them how unsatisfactory a spouse Robinson was.

The police officers then went to a house in De Laune street, Kennington, London, S.E., acting upon information supplied by Mrs. Robinson. There they found Mr. Robinson asleep in bed. He was promptly awoken and arrested.

Pathetic story

To begin with, he denied any knowledge of Minnie Bonati, or the trunk, or of recently having been at Charing Cross cloakroom. But at a second interview—and after being kept waiting for a long time at Scotland Yard—he broke down and told the full, somewhat pathetic story of his crime.

According to Robinson (who had been

UNRUFFLED . . . Minnie's husband, an Italian waiter (below), showed little emotion at his estranged wife's death.

John Frost Collection

The Daily Mail

TRUNK CRIME ARREST.

DETECTIVES ROUSE MAN FROM BED.

POLICE SEARCH AN OFFICE

OVERLOOKING A POLICE STATION.

After being roused from his bed in a house in De Laune-street, Kennington, London, S.E., by detectives and questioned at length at Scotland Yard, John Robinson, aged 36, a clerk, was yesterday charged with the murder of Mrs. Minnie Alice Bonati, whose dismembered body was found in a trunk in the cloak-room at Charing Cross Railway Station on Monday, May 10.

Robinson will appear this morning at Westminster Police Court. The charge is one of murdering the woman on May 4 in a block of offices at 86, Rochester-row, Westminster, S.W., which directly overlooks Westminster Police Court and Rochester-row Police Station, where the man is now under arrest.

On arrival at Scotland Yard Robinson was questioned and then detained. Later he was charged. When he had been at Scotland Yard for seven hours he was taken to Rochester-row Police Station.

Detectives from Bow-street, yesterday afternoon visited 86, Rochester-row and took a number of articles, including a

Topix

discharged from the Army in 1923 on medical grounds), he had been "accosted" by his future victim as he left his office late on the afternoon of May 4.

He took her back to his second floor room, where she complained of not feeling well and asked him for a pound. When he refused to give it to her, she became abusive, flew into a temper, and attacked him in the chair in which he was sitting.

Grisly act

"She bent down as though to pick something from the fireplace," he said in his formal statement, "and came towards me. I hit her on the face with my right hand . . . She fell backwards. She struck a chair in falling and fell over it.

"As she fell she sort of sat down and rolled over with her hand in the fireplace . . . . I returned to my office about 10 o'clock the following morning. I was surprised to find that she was still there. She was dead. I was in a hopeless position then. I did not know what to do."

Faced with this unenviable situation, Robinson again sat at his desk debating

THE ANSWER to the whole mystery lay in the Greyhound Hotel (below) where the killer's wife worked. Subsequent arrest and conviction were mere formalities.

TRUNK CRIME "DEAD END."

SCOTLAND YARD BAFFLED.

300 STATEMENTS TAKEN AND NO CLUE.

Two conferences were held during the week-end at Scotland Yard by the police officers engaged in trying to solve the mystery of the death of Mrs. Minnie Alice Bonati, whose dismembered body was found in a trunk at Charing Cross Station on May 10.

Two people were interrogated late yesterday afternoon, after which detectives were sent to Brixton to make certain inquiries.

Since the discovery of the body the officers in charge of the case have personally interrogated 120 persons, and in all more than 300 statements have been taken by the police.

Every possible line of inquiry has been exhausted, and Scotland Yard are now at a "dead end."

Inquiries have been made throughout the country with the object of tracing a man named "Jim," a chauffeur who is believed to have been associated with Mrs. Bonati six weeks before her death. This man has not yet come forward.

---

what his next move would be. He knew the police were only a few yards away, and finally decided to dismember the corpse and dispose of the pieces.

"I went to a big stationer's shop in Victoria Street," he continued, "and bought six sheets of brown paper and a ball of string, for which I think I paid 1s. 9d. . . . I went to a shop in the street nearer Victoria Station, and bought a chef's knife.

"I then went back to my office, and of course I did the job—that is, I cut off her legs and arms. I made them up into parcels and tied them up in the brown paper and string which I had just bought. I finished the job as quickly as possible before dinner."

Robinson's subsequent movements—on the morning of May 6—followed the evidence given by the taxi driver and cloakroom attendant. The knife he used in his grisly act was found where he had hidden it—under a tree on Clapham Common.

After completing and signing his statement, he was charged with murder and was tried at the Old Bailey later that summer. The case dominated the newspapers for the next few days, as thirty witnesses were called for the prosecution, and Robinson himself—who pleaded "not

guilty" – spent an hour and a half in the witness-box.

The verdict against him was almost a foregone conclusion, but even so the jury of ten men and two women were puzzled and intrigued by one of the murder's most remarkable features – the almost complete lack of motive. Robinson was duly found guilty, his appeal was dismissed, and he was executed at Pentonville on August 27. The "Great Trunk Murder" as it was called, was not, however, allowed to rest there.

Both at the trial itself, and at the police commission held afterwards, Chief Inspector Cornish was strongly criticized for making Robinson wait for over an hour in a room at Scotland Yard. It was then ruled that such "cat and mouse" tactics would not be used on a murder suspect

THE GREAT trunk murderer was duly executed at Pentonville prison (above), and the case vanished from the headlines. Few "left luggage" slayers ever escape.

again. In more ways than one John Robinson added his own chapter to the story of trunk murders which made such juicy – if bloody – reading for the crime-hungry public between the wars.

L'OGRESSE

**What kind of
odd, twisted compulsion
drove Jeanne
Weber to slay
young children?
And why did
the law allow
her to go free?**

MISERY gripped Jeanne Weber by the throat and turned her from a normal young woman into a homicidal maniac who found satisfaction in strangling babies.

DR. EDMOND LOCARD, the great French criminologist, once wrote that "the Weber case was a perfect example of the French knack of refusing to believe the obvious . . . the truth under everyone's nose" The centrepiece of this incredible forensic case was Jeanne Weber, daughter of a humble fisherman of a village in the Côtes-du-Nord in Brittany.

Jeanne—who was born in 1875—appeared to be a normal child in every way —other than possessing a streak of independence which manifested itself at 14 when she went into service with a respectable *bourgeois* family. She behaved impeccably, but on her half-days off managed to taste a little of life in a neighbouring town. This was enough. Longing for "romance" and "excitement", she left her job to wander throughout France.

She made her living by a series of casual jobs. Because of her low status she did not excite comment or interest in her progress, nor were her looks worth attention. She was a small, somewhat overweight teenager apparently without physical attraction.

She arrived in Paris in 1893, and eked out a livelihood in one of the poorest quarters of the town. In that year she met a man named Marcel Weber, who, to her surprise and delight, became romantically involved with her.

Weber was one of four brothers who lived in an ugly slum of brothels, tenements, and factories. His home was in the *Passage de la Goutte d'Or*—though anything less like a drop of gold did not exist.

Jeanne went to live there as Marcel's legal wife, and was soon absorbed into the life of the brawling Weber clan. She knew that the miserable street was close to the great Salpétrière Hospital, the Bretonneau Hospital and—like a premonitory warning—a madhouse.

Marcel was a heavy drinker, a habit his new wife quickly acquired. But at first this did not intrude into the hard, poverty-stricken life which she lived with her husband and three children.

Superficially in the area and conditions of the time, it appeared to be a happy marriage.

An early tragedy were the deaths—due to natural causes—of the Webers' two small daughters. What no one seemed to notice was Madame Weber's spiritual change. Death was no stranger in that sad slum, but Jeanne Weber took the deaths of her daughters very much to heart. Her outlook was affected, and to dismiss her own misery she drank more than ever—which did nothing to improve her unstable and melancholic character.

Curious incidents

The first "curious incident" in her history occurred when two children—Lucy Alexandre and Marcel Poyatos—died while under her nursing care. There did not seem to be any suspicious circumstances, nor did the doctors concerned find anything irregular about the deaths. (There was a high infant mortality rate in late nineteenth-century France.)

Then, one bitingly cold March morning the second "curious incident" took place at the home of Pierre Weber, brother of Marcel, and father of two little girls, Georgette and Suzanne. Madame Pierre Weber visited her sister-in-law, asking if she could come round to look after the children. One of them had not been well, and she had to take the family laundry to the local wash-house. Jeanne agreed to baby-sit, and went with Madame Weber to her apartment in the rue Pré-Maudit.

A neighbour, a Madame Pouche, happened to pass the open door of the Weber

164

BESTIAL baby sitter Jeanne Weber, the French ogress, strangles her last victim.

Mary Evans

apartment, and saw Georgette on Jeanne's lap, apparently in convulsions. Within minutes Madame Pierre had been rushed home to find her child's face blue and her phlegmatic sister-in-law massaging the child's chest. With prompt attention there was complete recovery, and the mother, feeling that there was nothing more to worry about, went back to finish her laundry.

An hour later, however, Pierre Weber rushed in a state of alarm to the wash-house and hurried his wife to the apartment — where Georgette seemed to have suffered a second seizure and had died from it. Her face was blue, and her small body convulsed. Madame Pouche was again present, exclaiming loudly at the marks on Georgette's throat. But neither the parents nor the doctor, when he arrived, regarded this as important.

Throat marks

Unbelievably, exactly nine days later, Madame Pierre Weber decided to leave her sister-in-law to look after three-year-old Suzanne while the family shopping was collected. The child was dead when the mother returned, a scarf wrapped loosely round her neck. The indefatigable Madame Pouche was on the scene again, openly accusing the seemingly imperturbable Jeanne, and drawing the attention of the doctor to marks on Suzanne's throat. This time he refused to accept the death as natural and informed the police.

Feeling there was no importance or urgency about the case, the officers arrived later with an official surgeon. They probed and searched but, despite the suggestive facts, did not consider either the death or the circumstances as suspicious!

The astonishing coincidences began to multiply. Two weeks later Jeanne Weber went to lunch with another sister-in-law, Madame Léon Weber, in the neighbouring Impasse Langlois; Madame Léon's daughter Germaine was exactly seven months old.

Like a film being re-run the story was repeated with uncanny similarity. Madame Weber returned from shopping to learn that her mother had rushed from her upstairs apartment when she heard screams below, and discovered Jeanne with her hands under Germaine's shift busily engaged in "massaging her heart". The baby had been taken upstairs, where she recovered, and was now sleeping peacefully.

Madame Léon — with touching faith or blind idiocy — then went shopping for Jeanne who "felt unwell". She returned to find Germaine suffocating. A doctor was called, but nothing alarmed him. Laughably, were it not so serious, Madame Léon again left the apartment, again the baby was found to be in a "fit" with

Jeanne massaging its chest. Then, for the third time, the mother departed, on this occasion with a neighbour. She came back to find that Germaine had undergone "another seizure" and had died.

That same night little Marcel Weber, Jeanne's own seven-year-old son, fell mysteriously ill and died of suffocation, which seemed to be caused by diphtheria — although there are no records to support such a diagnosis on the doctor's part.

But it was not until the next "curious incident" that the Webers felt there was something "odd" in connection with their relative by marriage. This time, on the afternoon of April 5, Madame Charles Weber and her son Maurice, just under one-year-old, paid a visit to Jeanne in the company of her bereaved sister-in-law, Madame Pierre.

Willingly they agreed to get some shopping for their hostess, but returned unexpectedly within a few minutes. Maurice

UPROAR . . . On her first arrest Jeanne Weber was almost lynched by a hysterical crowd screaming for her blood. In spite of the public outcry, the trial took place in calm and she was acquitted.

was blue in the face and choking. Madame Charles was no fool; she openly accused Jeanne, then rushed to the nearest doctor with her child, and on to the casualty department of the Bretonneau Hospital.

There she was seen by a Dr. Charles Saillant, who diagnosed the red marks on the baby's throat and stated that he was suffering from attempted asphyxiation.

Post mortems

By evening Maurice had recovered in the safety of the hospital and Madame Charles, wary and angry, related the curious family story of death. As a result of this, the police were informed and Jeanne Weber was arrested.

The Examining Magistrate before whom she was placed was a cynical and erudite man. When he heard the facts he sent for a highly-regarded medico-legal expert, Dr. Léon Thoinot, who examined young Maurice. The dead Weber children were exhumed.

Despite his reputation, however, Thoinot was a stolid, unimaginative man used to going strictly by the book — which is what he did. He examined Maurice, whose throat now showed no marks. The post mortems on the dead children

revealed nothing. There was no sign on the well-preserved bodies to indicate strangulation.

Medical proof

The Examining Magistrate, with the facts in hand could not accept that the bodies bore no suspicious indications. He re-checked every witness and asked Dr. Thoinot to go over his findings with the "greatest care". The result was the same, but the Magistrate went against the "evidence", and Jeanne Weber was put forward for trial.

Before this took place the judge concerned, deeply disturbed by the circumstances, still wanted medical proof. In January 1906 he asked Professor Paul Brouardel, a noted medical jurist, to check Dr. Thoinot's report. He did so and backed Thoinot completely — the children had not been strangled or choked to death.

The public appeared to have no doubts at all, nor did the press. By the time the trial opened Jeanne Weber had been dubbed the 'Ogresse de la Goutte d'Or'. The great Maître Henri Robert king of advocats, defended Jeanne with all his brilliance. He tied the prosecution and prosecution witnesses in knots on his way to gaining an acquittal for the "maligned" Madame Weber.

She was set free and remained out of the public eye until April 16, 1907, when nine-year-old Auguste Bavouzet, a peasant child of a village in central France, was taken ill and died, with a reddish mark around his throat. The doctor concerned was suspicious and informed the police. After investigation it was decided that the death was natural, and Auguste was buried in the presence of his father, his sisters, and his father's recently acquired housekeeper and mistress, Madame Moulinet.

Old newspaper

But the elder Bavouzet daughter, who thoroughly disliked the housekeeper, secretly searched Madame's handbag. There she found some old newspaper cuttings together with a picture of Jeanne Weber. She went to the police and hysterically denounced Madame Moulinet-Weber as her brother's murderess. This time a doctor and an expert pathologist made no mistake and announced that strangulation was the cause of Auguste's death.

The newspapers were frantically excited when Moulinet-Weber was arrested. France rang with the news, and Maître Robert — unwilling to admit that he had made an error — volunteered to again defend Jeanne. He even reintroduced Dr. Thoinot onto the scene, demanding that little Auguste should be exhumed.

Three months later Thoinot conducted the post mortem, concluding that Auguste Bavouzet had died of "typhoid fever". Thoinot then tore into the ignorant local medical men, and despite their efforts to achieve support against him, Jeanne Weber was released at the end of 1907.

The awful comedy resumed, but not for long. In May 1908 a man named Bouchery and his "wife" rented a room at an inn in northern France. Madame Bouchery made much of seven-year-old Marcel Poirot, the son of the landlord. When her husband was away on his work as a charcoal-burner she told Monsieur Poirot that she was lonely and nervous at night, and could Marcel sleep with her? Impressed by his guest's plight and politeness, the inn-keeper agreed — particularly as Marcel said he liked the new patron.

That night there were screams from Madame Bouchery's room. A lodger next door rushed in, followed shortly by Poirot. They found Marcel with a discoloured face, blood pouring from his bitten tongue, and blood-stained rags under the bed. Madame Bouchery had blood on her hands and her night clothes.

This time the doctor who was called immediately noticed fingermarks on the child's throat. When Madame Bouchery's day clothes were searched, a letter was found, addressed to Madame Jeanne Weber, signed by Maître Robert.

The police then made enquiries about the suspect. They soon discovered that Madame Bouchery-Weber had been briefly employed in a children's home, and that she had been dismissed when she was caught apparently trying to choke a sick child. Next she had been arrested as a vagrant, examined as to her mental state, and released as perfectly sane.

Horrible death

By now France was in a worse uproar than before. The whole Weber case was disinterred, picked over, and analyzed. Anxious to protect his reputation, Dr. Thoinot arranged for psychiatrists to examine Jeanne Weber. They did so and declared that she was "unbalanced". In October 1908 she was pronounced a "suitable inmate for close confinement" in a mental home.

An awkward and abusive patient, she was incarcerated for two years. She then died horribly, foaming at the mouth and screaming, clutching her own throat in a suicidal grip.

Thoinot and Robert, dogmatic to the end, claimed that Jeanne Weber was guilty only of the last murder. It was clear, they stated, that she had been "animated by a frenzy at being accused and arraigned for crimes she did not commit".

They personified the art of forensic science at its most obstinate and obtuse — a situation which could not exist among their successors today.

René Dazy

THE BEAST OF THE APOCALYPSE

A life-long pursuit of perversion had left poet Aleister Crowley with little more than a nice line in magic robes, a series of pretentious Tarot designs . . . and a carefully nurtured reputation as a degenerate monster. Now he had the nerve to sue for libel — only to find that he was the one on trial.

Both Radio Times Hulton

IT TAKES a lot to shock a judge, but Mr. Justice Swift had heard enough. For a moment his face bore the shadow of a man who had stared into the very abyss of Hell and seen its abominations. When he spoke, the revulsion was easily discernible behind the clipped, legal tones.

"I have been over 40 years engaged in the administration of the law in one capacity or another," he said. "I thought that everything which was vicious and bad had been produced at one time or another before me. I have learnt in this case that we can always learn something if we live long enough. I have never heard such dreadful, horrible, blasphemous and abominable stuff as that which has been produced by the man who describes himself to you as the greatest living poet."

The court muttered in approval. They, too, had gazed into the Pit. They had smelt the pitch and the sulphur, heard the cries of the damned and seen the monstrous regiment of demons rise gibbering from the nightmare world beyond the grave. For four days it had seemed that the Devil himself had been in the courtroom. And in a way, he had; though the man who had conjured up these frightful visions looked more like an English country gentleman than a messenger of Satan.

He was balding and thickset, and wore a tweed suit. Yet there was something about the face . . . not so much the puffy, debauched features as the eyes. The left eye was slightly larger than the right. They stared blankly, as if seeing some private, inner vision, and their colour was a strange yellow-brown, like the pages of some aged and dangerous manuscript.

They were the eyes of a necromancer, a high priest of the Black Arts. They were the eyes of the Satanist dubbed by the Press "The Wickedest Man in the World". They were the eyes of the self-styled

Beast of the Apocalypse, the Demon Who Bears the Name 666, who in the 13th chapter of *Revelation* "came out of the sea, having ten horns and seven heads, and on his horns ten diadems, and upon his heads names of blasphemy . . . And he opened his mouth for blasphemies against God." They were the eyes of Aleister Crowley, poet, prophet, degenerate, drug-addict, sex-maniac and mystic.

At 60, Aleister Crowley, the Beast 666, Frater Perdurabo, Prince Chioa Khan, the Master Therion and Prophet Baphomet, had drained the cup of evil to the dregs. "I have exposed myself to every form of disease, accident and violence," he boasted. "I have driven myself to delight in dirty and disgusting debauches, and to devour human excrement and flesh."

Demoniacal

This was the demoniacal figure who stood before Mr. Justice Swift in the High Court in London on April 14, 1934, awaiting the verdict of the jury. And yet Aleister Crowley was not on trial. After a lifetime of depravity, he was claiming damages for libel. For once, the Devil had failed to look after his own. Crowley was short of money, and a defamatory reference to his putrid life in a recent book had seemed like a gift from Hell.

That was not the only reason for the lawsuit, however; he had entered the courtroom hoping to vindicate his name, to strike a blow against mealy-mouthed convention, even to propagate his morally-bankrupt creed. "Do what thou wilt shall be the whole of the Law" was the message Crowley had preached to a jury almost sick with disgust. They were about to deliver their unique verdict . . .

It was Crowley's mother—an almost repressively religious woman—who had given him the name of the Beast when she realized that she had spawned a monster. At the tender age of 11 he had dedicated himself to a life of evil which was later to embrace every excess, from sexual perversions to live sacrifices. His first victim was the family cat. He was eager to discover whether it had nine lives. "I administered a large dose of arsenic," he recalled in his *Confessions*.

"I chloroformed it, hanged it above the gas jet, stabbed it, cut its throat, smashed its skull and, when it had been pretty thoroughly burnt, drowned it and threw it out of the window that the fall might remove the ninth life. The operation was successful. I was genuinely sorry for the animal; I simply forced myself to carry out the experiment in the interest of pure science."

His voracious appetite for women started when he was 14, when he seduced the kitchen-maid on his mother's bed while the family were at church. From

then on, he enjoyed an endless succession of whores and mistresses. Women were fascinated by his animal vitality and hypnotic eyes. A titled woman who stopped to look in a shop window in Piccadilly was overcome by the reflection of his eyes as he stood behind her. They had never met before, yet the woman immediately booked into a hotel with him for 10 days.

Crowley claimed to wear a secret aphrodisiac called "The Perfume of Immortality", which he rubbed into his scalp. It was made up of musk, ambergris and civet, and women found it irresistible, as did horses—they whinnied after him in the street. Men, however, often remarked on his "sweet, slightly nauseous odour".

Any woman was fuel for Crowley's blazing lust. They should, he said, be "brought round to the back door like the milk". There was certainly danger and excitement when Crowley was around, but his women paid dearly for their thrills. He drove both his wives into lunatic asylums and abandoned every one of his mistresses to either the bottle, the hypodermic syringe or the streets.

Sex was the most powerful element in Crowley's form of Black Magic, which might explain why he failed his degree at Cambridge University. By then, he had become obsessed with the occult; he embraced one sect after another, starting with the "Hermetic Order of the Golden Dawn", in which he was re-named Frater Perdurabo. It was only one of a series of preposterous titles he adopted. For each one, he invented a bizarre costume and hairstyle, culminating in a "horn" of waxed hair, which made him look more like an overweight unicorn than the "Great God Pan".

Dangerous

The blinding revelation that put Crowley's life on a new and dangerous path occurred on March 18, 1904, in the Cairo Museum. A few days earlier, his wife, Rose, had remarked, as if in a trance, "Horus is waiting for you." Crowley had never heard of Horus. Suddenly, as they were walking through one of the museum galleries, she cried out, "There he is!"

In a glass case was an image of the falcon-headed god Horus, painted on an ancient wooden obelisk; but what shook Crowley was the number on the exhibit label—it was 666, *his* number, the number of the Beast.

That night, in a state approaching religious exaltation, Crowley invoked the spirit of Horus, and his faith was rewarded. According to Crowley, Horus sent a spirit-guide named Aiwass who proceeded to dictate a series of precepts and prophecies.

Then, over several weeks Crowley incorporated the supernatural messages into a huge volume called *The Book of the Law*. The result was an almost unreadable ragbag of mysticism, poetry, prediction and pornography. But the ultimate meaning was clear: Mankind was on the brink of a New Dawn, and the prophet selected to lead the way was Aleister Crowley.

Pagan sex-cults

"Crowleyanity" had arrived, and the world was ready for the cult of "Do what thou wilt". Crowley certainly had psychic powers. He had an outstanding mind, and his knowledge of witchcraft, black magic, the occult and the ancient mysteries was encyclopaedic. He also had a profound belief in his destiny: and this is what made him dangerous, for there was something deeply compelling about the man. But, stripped of its mystique and mumbo-jumbo, his apocalyptic new system of universal magic was nothing more than a rehash of the pagan sex-cults discarded centuries ago in the advance of civilization.

Crowley threw himself into his new mission with manic fervour; the horror was that he was a Messiah of Madness, marching backwards to the Black Ages of cruelty, superstition and diabolism.

His behaviour became more and more outrageous. He filed two of his teeth into a point, so he could give women the "Serpent's Kiss" when introduced — one woman, bitten on the arm, went down with blood poisoning. He defecated on drawing-room carpets, and when his hosts protested, he claimed his excreta was sacred.

Crowley believed he could make himself invisible at will. Diners at the Café Royal in London were astonished when Crowley appeared one evening, dressed in a wizard's robes and wearing a conical hat. He glided noiselessly among the tables and left without saying a word. "There you are," he said afterwards, "that proves I can make myself invisible! Nobody spoke to me, therefore they couldn't have seen me."

He toured the world, collecting a retinue of gullible sensation-seekers, neurasthenics and occult cranks. At his temples of magic, newspapers referred in shocked tones to "nameless orgies" and "indescribable rites". His followers claimed that he could conjure up evil spirits, turn day into night and perform prodigious feats of second-sight and clairvoyance.

All his rituals, however, centred round sex. "I rave, I rape, I rip and I rend," he said in his *Hymn to Pan*. In the hocuspocus of Crowleyanity, references to "Magick", "opuses" and "my work" were euphemisms to cover ceremonial sexual acts with his followers, usually perverted and frequently with several partners at the same time.

Scarlet Women

There was always a "permanent mistress" to help in his rituals. Each one bore the name "The Scarlet Woman". The first was a skinny and neurotic New York singing teacher named Leah Faesi, whom he met in 1918. Crowley branded her on the breast with "The Mark of the Beast" — a cross within a circle — using a dagger heated in the fire.

All photos Radio Times Hulton

DEMON Crowley (left) drove his first wife Rose (above) to drink. His other women were even less lucky. He had started as a boy (far left) killing the family cat. . . .

It was Crowley's dream to found a "temple of black magic" where he could practise his rites undisturbed. The dream came true in March 1920, when he discovered an isolated villa, set amid olive groves near the fishing village of Cefalu, on the northern shore of Sicily. It was ideal. "My house is going to be the Whore's Hell," he said, "a secret place of the quenchless fire of Lust and the eternal torment of Love." Cefalu was to be the scene of Crowley's most atrocious excesses.

Crowley called it "The Sacred Abbey of the Thelemic Mysteries". On the floor of the inner temple was a magic circle, with an altar in its centre. A copy of *The Book of the Law* rested on the altar, surrounded by ritual vessels and objects, including the "Cakes of Light", a blas-

phemous mockery of the consecrated wafer, made of oatmeal, honey, red wine and animal or menstrual blood. Outside the circle were the thrones of the Beast and the Scarlet Woman, and the walls of the temple were covered in Crowley's own paintings, depicting every kind of sexual act in every possible position, and some impossible ones.

The gross and perverted ceremonies performed inside the Abbey soon became notorious. During one drug-induced ritual, the Scarlet Woman committed bestiality with a goat, after which its throat was cut by Crowley, allowing the blood to flow over another woman's back. The superstitious Sicilian peasants were terrified of the evil aura surrounding the Abbey—not to speak of the screams, the shrieks and the wailing gibberish that floated from the building after dark. The villagers crossed themselves every time they passed.

More sophisticated disciples flocked to the Abbey to take part in the orgies.

Among them was a 23-year-old Oxford University undergraduate named Raoul Loveday, and his wife Betty May, an artist's model. Loveday was destined to become the first of the Beast's victims. Even before he arrived at Cefalu, Loveday was a marked man. Strolling through the Egyptian Room of the British Museum, his wife had poked fun at a mummy of a high priestess of the wrathful god Amon-Ra. Loveday had been appalled and warned her that Amon-Ra destroyed all who offended her.

When they returned home, he prayed that the curse should fall upon him instead of Betty May. Later, looking through her wedding pictures, Betty May noticed that a mysterious, shadowy outline of a young man had appeared over Loveday's head in one of the prints. The man was lying horizontally as if dead. Despite these unnerving omens, Crowley found Loveday such a promising pupil that he renamed him "Aud", meaning "magical light". Betty May was less enthusiastic. She detested Crowley and was horrified by the sexual orgies, which were frequently watched by Crowley's legitimate and illegitimate children.

Living sacrifice

When Betty May reprimanded one of the little boys for smoking, he turned on her with a stick and shouted, "Leave me alone! Don't you know I'm Beast Number Two and can shatter you? I will, too. I will throw you into the ocean. I am getting ready to be the Great Beast of the Apocalypse when Crowley dies, and I'm going to split the world wide open."

Drugs, dissipation and loss of blood caused by self-inflicted wounds—scourges of the flesh were imposed by Crowley as part of the daily routine—gradually sapped Loveday's strength. One night, during a Black Magic ceremony, he was forced to sacrifice a live cat. As the Scarlet Woman held up "The Cup of Abominations" to catch the blood, Loveday slashed at the animal's throat.

The cut was not deep enough, and the cat wriggled out of his grasp and raced round the room, blood pouring from its neck. Trembling and overwrought, Loveday managed to catch it and despatch it with a second blow, although it meant leaving the "protection" of the magic circle. The Scarlet Woman handed him the cup and he drank the blood.

A few days later, Loveday fell ill. His condition rapidly deteriorated, despite mystic spells and incantations. A conventional doctor was called in from the village, who diagnosed acute enteritis, though Crowley believed Loveday had fallen victim to an evil spell after breaking the magic circle. Either way, on February 16, 1923, Raoul Loveday died. Betty May noticed that his body adopted the position of the ectoplasmic figure in the wedding photograph. Amon-Ra had taken his revenge.

The newspapers descended on Betty May the instant she returned to Britain. "A maelstrom of filth and obscenity," gasped the *Sunday Express*, going on to hint at "horrible sexual debauches" touching "the depths of depravity".

Quivering with moral outrage, the newspapers quoted the Scarlet Woman's solemn oath, as inscribed in the Abbey's *Record*:

"I will work the work of wickedness
I will be loud and adulterous
I will be shameless before all men
I will freely prostitute my body to the lusts of each and every living creature that shall desire it.

I claim the title Mystery of Mysteries, Babalon the Great and the Number 156, and the Robe of the Woman of Whoredoms and the Cup of Abominations."

It was all too much for the Italian authorities, and in May 1923, the Beast was expelled from the country, complete with bell, book, candle and Cup of Abominations. Crowley was at the height of his notoriety. But nobody wanted him. He was deported from France and, for a time, refused entry to Britain; he had become a Satan without a hell to go to.

The rise of Hitler

Slowly, the world began to forget about Aleister Crowley, the Scarlet Woman and the Thelemic Mysteries. A new Beast of the Apocalypse had risen in the west, who flaunted Crowley's favourite symbol of the crooked cross, or swastika. His name was Adolf Hitler, and his murderous rites were to make Crowley's contrived orgies look like nursery games.

Crowley devoted himself to publishing—usually at his own expense—pornographic and pseudo-mystical books, including *White Stains*, the wildly obscene *Snowdrops from a Curate's Garden* and *My Confessions*. One didn't have to read the books to guess their contents. The dust-jackets bore Crowley's signature, with the initial 'A' in the form of a huge phallus.

It was in his book *Magick*, under the heading "Bloody Sacrifice", that Crowley wrote, "A male child of perfect innocence and high intelligence is the most satisfactory and suitable victim." A tongue-in-cheek footnote added, "It appears from the Magical Records of Frater Perdurabo that He made this particular sacrifice on an average about 150 times every year between 1912 and 1928."

The reference was merely an example of Crowley's exhibitionism and sick humour, but many people took it seriously, and the rumour persisted that Crowley had practised cannibalism.

In 1932, the authoress Nina Hamnett,

GROSS AND PERVERTED ceremonies inside Crowley's Sicilian "abbey" soon gained notoriety—as did his pornographic murals (inset top). Introduction to the Beast was to prove fatal for young Raoul Loveday, pictured at right with his wife Betty May.

a former friend of Crowley's, published her autobiography, *Laughing Torso*, in which she wrote, "Crowley had a temple in Cefalu in Sicily. He was supposed to practise Black Magic there, and one day a baby was said to have disappeared mysteriously. There was also a goat there. This all pointed to Black Magic, so people said, and the inhabitants of the village were frightened of him."

Crowley saw the defamatory reference as a wonderful opportunity to line his pockets. Encouraged by an earlier lawsuit, in which he had succeeded in claiming £50 damages from a bookseller, he sued the publishers, Constable & Company, for libel. It was a step which Crowley was to regret for the rest of his life.

In the months before the trial, Crowley

ignored all the warning signs. It was essential to his case to represent himself to the jury as a harmless, ageing scholar whose views had been distorted and misunderstood. Not one of his former friends, however, could be persuaded to go into the witness box to testify to his character. One of them, novelist J. D. Beresford, wrote to Crowley urging him to drop the action.

"I haven't the least doubt that some very extraordinary and damaging charges will be made against you if you come to

indulgently as his counsel, Mr. J. P. Eddy, K.C., described Crowley as an "altruist, a white magician, whose life has been a crusade against black magic". Mr. Eddy went on to relate in expansive terms how Crowley had inherited a fortune of £40,000, how he was devoted to poetry, art, travel and mountaineering, how he had climbed the Alps and walked across the Sahara. The awkward question of the Abbey at Cefalu was easily disposed of. It was, said Mr. Eddy, "a little community for the purpose of studying white magic".

This was the story Crowley had told his solicitors. The pile of privately printed books by Crowley on the table of Mr. Malcolm Hilbery, K.C., Counsel for the Defence, told an entirely different tale. Mr. Hilbery had done his homework, and

court, the kind of charges that would spoil any chance you might have with a judge, who is a kind of professional moralist." But buoyed up by vanity and the lure of a quick financial killing, Crowley blundered on.

Even his legal advisers were getting nervous; after reading a copy of *White Stains*, his lawyer wrote, "I have no hesitation in saying that if the defendants are in possession of that book your chances of winning this action are negligible."

The trial opened on April 10, 1934, at the High Court. At first, things seemed to be going well for Crowley. He smiled

there was a steely tone in his voice as he rose to bait the Beast 666.

Counsel: Are you asking for damages because your reputation has suffered?

Crowley: Yes.

Counsel: For many years you have been publicly denounced as the worst man in the world?

Crowley: Only by the lowest kind of newspaper.

Counsel: Did any paper call you "The Monster of Wickedness"?

Crowley: I can't remember.

Counsel: Have you, from the time of your adolescence, openly defied all moral conventions?

Crowley: No.

Counsel: And proclaimed your contempt for all the doctrines of Christianity?

Crowley: Not all the doctrines.

Counsel: Did you take to yourself the designation of "The Beast 666"?

Crowley: Yes.

Counsel: Do you call yourself "The Master Therion"?

Crowley: Yes.

Counsel: What does Therion mean?

Crowley: Great Wild Beast.

Counsel: Do these titles convey a fair expression of your practice and outlook on life?

Crowley: The Beast 666 only means "sunlight". You can call me "Little Sunshine".

Crowley's flippancy, and the laughter which greeted his last answer, didn't deter Mr. Hilbery. He picked Crowley's book *Clouds Without Water* from the pile and read some of the erotic verses. Then he snapped the book shut.

Counsel: Have you not built a reputation on books which are indecent?

Crowley: It has long been laid down that art has nothing to do with morals.

Counsel: We may assume that you have followed that in your practice of writing?

Crowley: I have always endeavoured to use the gift of writing which has been vouchsafed to me for the benefit of my readers.

Counsel: Decency and indecency have nothing to do with it?

Crowley: I do not think they have. You can find indecency in Shakespeare, Sterne, Swift, and every other English writer, if you try.

Echoes of Oscar

There were echoes of Oscar Wilde in Crowley's arrogant answers, and also in the way the case was turning. Miss Hamnett and her publishers were no longer on trial for libel. It was Crowley who was having to justify a life of depravity.

Mr. Hilbery picked up another book of poems, and again there was a faint whiff of that momentous trial, 40 years earlier, when Oscar Wilde had clashed with the brilliant lawyer, Mr. Edward Carson. Carson had read one of Wilde's poems and demanded, "Is that a beautiful phrase?" Languidly, Wilde had replied, "Not as you read it, Mr. Carson. You read it very badly."

Now Mr. Hilbery went through the same routine. "Is that not filth?" he asked, after reading one of Crowley's poems. Crowley turned Wilde's answer on its head. "As you read it, it is magnificent," he said.

Aleister Crowley, however, was no Oscar Wilde, and Mr. Hilbery refused to be put off.

Counsel: Are you known as the author of these poems?

All Radio Times Hulton

Crowley: They have had a very small circulation. I regret that my reputation is not much wider than it is.

Counsel: You would like to be still more widely known as the author of these, would you?

Crowley: I should like to be universally hailed as the greatest living poet. Truth will out.

Having established Crowley as a pornographer, Mr. Hilbery turned to the Beast's so-called experiments in "white magic". In the space of a few minutes Mr. Hilbery succeeded in turning white into black. He questioned Crowley on quotations from his own books on magic and the occult.

Counsel: You say here, "I had two temples; one white, the walls being lined with six mirrors, each six feet in height; the other black, a mere cupboard, in which stood an altar, supported by the figure of a Negro standing on his hands. The presiding genius of the place was a human skeleton . . ."

Blood and birds

Hurriedly, Crowley interjected, "Yes, the skeleton was £5 from Millikin and Lawley's, the medical shop."

Counsel: ". . . which I fed from time to time with blood, small birds, and the like . . ." Was that true?

Crowley: Yes.

Counsel: That was white magic, was it?

Crowley: It was a very scientific experiment.

Counsel: ". . . the idea was to give it life, but I never got further than causing the bones to become covered with a viscous slime . . ."

Crowley: I expect that was the soot of London.

Despite Crowley's supercilious replies, he could see the case slipping away from him. There was no stopping Mr. Hilbery. Crowley's debauched life was, literally, an open book. The voice of Mr. Hilbery continued remorselessly, quoting Crowley's words on human and animal sacrifices, on transubstantiation, on his ability to invoke evil spirits and summon up supernatural darkness in the middle of the day.

Mr. Hilbery read from one of Crowley's own articles in the *Sunday Dispatch*, where he had said, "They have called me the worst man in the world. They have accused me of doing everything from murdering women and throwing their bodies in the Seine to drug peddling."

Counsel: Is that, then, your general reputation?

Crowley: Any man of distinction has rumour about him.

Counsel: Does any man of distinction necessarily have it said about him that he is the worst man in the world, by way of rumour?

Crowley: No, not necessarily; he has to be very distinguished for that.

Counsel: You wrote, ". . . James Douglas described me as a monster of wickedness. Horatio Bottomley branded me as a dirty, degenerate cannibal . . ." You never took any action against any of the persons who wrote and published those things about you, did you?

Crowley: No.

Counsel: And then comes this silly little paragraph in this book, and you run to your lawyer with it, according to you, to bring an action for injury to this reputation, the reputation of being the worst man in the world. Is that the case?

Crowley: I also have the reputation of being the best man in the world.

Relentlessly, Crowley was being crucified. Now Mr. Martin O'Connor, representing the authoress, Nina Hamnett, rose to hammer in some more nails. The first one was both sharp and unexpected. Mr. O'Connor produced a bill from Mrs. Rosa Lewis, covering a stay by Crowley at her hotel, the Cavendish, in Jermyn Street, London.

Counsel: I understand you to say that you are a gentleman who sees visions. Is that right?

Crowley: Sees visions, yes.

Counsel: Were you summoned for the amount of this bill by Mrs. Lewis in the Westminster County Court in April 1933?

Crowley: I have no information on the subject.

Counsel: What?

Crowley: I do not know. People do all sorts of things like that, and I never hear of them.

Counsel: That is peculiar, and I will tell you why. County Court summonses have to be served personally.

Shade of yellow

Crowley: Yes, but I still do not know. Someone gives me a paper, and I put it in my pocket. I think no more about it. A fellow gave me a Judgment Summons only yesterday. I have never seen one before. It was a very nice shade of yellow.

Counsel: You say that you have visions. Conjure up a vision of when you are going to pay Mrs. Lewis the £24 for which she had judgment against you last April. Now throw a vision. Tell My Lord and the jury when the vision tells you that you are going to pay Mrs. Rosa Lewis the amount for which she has judgment for your board and residence.

Crowley: If I am bound to pay her, I shall pay her.

Counsel: When?

Crowley: When I can.

Having failed to induce Crowley to demonstrate one of his supernatural gifts, Mr. O'Connor generously allowed him the chance to try another.

Counsel: You said yesterday that as the result of early experiments you invoked certain forces with the result that some people were attacked by unseen assailants. That is right, is it not?

Crowley: Yes.

Counsel: Will you try your magic now on Mr. Hilbery?

Crowley: I would not attack anybody.

Counsel: Is that because you are too considerate or because you are an impostor pretending to do things which you cannot do?

Crowley: I have never done wilful harm to any human being.

Counsel: My friend, I am sure, will consent to your harming him. Try it on.

Court into temple

Before Crowley could conjure up the 316 demons to drag Mr. Hilbery down to the Underworld, the Judge intervened. "Mr. O'Connor," said Mr. Justice Swift, "we cannot turn this court into a temple." Mr. Hilbery's soul was saved, but Mr. O'Connor couldn't resist one final challenge.

Counsel: You said you have succeeded in rendering yourself invisible. Would you like to try that on? You appreciate that if you do not, I shall denounce you as an impostor?

Crowley: You can denounce me as anything you like. It will not alter the truth.

The Beast 666 stepped from the witness box, visibly angry and angrily visible.

The full enormity of Crowley's evil and depraved "magick" was brought home to the court by Betty May, the wife of the Oxford undergraduate who had died at Cefalu.

She described the perverted rituals at the Abbey of Thelema, the constant use of drugs, the blasphemies and obscenities, the animal sacrifices, the pornographic paintings round Crowley's room, known as "The Chamber of Nightmares".

Witness: The pictures were terrible.

Counsel: Do you mean they were indecent?

Witness: Most!

On the fourth day, halfway through Mr. O'Connor's closing speech, the jury started muttering among themselves. The Judge spotted them and halted counsel in mid-sentence.

Judge: I thought you were speaking to each other.

Foreman of the jury: My Lord, I was whispering to my fellow juror.

Judge: There is no reason why you should not whisper to him.

Foreman: May I be given an opportunity to do so?

SHOCKED DENUNCIATION of the Beast and his way of life by Justice Swift confirmed the jurors' decision to stop the trial: "I have never heard such dreadful, horrible, blasphemous, abominable stuff."

Judge: I have stopped learned counsel so you might speak to each other, if you want to do so.

Foreman: I think it is unanimous among the jury to know whether it is a correct time for us to intervene?

It was clear the jury wished to stop the case there and then. But as Mr. O'Connor had already started his speech, it automatically meant that Mr. Eddy had the right to put the case for Crowley. The jury heard him out, but their minds were already made up. Mr. Justice Swift's shocked denunciation of the Beast and his way of life only served to confirm their opinion.

When the Judge ended by asking the jury, "Do you want the case to go on?" there was not a second's hesitation.

Syndication International

John Frost

THE DAILY MIRROR   Saturday, April 14, 1934

JUDGE'S SCATHING COMMENT
ON ALEISTER CROWLEY
"Abominable Stuff by Man Who Poses as Greatest Poet"—Jury Stop Libel Suit

There was a dramatic end in the King's Bench Division yesterday to the action in which Mr. Aleister Crowley, the author, claimed damages against Miss Nina Hamnett, authoress of a book entitled "Laughing Torso," and the printers and publishers, for alleged libel.

Mr. Crowley complained that passages in the ...

Miss Nina Hamnett, who was one of the defendants, photographed yesterday.

Footballer's Broken Leg

"No," said the foreman. Without leaving the courtroom, the jury returned a verdict in favour of Nina Hamnett and Constable & Company. There was not even the derisory farthing damages for Crowley, although the libel still stood and had not been disproved by the defence.

It was a unique and contemptuous verdict. Crowley left the court a dazed and bewildered man, his reputation ruined, his future bleak and unpromising. In just over 10 years' time he was to die in obscure poverty in a boarding-house in the far-from-devilish seaside resort of Hastings, a physical wreck, dependent on a daily dose of 11 injected grains of heroin, enough to kill a dozen men.

But there was still a spark of the old Beast 666 left. Outside the court, a 19-year-old girl, who had been following the case, dashed after him. "That verdict," she sobbed, "it's the wickedest thing since the Crucifixion. Is there anything I can do to help?" The old urge flickered in the 60-year-old mystic as he gazed down at her. "Couldn't I," she pleaded, "be the mother of your child?"

The girl got her wish.

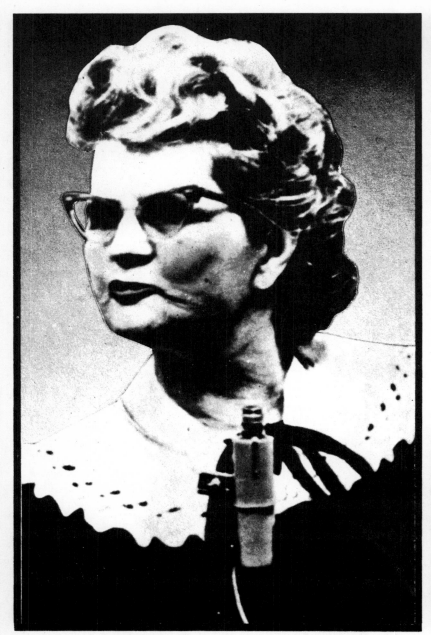
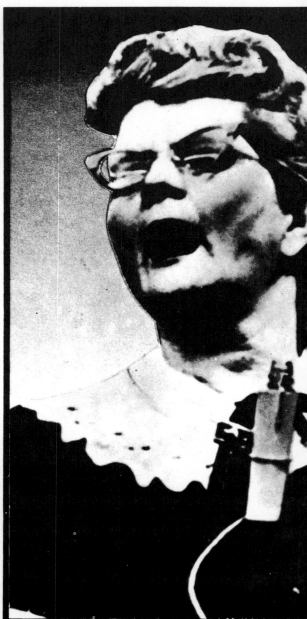

MOTHER DUNCAN'S DEVOTION

MIDDLE-AGED Mrs. Elizabeth Duncan, an outwardly respectable divorcée, devoted mother of a successful grown-up son, went shopping in the downtown area of Santa Barbara, California. Like so many other women among the 59,000 people of this opulent Pacific coast city, careful spender Mrs. Duncan was keeping alert eyes open for a bargain. But her quest, that December day in 1958, was not for a new chic hat, a becoming housecoat or a memorable evening gown. She was out to buy the services of a killer who would "eliminate"—as she delicately put it—her newly-acquired daughter-in-law.

Many women like to have the company of a friend on a shopping spree and Mrs. Duncan was no exception. With her as she bustled along Santa Barbara's State Street was her close friend and confidante, Mrs. Emma Short. To the casual passer by they appeared to be no more than two rather nice, mature citizens, Mrs. Duncan nearly sixty, her friend Emma in her seventies.

But their animated, low-voiced chat was about purchased death. Mrs. Short fully shared her friend's secret and for a homely old pensioner she was remarkably complacent about it. Her only reaction, as she could later recall it, was that, although she was keeping Mrs. Duncan company, "I didn't approve of her plan to kill her daughter-in-law".

Twisted woman

The "market-place" to which their dangerous mission took them was a seedy, run-down beer parlour on State Street, called the Tropical Café, owned by an illegal Mexican immigrant, Mrs. Esperanza Esquivel. Wily Mrs. Duncan had chosen it carefully. Mrs. Esquivel lived in fear that the police would discover that she had no legal right to be living and operating a business in the United States; already, on a quite separate brush with the law over the alleged receiving of stolen property, Mrs. Duncan's lawyer son, Frank, had represented the Mexican family's interests.

As Mrs. Duncan saw it, Mrs. Esquivel owed her a favour and, moreover, she seemed the likely sort of person to know drifting, café-haunting customers ready to offer their services as hired killers.

It was all incredibly cold-blooded yet it all fitted the psychopathic personality of Elizabeth Duncan. For, despite outward appearances, she was a dangerously twisted woman. In the course of her life she had had many husbands—probably 20 or more, but even she was not certain—some taken in legal marriages, others bigamously. She had married most of them in the hope of acquiring their money, for she was also a diligent, if not very skilful, confidence trickster.

The only man who had brought her any

lasting joy was Frank Low who had fathered her son, Frank, in 1928. She quickly tired of Mr. Low and illegally "married" a Mr. Duncan, whom she also deposed in favour of yet another "husband", but she raised her son as Frank Duncan. Young Frank she doted upon and wrapped in a suffocating mother love, obsessed with the anxiety that he would one day leave her.

Major quarrel

"Frank." she told her own doctor, who was concerned about the effects on the boy of her neurotic obsession, "will never leave me. He would never dare to get married." Surprisingly, in view of this crushing maternal weight, Frank Duncan showed remarkable independence. An intelligent, lively-minded boy, he did well educationally, made his way through law school and ended up as a successful lawyer with bright prospects.

Somehow he survived the embarrassment of being followed around from court to court by his energetic, clinging mother and listening to her vigorous and sustained applause every time he won a case. Lawyer-colleagues, gossiping together while juries deliberated, expressed the private view that the sooner Frank Duncan found himself a wife and escaped to complete personal freedom the better off he would be.

In the few quiet moments of meditation that he could snatch for himself, Frank began to think along similar lines. He was more than ready to throw off the yoke that bound him and, in 1957, he and his mother had their first major, stand-up quarrel. In his exasperation he ordered her out of their apartment. She, prepared to go to any lengths to remind her son of his permanent servitude, responded by taking an overdose of sleeping pills.

Loving Mother Duncan survived, but her action was to have terrible and far-reaching results for herself and three other people. For she was taken to a nearby hospital and there given into the care of a dark-haired attractive nurse, Canadian-born Olga Kupczyk, 29-year-old daughter of a railroad foreman.

Olga was one of the first people Mrs. Duncan saw when she emerged, pallid and shaken, from her coma. And Olga was almost the only person in the hospital, even including his mother, to whom Frank paid immediate attention on his first bedside visit to the patient. The attraction was mutual and the devastated mother, watching the alarming, affectionate glances between son and nurse, now saw that her worst fears were being realized. Her rival, long dreamed of with dread, had taken human shape and soon Mother Duncan would no longer be Frank's only and eternal love.

Within a few months the web that was being spun between the three principals in the drama tightened with the disclosure that Olga had become pregnant and a hesitant Frank found it necessary to inform his mother that he was considering marrying the girl. Mrs. Duncan, now restored to normal, angry health, was driven into a frenzy of rage, saw the nurse and told her with vehemence: "I'll kill you before ever you marry my son. You are not a fit person to live with my son."

Determined as he seemed to lead his own life, Frank Duncan was nevertheless still too conscious of his mother's vulnerability to make a decisive, precipitate break. Accepting the quite exceptional patience of his betrothed, he secretly married Olga but, from his very wedding night, left her at a late hour each day to return home and sleep at his mother's apartment. Later he remarked, ruefully, "Quite frankly, I was going back and forth like a yo-yo."

Screaming tirade

But it was impossible to under-rate a woman of such tenacity as Elizabeth Duncan. Within a day or so she had learned of the marriage and determined that it would not last. Her first move was to insert an advertisement into a local newspaper declaring: "I will not be responsible for debts contracted by anybody other than my mother, Elizabeth Duncan on, or after, June 25, 1958. Frank Duncan."

The advertisement came as a surprise to Frank but, still anxious to dampen the fires of fury, he felt it unnecessary to do more than to admonish his mother for interfering in his private affairs. As far as Mrs. Duncan was concerned, he had no private affairs and she presented herself, without warning, at Olga's apartment and launched into a wild tirade which was ended only when Olga summoned the help of her landlady who persuaded Mother Duncan and her son to leave.

Clearly, poor Frank had not launched himself upon wedded bliss but his mother was only yet in the early stages of her campaign to separate husband and wife. Her first improbable scheme was to kidnap Frank, while he was visiting his bride, and whisk him away to a hideout in Los Angeles. She even bought some rope with which to secure her rebellious son and confided her plan, inevitably, to her good friend, Emma Short. But in her more lucid moments even Mrs. Duncan was forced to acknowledge that the scheme was preposterous and she abandoned it.

What she could not, or would not,

AUTHORITIES uncover the body of Olga Duncan (right). Hired killer Luis Moya (left) was one of the two men who contracted to dispose of her for a fee.

abandon was her vitriolic hatred of Olga. She assured Mrs. Short that she would disfigure Olga with acid but then, on second thoughts, proposed that she should strangle Olga with Emma Short's assistance. The idea was that Mrs. Short should induce Olga to come to her home where Mrs. Duncan would hide in a cupboard. When Emma Short had invited Olga to take a comfortable seat, with her back to the cupboard, Mrs. Duncan would spring out and strangle the girl.

As the monumentally acquiescent Mrs. Short later explained: "The idea was that she should then hang her up in the cupboard until the evening. Then she would put a blanket around her, tie her with a rope and put a stone to the rope and take her to the beach in a car and throw her over the wharf." According to her own narrative, Mrs. Short's response was curious. "Do you realize," she told her bloodthirsty friend, "what you are trying to do? She will never stay in my apartment all night!"

Faced with Emma Short's reasonable objection to being saddled with the annoyance of a corpse in a cupboard, Mrs. Duncan turned her mind towards

EXACT details of the crime and location of the body were provided by Augustine Baldonado (below), the second of the amazingly incompetent killers.

more businesslike and better-organized methods of disposal. She would put the "job" out on hire and, for a mutually agreeable sum of money, hand over the technical details of her daughter-in-law's death to a third party. And so it was that the two old ladies, Elizabeth and Emma, found themselves in the steamy premises of the Tropical Café on State Street.

Apprentice killers

Mrs. Duncan turned her glib tongue to the immediate task of convincing the Tropical's owner, Mrs. Esquivel, of her problem — adjusting the facts to suit the situation. Her daughter-in-law, she confided, was blackmailing her and unless she could be removed, her son, Frank, might well be the victim of Olga's wrath. Perhaps Mrs. Esquivel had some friends who might not object to "removing" a bothersome person?

Mrs. Esquivel, adopting the view that the customer, however eccentric, was always right, knitted her brows in thought and finally pronounced that there were

180

For once, Emma Short was excluded and left to sit on her own, sipping coffee at an adjoining table. But the trio of Mother Duncan and "the boys" moved swiftly to the heart of the matter. As young Moya subsequently reported: "After we got down to brass tacks we just started making suggestions of how much money it would be worth to her to eliminate her daughter-in-law, and when it could be paid and how much, and there were suggestions made of how to get rid of her body. At first Mrs. Duncan just wanted to pay $3000, but I finally boosted the price up to six . . . She agreed to pay $3000 right away and then the remainder after Mrs. Olga Duncan was eliminated."

Mother Duncan was full of suggestions for the actual commission of the

"elimination". Once again, it involved rope, with the addition of sleeping pills and a final neat touch of acid "to disfigure her in general and her fingerprints . . ." Finally, "the boys" agreed to accept the assignment and promised to proceed as quickly as possible to fulfil it.

There remained, of course, the question of money. Mrs. Duncan omitted to mention that, far from having $6000 at her disposal, she had not the remotest chance of laying her hands on the initial $3000, or anything like it. But Moya and Baldonado were among two of the most gullible apprentice hired killers in criminal history. They listened to Mother Duncan's promises, finally accepted a ludicrous cash advance of $175 and naively agreed to receive the balance after the "contract" had been completed.

Mrs. Duncan left the café in high spirits, informing reliable old Emma on the way back home, "I think they are going to do it."

Moya and Baldonado wasted no time. They hired a 1948 Chevrolet for $25,

SMILING contentedly, Mrs. Duncan gazes at her grief-stricken son during the trial. Her friend Emma Short (right) knew about the murder but said nothing.

"a couple of boys" but whether they would be available or not she did not know. Perhaps if Mrs. Duncan could return the following day she would introduce them to her?

Mrs. Duncan duly returned with the imperturbable Emma still tottering in her wake, and was introduced to two unemployed young men, Luis Moya, Jr., 21, and his inseparable companion, Augustine (Gus) Baldonado, 26. Both were drifters, who had been in and out of the hands of the police, but neither of them had any history of violence.

Almost certainly they had never met any matronly old body with such a persuasive tongue as Mrs. Duncan before and they solemnly sat down at one of the café's grubby tables with her and discussed her proposition as others might discuss a real estate deal.

borrowed a ·22 pistol from an obliging friend and bought some ammunition to fit it. Soon after 11 p.m. on Monday, November 17, 1958, they drove to Santa Barbara's quiet suburban Garden Street and parked outside number 1114, the house in which Olga Duncan lived.

They waited to ensure that all was quiet and then young Moya went into the building, up the stairs and knocked on Olga's door. She appeared in housecoat and slippers and politely Moya launched into the killers' well-rehearsed script. Frank, her husband, he said, was downstairs in the car. "I met him in a bar and he's pretty drunk and has quite a large amount of money with him and he told me to bring him home. But I need help to bring him up."

Immediately Olga offered that help and followed Moya back down to the street. Baldonado had meanwhile stretched himself out on the back seat of the car, face downwards, to simulate the drunken, passed-out form of Frank Duncan. Moya opened the car door and Olga put her head in, reaching towards what she took to be her inert husband. As she did so, Moya struck her a blow on the side of the head with his pistol and pushed her on to the car floor as the suddenly active Baldonado dragged her towards him. In a moment the car door had shut and Moya was driving fast away towards the beach.

But the two young hoodlums had not made a very professional start to their killer careers. Olga, who was only dazed, came to her senses, began to scream and struggled to escape from the fast-moving car. Baldonado grabbed at her and tried to quieten her but she was a well-built, strong young woman and she fought against him valiantly.

"I can't hold her," the breathless Baldonado gasped and, as he was forced to brake at a stop sign, Moya leaned back across the front seat and struck viciously several more times at Olga's head with the pistol. Quiet at last, her blood spilling into the car, she slid to the floor.

Damaged mechanism

Now the second part of the makeshift plan worked out by the two killers began to go wrong. They had intended to dispose of the body somewhere around the Mexican border but, shaken by events, they changed their minds and decided instead to head for the mountains, south of Santa Barbara, and rid themselves of their victim with the utmost speed. Thirty miles down Highway 150 they found a darkened roadside culvert, parked beside it and, seeing that the road was deserted, dragged Olga Duncan out of the car.

She was still breathing and Moya drew his pistol once again, this time to put a final, despatching bullet through her head. But the use of the gun earlier as a club

had damaged the firing mechanism and, while Moya struggled with it in vain, Baldonado bent over the reviving woman in the darkness, searched for her neck and strangled her. When she had ceased to move, Moya picked up a rock and used it to deliver the *coup de grâce*.

So pathetically inept were the two young murderers that they had brought no tools with which to dig a grave and conceal the body. Both jumped down into the culvert and began scrabbling the dirt away with their bare hands, gouging out, after much sweated effort, an insecure and shallow pit into which they slid their victim's bloodied body.

Cryptic question

Blood dominated their thoughts as, at last, they drove back to Santa Barbara, for there was blood everywhere. It saturated their clothes, it lay in thick pools on the car seats and it seeped and trickled between their feet. Back in the city they spent anxious hours getting rid of their bloodstained clothes and tearing out the blood-covered seat coverings. They had accidentally started a fire in the car with a lighted cigarette, they explained to the Chevrolet's owner.

For a time it looked as though the clumsy murder might escape detection. A distraught Frank Duncan, calling at Olga's apartment and finding lights blazing and doors unlocked, summoned the police, but their best assessment was that this was a missing-person case. No doubt Mrs. Olga Duncan would return, or be traced, before long. No one came forward to offer any useful information, not even Emma Short who knew the almost certain answer to the mystery.

Two days after the murder, Luis Moya telephoned Mrs. Elizabeth Duncan at her home and reported that the "con-

tract" had been duly carried out. "You don't have to worry about her any more," he said before coming to the principal reason for his call: "Are you going to be able to accomplish your end?" Mrs. Duncan was in no doubt as to what that cryptic question meant. The labourers now wished to make it clear that they were worthy of their hire but, worthy or not, Mrs. Duncan had no money for them and no intention of meeting the full bill.

She had her story well prepared. "The police have been up to the house asking about Olga's disappearance," she explained. "So I can't draw any money out of the bank." She had a little money —around $200—and that would have to suffice for the moment. A few days later she met the two boys, accompanied by faithful Emma Short, and handed over an envelope to Moya. On opening it later he found it contained only $120.

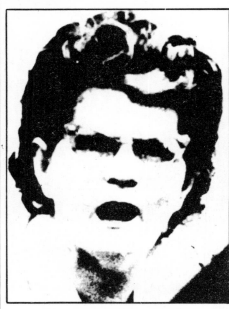

ALL THREE killers (this page) were slated to die on the same day—in the gas chamber at San Quentin, California, but Mrs. Duncan appeared unperturbed.

Infuriated by what was now clearly a rather nasty con-trick, the two killers began to pester Elizabeth Duncan for their pay-off to such a wearing extent that she decided to indulge in a piece of table-turning blackmail. She told the police that *she* was being blackmailed by two Mexicans, whose names she could not reveal but who were threatening to kill her and her son, Frank. Her theory was that once the killers heard of her action they would quietly leave town and she would be rid of them, just as she was now rid of her daughter-in-law.

It was Mother Duncan's last and clumsiest move. The police, by now aware of the bad blood that had existed between

mother and daughter-in-law, began to look more closely at Mrs. Duncan's wide-ranging activities. They questioned Emma Short, because of her known close association with Elizabeth Duncan, and at last old Emma began to talk. Astonished policemen sat wide-eyed as they heard her tell of the "contract" meeting at the Tropical Café and her explanation that she had not thought it necessary to pass on the information before murder was committed.

Side by side

From that point on, events moved swiftly to an inevitable climax. Baldonado and Moya were picked up and Baldonado dictated a confession which included precise details of the roadside grave of Olga Duncan. Mother Duncan's arrest followed as a matter of routine and by the time they came to talk to her at length the police were convinced that she was one of nature's pathological liars. Almost nothing she said rang true—except her blinding devotion to her son.

All three, the female instigator and the two hired killers, were found guilty and sentenced to death. Mrs. Duncan still had hopes of survival and her lawyer son repaid her distorted devotion by fighting, after a long series of appeals, for a final stay of execution. But even his energy and skill could not prevail against the course of the law and the murder trio went to the gas chamber at San Quentin on August 8, 1962. Moya and Baldonado died together, strapped into death chairs placed side by side.

Mother Duncan died alone. Her son could not be with her for, up to that final, eliminating moment, he was still pleading her case. Her last words, as the door of the glass and steel gas chamber was opened, were: "Where is Frank?"

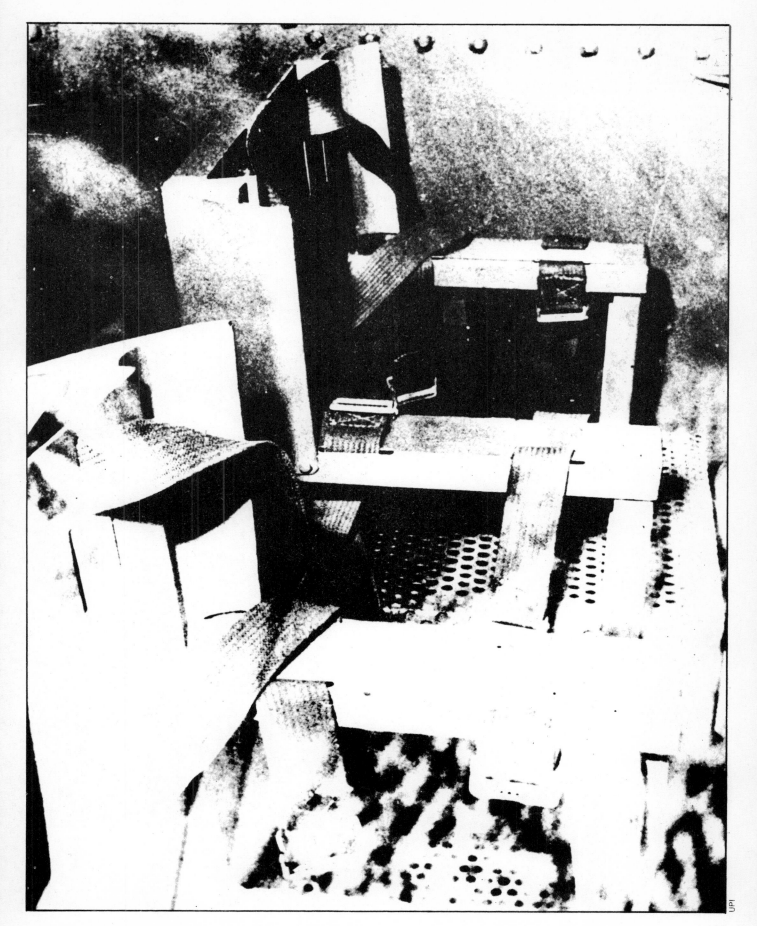

THE MISSING BODY OF

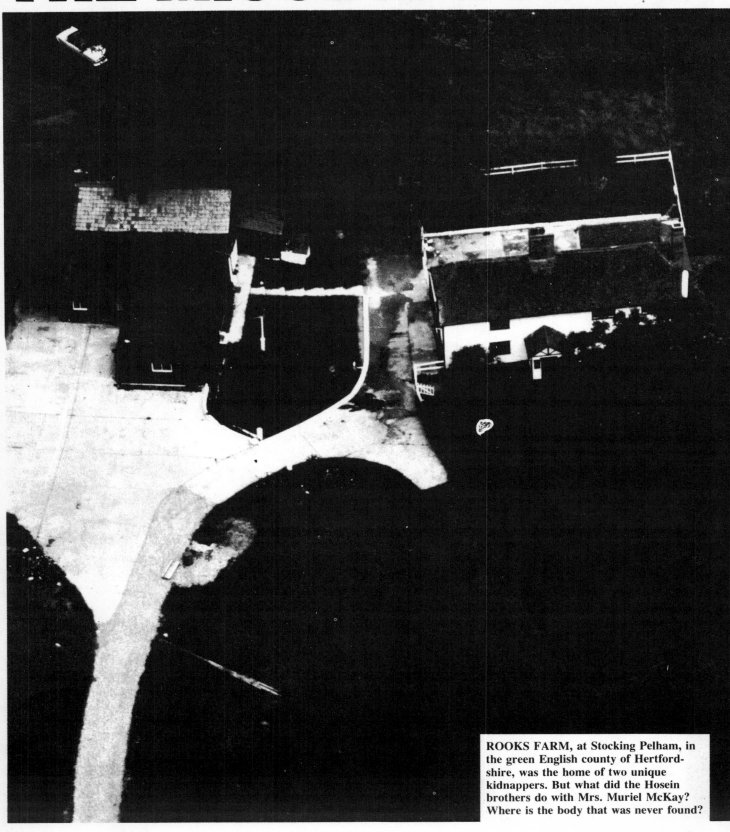

ROOKS FARM, at Stocking Pelham, in the green English county of Hertfordshire, was the home of two unique kidnappers. But what did the Hosein brothers do with Mrs. Muriel McKay? Where is the body that was never found?

STOCKING PELHAM

On this farm,
a woman was imprisoned
for more than a month...
then she vanished
without trace.

Two brothers were
charged with her murder.
They had planned to
seize the wife of a
newspaper millionaire,
and demand a £1 million
ransom. They got the
wrong woman ...

The Mrs. McKay "missing body" trial ... it was unique in British legal history

NO trial in Britain since the abolition of hanging for murder received more advance publicity than the court room drama which opened in London's Old Bailey on September 14, 1970. The two men who were brought up from the cells below the building to take their places in the dock of the historic No. 1 Court were brothers from Trinidad named Arthur and Nizamodeen Hosein. Although born in the former British colony, they were strictly speaking not West Indians but Indian Moslems whose family had originally come from the sub-continent of India.

Their father Shaffi Hosein was a respectable, hard-working tailor who had settled in Trinidad and owned the house where the family lived near Port of Spain. A deeply religious man, Shaffi also officiated as Imam in the Mosque which served the needs of the local Indian Moslem community in his village. The two boys, Arthur aged 34, and Nizamodeen, 12 years younger, had been brought up according to the teachings of the Koran, the Moslem bible.

The local squire

Together with their sister Hafiza and Arthur's wife Elsa and her two children, they lived at Rooks Farm, Stocking Pelham, near Epping, in Hertfordshire. This was a small property of some 12 acres, which Arthur had bought for £14,000 with the aid of a mortgage in May 1968. It was largely uncultivated and the only livestock consisted of a few pigs, calves, and chickens. Incidentally, pig keeping hardly commended itself to Arthur's father, since the pig is considered unclean by good Moslems. For finance Arthur depended on his sewing machine with which he used to produce trousers for London's East End tailors. Nevertheless, Arthur Hosein, who possessed delusions of grandeur, fancied himself as the local squire and spent freely in the neighbouring bars. He even tried, without success, to join the local hunt. At his trial he gave his occupation as "fashion designer". He was known in the neighbourhood as "King Hosein".

Both brothers were charged with murder, kidnapping, blackmail, and sending threatening letters. Their victims were an attractive, 56-year-old Australian married woman named Muriel Frieda McKay and her husband Alick. One reason, the principal one, why the trial had already received such extensive press coverage was that Alick McKay was the Deputy Chairman of the *News of the World*, which

"ALICK, DARLING" . . . the wife of Alick McKay was snatched from her home, and never seen again. Mr. McKay was Deputy Chairman of the biggest-selling newspaper in Britain.

has the largest circulation of any English newspaper. The *News of the World* had recently been bought by another Australian, the young millionaire Rupert Murdoch.

The story which the stern and tight-lipped Attorney-General Sir Peter Rawlinson, who led the prosecution, recounted to the jury of nine men and three women was an extraordinary one. The Hosein brothers, he said, had devised "a brutal and ruthless scheme to kidnap a wife and by menaces to extort from her husband a vast sum of money."

Chauffeured Rolls

Arthur Hosein had noticed a luxurious chauffeur-driven Rolls Royce driving round London. He took a note of the registration number ULO 18F and determined to trace its owner. This he was able to do at County Hall, the headquarters of the Greater London Council where particulars of all motor vehicles in the metropolitan area are filed. At his brother's prompting, Nizamodeen made the inquiry in person, giving a false name in the application form he filled out. The reason for his inquiry, he told the counter clerk, was that the Rolls had sustained minor damage in a collision with his own vehicle and he was anxious to get into touch with its owner. As a result he learned that the car belonged to the *News of the World* and was allotted to the chairman for his use.

The brothers then proceeded to follow the Rolls one evening from the *News of the World* offices off Fleet Street to the prosperous London suburb of Wimbledon, where it deposited its occupant, whom they took to be Rupert Murdoch, at the door of a fine Georgian-style house in Arthur Road, No. 20, known as St. Mary House. However, the man in the Rolls was not Rupert Murdoch. Rupert Murdoch had left England with his wife a short time before on a business trip to Australia and lent the car to the deputy-chairman, who was in charge of the paper during his absence. The man in the Rolls was Alick McKay, and he owned St. Mary House.

Gagged and trussed

During the late afternoon of Monday, December 29, 1969, the Hosein brothers used some pretext to get into the McKay house, since Muriel McKay always left the door on the safety chain. Having overpowered her, they took her away with them. "It was obvious," said the Attorney-General, "that they thought they were abducting Mrs. Rupert Murdoch, but she was safe and at home in Australia."

When Alick McKay returned an hour or so later, he found several articles which the intruders had left behind. They were some sheets of a newspaper, a roll of twine, a piece of sticking plaster tape, and a billhook. This latter is an implement resembling a small axe, which is used by farmers for hedging and ditching work. The telephone was on the floor, but had not been ripped away from the wall. Muriel McKay's reading glasses, hand-bag, wallet, keys, and cheque book were lying scattered about the stairs. Some short time before, the house had been burgled, and Alick McKay now thought that the burglars had returned and used some of the twine to tie up his wife before abducting her.

The picture which Sir Peter Rawlinson presented to the jury was a horrifying one. "Can you imagine the horror of a woman, one minute beside the fire waiting for her husband to return, and minutes later —gagged and trussed—then driven away in the darkness?"

Five hours later the phone rang in St. Mary House. Alick McKay heard a voice at the other end of the line identifying himself with "Mafia Group Three from America," or M3 for short. "We tried to get Rupert Murdoch's wife," said the caller. "We could not get her so we took yours instead. Have one million pounds by Wednesday night or we will kill her!"

During the next few weeks there were 18 calls from the kidnappers, most of which were taken by Alick McKay's son Ian—who moved into the house in order to spare his father, who was suffering from a serious heart condition, since the excitement of continuing to speak to the kidnappers on the telephone might prove fatal.

"Frankly we want to know if she is alive and well," said Ian McKay in response to one call. "We have the money. But why should we give you the money if we do not know if she is alive?"

"I have told you what she is wearing," M3 replied. "What do you want me to do? Take her clothes off and send them to you? If you do not cooperate you will get her dead on your doorstep."

A request by Ian McKay to speak to his mother, or have her voice taped as proof of her continued existence, was ignored. Three letters had been received from her, Sir Peter went on, two addressed to her husband and one to her daughter Dianne. ("Alick darling, I am blindfolded and cold. Only blankets. Please do something to get me home.") But when Ian McKay continued to press for proof that she was still alive, he was told that she would not be allowed to write again.

Never murdered

"It's because you have not got her," Ian shouted over the telephone to M3. "You have got a corpse. You are trying to trick us. How many other people have you kidnapped before?"

"We have never murdered anyone as yet," was the ominous reply, "but there will always be a first time."

A further letter, postmarked January 9, 1970, was addressed to the editor of the *News of the World*. Written in block letters on a single sheet of white lined paper,

the message, which bore no signature, asked the editor to inform Mr. Alick McKay that they had his wife, that he would get some proof, that they wanted a million pounds, and that if Mr. McKay failed to cooperate his wife "would be disposed off" [SIC]. In fact some pieces of the dress, coat, and shoes, she was wearing at the time were later sent to the unfortunate husband.

Meanwhile, a sheet of paper similar to that on which the *News of the World* letter was written had been found by the police in Nizamodeen's bedroom at Rooks Farm. The sheet had been torn from an exercise book and exactly matched the letter. In addition, there were two ransom notes which a handwriting expert stated were in Arthur Hosein's disguised handwriting, and one of these notes had impressions of Arthur's thumb and one of his fingers. Apart from this, a palm print found on the newspaper lying on the floor of St. Mary House on the night of the kidnapping was positively identified as being that of Arthur Hosein.

In this instance the English police were up against a completely novel kind of crime. In no case since that of King Richard the Lion Heart in the twelfth century had the kidnapped person been held to ransom.

It was otherwise in America and the European continent where the F.B.I. and the police authorities have learned from

"I APPEAL" . . . Mr. McKay pleaded with the kidnappers for news of his wife, at a Press conference. With him, daughter Dianne. Son Ian (above) rallied the family during the search.

experience to put the safety of the kidnapped person first, and the capture of the abductors second, and do not usually take action against the kidnappers until after the ransom money has been paid and the victim released. This procedure has as a rule worked well in practice, although there have been exceptions, of which the case of the Lindbergh baby in 1932 is the best known. But in America and the continent the kidnapping is normally the work of professionals who leave notes plainly stating their ransom requirements at the time the victim is taken away.

The amateurish Hosein brothers left no such message behind at St. Mary House, and with hoaxers frequently calling up the house as a result of the newspaper publicity, the police were hampered in their investigations through being unable to say whether Muriel McKay had, in fact, been abducted at all. Indeed, there was a suggestion that she had gone off to Australia on her own.

Enormous publicity

Furthermore, for the first two weeks in January 1970 no word was heard from the kidnappers, who were no doubt alarmed by the enormous publicity which Muriel McKay's disappearance had attracted. Then, on January 14, the telephone calls from M3 were resumed. Six days later Alick McKay received a letter containing directions for his son Ian to go to a certain telephone call box outside London on the Cambridge Road on the evening of February 1, where he would get a call at 10 p.m. telling him where to proceed with the money. This was followed by a second letter on January 26 repeating the directions, and enclosing a letter from Muriel McKay with the pieces of her clothing. In this letter M3 threatened that she would be "executed" if her son failed to keep "our business date without any error".

The date was kept—by Detective Sergeant Street who posed as Ian McKay. He took the call and was told to proceed to another telephone box on the road and wait for another call. The second call duly came through at 10.45, and "Ian" was told to look on the floor where he would find a used packet of Piccadilly cigarettes with further instructions. A note inside the packet ordered "Ian" to travel to a place called High Cross, beyond which he would see a road junction. At the side of the road there was a bank marked by some paper flowers, and this was the point where he was to leave the suitcase with the ransom money.

The Detective Sergeant did as he was instructed, while another police officer kept watch. But no one came to collect the suitcase, although the paper flowers were there. The result was that the police

eventually collected it themselves and took it back to Wimbledon.

Next day Ian McKay had a call from M3 accusing him of doublecrossing the kidnappers by going to the police, since they had seen a police car in the High Cross area the previous night. Later the same day M3 called again, this time saying he would do no more business with Ian McKay, but must deal with his father—who was instructed to pack the money into two smaller suitcases on February 6, and follow a similar call box procedure. This eventually led the police to Bishop's Stortford in Hertfordshire, where the suitcases were to be placed near a hedge by the side of a road leading into the town.

Here the kidnappers' luck ran out. A security officer, who had nothing to do with the investigation, happened to be driving past with his wife, and his suspicions were aroused by the sight of the two suitcases at the side of the road. He went to a call box and telephoned the local police, after which he returned and kept watch over the two cases. Meanwhile the Hosein brothers had been cruising round in Arthur's Volvo car, and noticing several police in the area, they thought it too risky to stop and pick up the suitcases. Thereupon they drove off—but not before the police had noted the Volvo's registration number. The number was checked; it was found to belong to Arthur Hosein, and it led the police to Rooks Farm.

No trace of Muriel McKay was found at the farm, but there were various articles there which connected the brothers with the abduction. These included paper flowers, which corresponded with those left at High Cross. It appeared that

190

THE MOST thorough and prolonged searches . . . whether Mrs. McKay died on the farm, and how she met her death, remains a mystery.

Nizamodeen's girl friend, Liley Mohammed, who worked as a hospital nurse, had shown Arthur's sister Hafiza how to make them—a process Liley had learned from a patient in the hospital. All this amounted to enough to incriminate the brothers as the kidnappers, and they were consequently arrested.

The first prosecution witness was Alick McKay, who looked very pale and shaky. He described the last time he saw his wife, which was the morning of her disappearance. "She was a very bright person."

Alick McKay was followed by a string of other witnesses who confirmed every point in the Attorney-General's story. Everyone who had spoken to M3 on the telephone—the operator who connected the first call, the editor of the *News of the World*, and various members of the McKay family—all testified.

Then the fingerprint and handwriting experts identified the prints and writing on the various articles exhibited in court as belonging either to Arthur or Nizamodeen Hosein. Finally, a neighbouring farmer in Hertfordshire swore that he had missed his billhook after visiting Rooks Farm in October 1969. When shown the billhook which had been found in the McKay house, he waved it from the witness box and exclaimed: "That's my bill. I defy anyone to say it's not!"

Both brothers gave evidence in their own defence, and denied all knowledge of the charges. But each tried to put the blame on the other for any suspicious happening or circumstance on which he was questioned.

Questioned about the billhook, Arthur said he could not recognize it and he thought the farmer had made up the story about it. However, he did admit, on being pressed, that he had borrowed a billhook to cut up a calf which had been brought to the farm. From time to time Arthur burst out into wild accusations against the police, who he said had frequently beaten him up after his arrest.

Nizamodeen, on the other hand, said he had been "scared stiff" of his brother.

He admitted going to County Hall and making inquiries about the Rolls, of which Arthur, he said, had supplied him with the registration number. It was Arthur, too, who told him to give the counter clerk a false name and address. His brother did not say why he wanted this information, Nizamodeen added, and he "did not give it another thought".

In his summing up of the evidence, the judge (Mr. Justice Sebag Shaw) mentioned every relevant point. "Each one perhaps is small in itself," he told the jury, "but from them it may be that an edifice is slowly erected by one tiny brick after another tiny brick."

It was clear that the jury thought so too. After an absence of just over four hours, they returned a verdict of guilty on all counts, but they recommended Nizamodeen to leniency.

Denounced judge

Asked by the judge whether they had anything to say before sentence was passed, Nizamodeen remained silent. But Arthur burst into a hysterical denunciation of the judge for his partiality. In

passing sentence, the judge addressed grave words to the men in the dock: "The kidnapping and detention of Mrs. McKay was cold-blooded and abominable. She was snatched from the security and comfort of her home and so long as she remained alive she was reduced to terrified despair.

"The crime will shock and revolt any right-minded citizen and the punishment must be sanguine so that law-abiding citizens will be safe in their homes. There cannot have been a worse case of blackmail. You put Mrs. McKay's family on the rack for weeks and months in an attempt to extort money from them by monstrous demands."

Both brothers were then sentenced to life imprisonment for murder. On the

other charges, Arthur got 25 years and Nizamodeen 15 years for kidnapping, and both got 14 years and 10 years respectively for blackmail and sending threatening letters—all the sentences to run concurrently.

Among the spectators in the crowded court was old Shaffi Hosein, who had come over from Trinidad for the trial. "I still cannot believe my boys would have done this," he said with a stupefied look. "I am sure they are not guilty."

However, it is abundantly clear that both brothers were convicted on overwhelming circumstantial evidence. Yet there is one puzzling factor about the case. Muriel McKay's body was never found. Not the slightest trace of her was discovered at the farm, or in the large surrounding area, in spite of the most thorough and prolonged searches.

There was a gruesome story current at the time that after they killed her the brothers cut up her body into pieces which they then fed to the pigs on the farm. But this is entirely unsupported by the evidence. Had it been so, some bones must have remained, but nothing of this kind was ever forthcoming. Nor was anything in the way of bones found in the large stove and chimney in the farm house, where it was likewise suggested that she had been cremated.

On the other hand; she may have died

from exposure during the bitterly cold weather at the time of her kidnapping, and her death may have been accelerated by lack of the drugs which she had been taking under medical prescription. It is possible too that she may never have been at the farm at all, but held in some hideout, perhaps in nearby Epping Forest, and after her death her body was weighted and dumped in a river or the sea.

Reprisals danger

Exactly how Muriel McKay met her death remains a mystery. How long it will remain so depends largely on Nizamodeen Hosein, who may conceivably be persuaded to solve it in return for an early parole by the prison authorities. Asked by Elsa Hosein, when she visited him in prison whether there was a third party in the case, Nizamodeen replied enigmatically:

"Arthur says that we must never talk about that, because if we do the children will be in great danger. There would be reprisals."

THE MEN WHO WALK ALONE: A lost wife, a shattered life . . . Alick McKay (centre), pictured leaving court. Parted, prisoners . . . the brothers Nizamodeen (far left) and Arthur Hosein (above).
Was there another person involved in the puzzling case of Mrs. McKay? The brothers remained enigmatic . . .